THE CHRISTIAN ASHRAM MOVEMENT IN INDIA

This book is one of the first to present a definitive history of the Christian Ashram Movement. It offers insights into the development of the Movement, Europe's Orientalist view of Eastern mysticism and how the concept of the "ashram" spread beyond the borders of India.

Drawing extensively from ashram literature and the author's field research, the book critically analyzes the notions of inculturation in the encounter between Christianity and Hindu spirituality and ritualism. It looks at how the Movement grew out of the colonial encounter and how it evolved through the years, which was contingent on developments within Christian churches outside India. The volume also discusses the reinterpretation of the idea of the "ashram" by Christian theologians, the introduction of elite Brahmanical concepts within the Movement and the unique theological perspectives which were nurtured in these ashrams.

The book offers an alternative perspective to the generally perceived history of Christianity in India. It will be of interest to scholars and researchers of religious studies, Christianity, sociology, social anthropology and religious history.

Zdeněk Štipl is an assistant professor of Indology at the Faculty of Arts, Charles University in Prague. He teaches Sanskrit, Indian history and religion. His research interests include Christianity in India and the Sanskrit Puranas. He has been travelling in India extensively since 1996.

THE CHRISTIAN ASHRAM MOVEMENT IN INDIA

Zdeněk Štipl

LONDON AND NEW YORK

CONTENTS

Introduction ... 1

1 Preliminary notes on Christianity in India ... 7

2 Inculturation of Christianity ... 46

3 History of the Christian Ashram Movement ... 67

4 The phenomenon of the Christian ashram ... 168

Conclusion: interpretive possibilities of the Christian Ashram Movement ... 200

Index ... 207

INTRODUCTION

This book deals in the broadest sense with the relation of Christianity towards Hinduism. This relation was newly constituted in the modern era and subsequently was also complicatedly developed in the form of the so-called Christian Ashram Movement. The Movement represents a remarkable experiment with inculturation through which Christianity attempted to penetrate the cultural and religious world of India. Despite its almost two thousand years' presence, Christianity in this world has remained in the position of a foreign religious element that is even perceived in some cases as undesirable. The history of Christian ashrams spans nearly the whole of the 20th century, and their idea cuts across church denominations. In the beginnings of the Movement, ashrams emerged in particular in South India and were established mainly by Protestant churches. They were, however, soon joined by the Syrian Orthodox Church, and from the middle of the century, the initiative was taken over by the Catholic Church. The latter became the leading spirit of the Movement after the Second Vatican Council at the end of the 1960s. In their heyday in the 1970s and '80s, the existing ashrams numbered over a hundred, and they were found in virtually all language regions of India. The ashram idea even spread to surrounding countries and far beyond the borders of India (Nepal, Sri Lanka, the United States, Great Britain, France, Spain etc.).

The topic of Christian ashrams and the Movement has already been elaborated upon in several books dealing with the studied aspect of Christianity in India. It also received well-deserved mentions in subchapters of voluminous synthesizing works dealing with the modern historical development of Christianity in India. Quite unsurprisingly, the topic of ashrams appeared in collections compiled in the ashram or broader Christian environment and also in a remarkable number of scholarly as well as popularizing articles in periodicals published both in India and outside the country. A large part of these contributions consists of apologetic works written by the promoters of ashrams and the Movement. They may be ashramites themselves, theorists and ideologues of Christian inculturation or sympathizers, who, despite standing outside the Movement, overtly or covertly express their support for the Movement through their moderately critical attitudes.

INTRODUCTION

Except for numerous generally informative contributions acquainting readers with the ashram phenomenon and its meaning for Christianity in India, the theme of ashrams can also be found in the works dealing with Christian spirituality. It was for the formulation of its new form, which appeared in India during the 20th century, that very strong inspirational impulses arose from ashrams. Ashrams and specific individual aspects of life in them also hold their inalienable position in the theological literature of the Catholic Church. By this, we mean the minor and more extensive works emerging in particular during the intellectually fruitful period immediately before the Second Vatican Council and in the two decades after its end. For reasons that will be explained adequately in our book, the topic of ashrams and their possible role for Christianity in India virtually disappeared from the thinking developed by the contemporary generation of Indian theologians. There are also some interesting biographical works dedicated to some of the leading figures in the Movement. It therefore stands to reason that in researching their life stories or lifework systematically, these works bring to light a great deal of new knowledge and observations concerning the Christian ashram phenomenon and the historical development of the Movement. The three monographs in the strict sense of the word that have been written so far are the pioneering works of Helen Ralston (1987), Paul Pattathu (1997) and Ernst Pulsfort (1989). All of them can definitely be considered erudite research output. In the case of H. Ralston and E. Pulsfort, this output is additionally based on field research of the ashram scene. However, both date back as far as to the 1980s, which is when the Movement reached the peak of its development. The extensive and ambitiously conceived work of P. Pattathu is to a certain extent affected by the fact that the author himself, an Indian Catholic priest, became actively involved in the Ashram Movement soon after he completed his work.

This book aims to view the whole Christian Ashram Movement in the historical context of the development of Christianity in India. It offers the perspective from which the Movement is seen as a remarkable and extraordinarily prolific phenomenon in this development. This phenomenon can be, moreover, critically evaluated in addition to the mere presentation or defence of its meaning, as used to be the case earlier, because today the Ashram Movement seems to be over. The general method that I have followed, in particular in the main part of the book dealing with the history of the Movement, is therefore to study the Movement as a development process, because it is not really something that is static and could be taken out of the historical context, analyzed and described. It was the complicated genesis of the ashram phenomenon in the course of the 20th century that transformed it into a genuine movement, with a beginning, peak and end phase that can be quite clearly identified and therefore named. This approach, which is, as I hope, innovative in comparison with all the previous works, also enables defining individual phases of the inner development of the Christian

INTRODUCTION

Ashram Movement and this specific type of inculturation of Christianity in India. There is always a corresponding theological relation to the non-Christian religious tradition and its contemporary reality underlying these phases. This book identifies the development of this relation, thus creating a meaningful framework for the periodization of the Movement. Following the analysis of the ashram phenomenon and its main constitutive features, which is based on studying the sources originating in the ashram environment and on many years of field research, the book further presents a set of differentiating characteristics of Christian ashrams. Thanks to these, the newly designed typology can be applied to the ashram phenomenon.

The first part of the book offers a brief overview of the history of Christianity in India. However, it is presented here not in the form of specific historical events taking place in its course and creating its actual content but from the perspective of defining individual phases of the development of the relation of Christianity to the religious and cultural otherness of India. This perspective is absolutely essential for the origin and significance of the Movement, its roots as well as possible impacts. It is through this perspective that the Movement takes on its meaning. This introductory part is concluded with a presentation of a critically conceived complex of characteristic features of Christianity in India. These result from its historical development in some cases or, the other way round, are its causes or by-products in others. They do, however, always significantly contribute to the form of Christianity in India as well as to the relationship of Christians towards the religious and cultural context in which their everyday and religious life takes place. Therefore, these features always inevitably constitute the form of the religious self-identity of Indian Christians.

The second part represents the thought concept of inculturation into the general framework of which Christian ashrams and the Movement can be included. Here, not only is the problematic definition of the content of the term "inculturation" thematized but also the considerably different approaches to its function. Also mentioned are the diverse opinions on the subject that inculturation should deal with and also on the individual phases that the inculturation process should go through if it is to bear the expected fruit. The theory of inculturation that is outlined in this part is almost consistently based on the works of Indian theologians because their opinions are relevant for the topic of ashrams. Furthermore, the methods and goals of inculturation in India differ considerably from the similar situation that Christianity faced and still faces in other countries of the world (in particular in Africa and Latin America). The second half of this part presents selected points of the critical analysis of the most important themes, functional principles and the meaning of inculturation as such. This criticism is based on an analysis of official documents of the Catholic Church. Its approach led to the systematic elaboration of the inculturation concept. For a certain period of time, it even constituted an integral part of the Church programme through which the Church aimed to establish its relation to other religious traditions in a completely new way in the second half of the 20th century. The antinomies of thought present in these documents, together with the outline of the later development of the relationship of the Church to inculturation, are the theoretical stakes demarcating the space where the Movement takes place and by which it is concurrently limited.

The third and most extensive part deals with the history of the Christian Ashram Movement itself. Its clear ambition is to present a comprehensive and definite description of the origin and development of the idea of the Christian ashram. Every attempt has been made to include every significant personality or event in the scope of the chosen coverage, and the whole Movement is placed, hopefully in a meaningful manner, in the context of the development of Christianity in India in the 20th century. No other work has offered such a complete picture of the history of the Movement so far, and so this part can be considered, hopefully justifiably, the most contributive. The applied historical method of synthesis and description seems to be the most appropriate for the defined objective.

The fourth part consists of an analysis of the ashram phenomenon. Attention is paid first to the inspirational model for the Movement, which is the ideal and considerably idealized concept of the ancient ashram. Far more important, however, seems to be the reinterpretation of such a concept in the context of the needs and possibilities of the Christian churches in the 20th century. A brief overview of several different definitions of the ashram from the pens of Christian authors is followed by a critical analysis of its constitutive traits and characteristics. They can be described as types of the essential given features of every ashram. The variety of approaches to these features eloquently points to the fact that the ashram phenomenon itself has undergone a fairly dramatic development and never represented an idea that could be unequivocally grasped. This variety of the means and ends that were attributed to ashrams and also the external and internal forms of individual ashrams at the same time are sources that raise an opportunity to classify them into several categories and according to different perspectives.

The briefly introduced structure of this book aims to follow the reliable method of a logical procedure. In its framework, individual parts gradually respond to generally formulated sub-questions, which are mutually contingent and interconnected. The first part seeks answers to the question "why" when it indirectly outlines the reasons and motives for the emergence of the Movement in the context of the history of Christianity in India. The second part explores the ideological background of the Movement, its theoretical and theological anchoring in the religious tradition and attitudes of Christians and churches, which were newly formulated in the 20th century. The third part depicts "how" and "when" the Movement emerged, or rather how it developed in the specific time. The fourth part characterizes the content of the Movement itself because it answers the question of "what" the Christian ashram is. In the conclusion, the main causes of the failure of the Movement are outlined. But also briefly mentioned are other possible interpretive perspectives through which the Movement can be seen and evaluated and the whole theme can be further developed as a subject of research.

This book came to its existence over quite a long period of time. My first contact with the phenomenon of the Christian ashram took place by concurrence of many circumstances in 1998. Its most important result was that I became acquainted with the personality, life story and theological and spiritual-popularizing work of the French Benedictine, Henri Le Saux, better known under the Indian name Abhishiktananda. A considerably unsystematic, mostly rather random collecting of materials, in particular the ashram literature available in Indian Christian bookstores, continued with varying intensity until the year 2008. My interest in the Movement at that time was driven by purely personal reasons. Over this decade, I also visited several Christian ashrams during frequent trips to India and made personal contacts with some representatives of the Movement. After 2008, the research on the ashram scene had already been carried out according to the ex-ante set systematic plan as part of a Ph.D. project. The field research conducted in four stages up to 2010 can undoubtedly be considered of the utmost importance. During it I visited more than thirty Christian ashrams run by various churches and located in twelve states of India. The length of stay in each of them ranged from a single day to two weeks and in several cases also repeatedly. The manner or method of studying the ashram phenomenon lay in my personal participation in the daily activities of a respective ashram, but also, to the same extent, in semi-structured interviews with ashramites, whether they were permanent residents or temporary visitors to an ashram. The central themes of these interviews were mostly questions about their personal motivation, spiritual and practical experience with the ashram way of life and also with specific ashrams. Valuable impulses for the further direction of the research very often came from the leading figures of ashram communities. Thanks to their openness, I learned about new ashrams that had been unknown to me until then, as well as about personalities active within the Movement in some of its developmental stages. In this context, it is certainly worth mentioning that none of the ashrams, including those that have existed for many decades, systematically built up their archives, where they would collect important documents concerning the origin and development, personal correspondence of founders and so on. However, on the other hand, a number of ashrams, especially Catholic, have very well or even excellently equipped libraries. In addition to the broadly conceived Indological and scholarly works as well as literature on comparative religion, they also contain works concerning the Movement or the ashram phenomenon. In particular, thanks to a stay in the libraries of the *Sameeksha* ashram in Kerala, the National Biblical, Catechetical and Liturgical Centre in Bangalore, the *Vidyajyoti* Catholic Theological Faculty in Delhi and the School of

INTRODUCTION

Oriental and African Studies in London, I hopefully managed to embrace the entire scholarly literature dealing with Christian ashrams. The helpfulness of many ashramites then allowed me to gather a substantial part of the written materials originating in ashrams themselves. These are, due to the many minor works in the form of information brochures comprising just a few pages, extremely confusing. It is the ashramites from the Christian ashrams in India whom I would like to thank most. This book would have never been written without their rare willingness to share their own spiritual world.

References

Pattathu, Paul. 1997. *Ashram Spirituality*. Indore: Satprakashan.
Pulsfort, Ernst. 1989. *Christliche Ashrams in Indien, Zwischen dem religiösen Erbe Indiens und der christlichen Tradition des Abendlands*. Altenberge: Telos-Verlag.
Ralston, Helen. 1987. *Christian Ashram: A New Religious Movement in Contemporary India*. Lewiston/Queenston: The Edwin Mellen Press.

1
PRELIMINARY NOTES ON CHRISTIANITY IN INDIA

The history of Christianity in India has already been told on thousands of pages in dozens of voluminous synthesizing works. It stands to reason that key events keep recurring throughout them, while their interpretations differ here and there, as does the emphasis placed on specific persons or churches. This happens in particular in connection with the changes of the political, cultural and religious context of the period of time when the works were created. Thus, the crucial "driving forces" are paraded in front of the reader whether in the form of orders and missionary organizations or exceptional individuals. The latter often appear at the turn of historical periods (Francis Xavier), standing out with their original approach (Roberto de Nobili) above their surroundings and, as a matter of fact, also the times, or changing through their decisions the confessional status quo of a specific church or community (Mar Thoma I or, in the opposite sense, Mar Ivanios). In this overview, the history of Christianity in India would seem to be in particular segmental histories of the individual churches that penetrated India and in later development stages were directly established in its territory. Although Christians with their total representation in Indian society constitute a minority group (about 2.3 percent),[1] the number of churches operating in India today can be counted in tens, if not even hundreds. With some amount of justified exaggeration, it could even be stated that hardly any of the forms of Christianity that appeared in the global context of its development also failed to reach the Indian subcontinent (Frykenberg 2008: 5). It is the heterogeneity of Indian Christian churches, the variety of the expressions of their religious life and also the complexity of the network of the mutual relationships existing among them that leads a number of contemporary researchers to think that it is not possible to talk about a single monolithic Christianity in India but about many various Christianities (Bauman and Young 2014: ix–x).

Christianity in India has never had any trouble catching the attention of historians. The first, often multi-volume, series on the history of Christianity in India had already emerged during the 19th century. Their authors were Anglican pastors, (former) missionaries and also retired officers who had worked for the East India Trading Company (e.g. Hough 1839). These mostly apologetically approached works saw the advent of Christianity in India as an inevitable phase in the development of religious thinking, as a transition from imperfect or in principle completely misguided archaic religious ideas towards the fullness of truth revealed in the person and teaching of Jesus Christ. The evidence and by-product of this qualitatively culminating development and also the cause of such a point of view was supposed to be, quite logically, the territorial expansion and subsequent dominance of Britain as a victorious colonial power. This supposition was based on the view of Britain's officials and subsequently also historians that their country was bringing to India the light of religious cognition alongside numerous civilizational achievements. The influence of the Indian cultural and religious context in which churches had to operate was more or less ignored or immediately regarded as damnable at the time. After all, it followed from the logic of the development that it was inevitably predestined to gradually, spontaneously perish.

The trend set by historians of high colonialism to a considerable degree continued for most of the 20th century. As part of it, the history of Christianity in India was seen and presented as the history of successes or failures of missions, the fates of exceptional individuals that had been their bearers and the particular churches to which these individuals belonged. The history of Christianity in India was thus seen strictly in the context of missiology, as the history of missions (Bauman and Young 2014: ix). The actual identity of Indian Christianity, what these missions, individuals and churches had left behind them in India and what was often further developed spontaneously through impulses from the Indian cultural and religious environment, had seemingly remained completely unaddressed. Despite the growing production of scholarly literature dealing with Christianity in India, the historiographic approach to its history, seen in its complexity, that had been formed in the previously described manner and is by its very nature Eurocentric did not change much until the 1980s. Then the monumental, although unfinished, work by Stephen Neill (1984, 1985) appeared. Thanks to his lifelong collecting and studying of sources, his stay in India lasting for several decades and last but not least his vast erudition, Neill was the first who tried to approach historical developments across individual churches, regardless of his own denominational affiliation. It was the latter which, on the contrary, had limited many previous authors to such an extent that they had overlooked, if not even systematically ignored, the developments in churches other than their own. At the same time, Neill also turned his attention to the influences coming from the Indian environment which Christianity, in particular its individual churches in respective cultural regions of India, was exposed to. After all, these influences contributed to the many various forms of Indian Christianity, and so their share in its resulting plurality, which was becoming differentiated, is comparable to that of specific characteristics of the churches, even before the latter came to India.

It was only from Neill that the process of seeking the history of "Indian Christianity", not merely "Christianity in India", started. And although he himself, in the words of a sympathetic critic and also admirer, did not manage to completely get over his strong ties to the Anglican Church, which some of his judgements and observations were affected by, and a certain colonialist approach to the studied topic (Frykenberg 2008: 18–19), Neill's numerous successors oriented their subsequent research exactly in this direction. As yet, the last significant contribution to the topic of the complex history of Indian Christianity is a voluminous synthesizing work by Robert Eric Frykenberg from 2008. It is the result of the author's longstanding research interest in intercultural communication and the relations of missionaries to the autochthonous religious traditions of India. In this work, due attention is paid in particular to the significance and influence of educated converts and also mass movements, which were not led by outstanding missionaries but on the contrary by the Christian laity. Even though Frykenberg's work has undoubtedly already become a standard in the academia, unfortunately it covers development in the 20th century only minimally. However, the trend of activating the laity culminated in the course of this century, significantly affecting the current form of virtually all big churches.

The current increased interest in indigenized, inculturated and folk Christianity is largely connected to the political and social emancipation of underdeveloped and ostracized segments of Indian society. These have been overlooked for a long time, even though a substantial percentage of Indian Christians come from their ranks. It is this laity, so far considered rather a passive mass and a mere object of missionary activities, that has been in the spotlight of contemporary researchers through a number of subordinate studies. These researchers recognize in them authentic bearers and mediators of spontaneous, not centrally managed and planned indigenization/inculturation. Its description and analysis, in terms of case studies (e.g. Raj and Dempsey 2002) and also macro history approached in a complex manner, searching the roots and development stages of the process of naturalization of Christianity in India (e.g. Collins 2006), seems to be the mainstream of the scholarly interest in Indian Christianity today.

Christianity in context – changes in relationships towards the surrounding environment

To present history from just one point of view is essentially insufficient, the more so if such a view is determined, sometimes even motivated, by some ideology or a religious belief. It is the relationships between individual religions and the concentrated observation of their development, whatever it happens to be in the course of history, that are absolutely crucial for a pluralistic culture and society of the Indian type. A good many studies have already dealt with interreligious dialogue, Christianity and Hinduism in this case, whether it was really implemented or only hypothetically considered. In his so far unsurpassed work, Wilhelm Halbfass (1988) approached this dialogue as a general philosophical and hermeneutic issue of the encounters between Europe and India throughout their historical development. Richard Fox Young (1981) focused on the interaction between the opinions of the apologists of both religions in the 19th century, which took place over specific texts and the theological questions arising from them. Bror Tiliander (1974) analyzed the conceptual religious terms of Hinduism and pointed out their possible theological parallels or, on the contrary, fundamentally irreconcilable differences with the Christian concept. Hans Küng with Heinrich von Stietencron (1987) introduced the mind-sets of both religious systems, drawing attention in particular to the specific difficulties related to different understandings of the very content of the term "religion", and then they tried to examine and propose opportunities for mutual understanding that would enrich both engaged sides. The issues handled relating to interreligious dialogue in terms of methodologies and opinions may be almost as plentiful as the scholarly literature dealing with them.

For introducing the topic of the Christian Ashram Movement, much more important than the interreligious dialogue itself is, however, the question of the relation of Indian Christians to the foreign religious environment in which they had and still have to move. If we try to view the history of Christianity in India from the very perspective of its interaction with the majority Hinduism, several different approaches will unfold in front of us. With a certain degree of simplification, they can perhaps be perceived even as the sub-phases of the development of this history that can help us create its clearly arranged periodization. At the same time, these phases always inevitably follow from the context of the respective period of time and are for the most part inseparably linked to the development of Christianity outside the territory of India. Indeed, the far-reaching cultural, religious and political changes in Europe were later reflected in Indian reality, especially in changing perspectives on it. These phases also faithfully reflect the pre-understanding of the Indian religious world of that time and various expectations connected with it. The meaningful periodization of the history of Christianity in India, the goal of which is to be only a rough overview, will concurrently set the historical framework of the Christian Ashram Movement and indirectly identify the causes of its origin, conditions of its development and subsequently also the reasons for the decline of ashram activities.

The price of the natural integration of the Saint Thomas Christians

The first and longest stage in the development of Christianity in India and the associated first way of approaching the Indian religious and cultural context relates to the existence of a small Christian community in the territory of today's Kerala in South India, dating as far back as to the first centuries after the beginning of the Common Era. The questions that have not been convincingly answered so far regarding the origins, exact date of the formation of the community and historical relevance of the traditional legend concept that considered Thomas, Christ's disciple and apostle, the founder of the community are not important for our topic (for a summary of these subjects, see Brown 1956: 49–51). Much more interesting are the relationships to the environment surrounding the early Indian Christians, which they therefore inevitably came into daily contact with. The influence of this environment on the doctrine and the overall lifestyle of the Saint Thomas Christians, as they had called themselves for centuries, or also Syrian Indian Christians (Fernando and Gispert-Sauch 2004: 61), or Nestorians (Frykenberg 2008: 105), as they used to be and still are often inaccurately called by the outside world, is particularly remarkable. Although unintelligible to an overwhelming majority of believers, Syriac as the exclusive language of the Christian liturgy had remained in use until the arrival of the Portuguese at the end of the 15th century. On the contrary, their living in the middle of the Hindu religious culture and in particular everyday encounters with the ritual rules of the caste system created a completely new identity for the small but internally probably quite differentiated Christian community (Amaladas 1993: 16). The local Hindu environment had left significant marks on its habits related, for example, to clothing and diet matters and also influenced some elements of the liturgy, which we have learned about from the fragmentary news left behind by European travellers (Frykenberg 2008: 109, 113). But, above all, this environment with its typical inclusivistic approach to every otherness included the Saint Thomas Christians in the caste structure (Visvanathan 1993: 3). They were engaged mostly in trading activities, and in some ports along the south-west coast they controlled overseas trading for centuries; in some areas, they were perhaps even blood relatives of the local royal houses. Their economic status thus ensured them a respected position in the caste hierarchy (Bayly 1989: 8; Amaladas 1993: 18; Frykenberg 2008: 112).

The Saint Thomas Christians from Kerala lived in cultural and political isolation from the Christian world, which was only occasionally broken by a traveller from Europe or a new migration wave of fellow-believers fleeing the religious persecution in the Middle and Near East. This isolation lasted for more than one thousand years, and the small Christian community probably did not develop its own theological thinking during it. So that they could live in peace and prosperity in the middle of the majority religion, the Saint Thomas Christians accepted its basic condition, the logical attribute of the caste system, always determining every man his specific place and status in society. They became yet another of the Indian endogamous religious communities when the seemingly indispensable creedal necessity to spread the Gospel, which means a call for religious conversion, disappeared from their Christian practice (Brown 1956: 173–174; Forrester 1979: 100–101).[2]

It is this conversion that actually changes the status of man before God, but also in the eyes of other people. The question remains as to whether the resulting state can really be considered "a dialog in life [meaning: between the two religions]" (Amaladas 1993: 16) or just another example of the strong Indian influence on all extraneous elements that happen to emerge in the territory of India. In any case, the Saint Thomas Christians can be classed as being a fully integrated Indian Christian community, the presence of which has not left any significant marks on the coexistence in a complicated multi-religious environment.

The power-motivated invasion of European Christendom under the Portuguese Padroado

An entirely new stage in the development of Christianity in India set in after the arrival of the Portuguese. The earlier period was characterized by the absence of regular, firmly established contacts between Christian Europe and India. With the arrival of the first Portuguese fleet in 1498, the religious and political situation in Europe, however, began to be reflected in the manner of how Christian missionaries approached the religious context of the country to which they were bringing their conception of Christianity. The main motivation of the Portuguese expeditions of discovery was the spice trade or rather the abolition of the monopoly that Arabian merchants had over it in the western part of the Indian Ocean. In addition, the search for Christian allies in the rear of the expanding Ottoman Empire also played a vital role, in particular after the fall of Constantinople in 1453. This was fuelled by a vague notion of the existence of an ancient Christian community in South India and also by the legend about the mythical kingdom of Prester John, which was extremely popular in Europe at that time (Neil 1984: 91; Halbfass 1988: 22). The traumatic experience with Islam, which the Christians in the Iberian Peninsula had carried with them from the time of its reconquista, left its mark on the general character of the expeditions of discovery, the relationship to the foreign religious environment and the future forms of interacting with it (Frykenberg 2008: 119–120). The aggressive asserting of Portuguese trade interests was thus accompanied by religious intolerance and attempts to spread Christianity or rather the militant form of Catholic Christianity alongside the influence of power (Ibid., 127). As became apparent, the role of the Church had been crucial in creating the reconquista identity of the Portuguese kingdom and missionaries who were leaving it for the newly discovered territories.

The domination and religious patronage of the Portuguese king (so-called *Padroado Real*) was confirmed by several papal bulls from the middle of the 15th century. They authorized the king to represent the Catholic Church in newly discovered countries, conquer them, subjugate their misbelieving inhabitants and turn them into devout Christians (Robinson 2003: 300). The tool of this mission became Catholic orders, out of which Franciscans were the first to reach India. They were soon followed by Jesuits and Dominicans, who set up the infamous Inquisition in Goa, the bastion of ecclesiastical and political power of the Portuguese in India, in 1560 (Kuriakose 2006: 34). This institution of God's jury in India had never expanded to such hideous proportions as in the Catholic countries of Europe (Frykenberg 2008: 134). Nevertheless, its task in India was similar – to see to the purity of belief of Indian Christians and also to fight against any attempts to implement ancient ritual practices into Christianity in the territory under the direct rule of Portugal (Henn 2014: 50–52). The Inquisition's apparatus of repression put no less force and zealotry into inveighing against the practising of mere regional customs that were in a way connected with religion and also punished the resistance of heterodox persons against missionary efforts aimed at new religious conversions (Kuriakose 2006: 61–64).

During the first period of their activities in India, which means for a major part of the 16th century, Portuguese missionaries did not show any considerably systematic interest in understanding the cultural and religious determinateness of the surrounding environment. The intellectual awareness of the religious world of India was minimal in Europe at that time. It was limited to a considerably vague notion that there might be certain hidden elements of Christianity in Hinduism that were, however, deformed and suppressed after the arrival of Islam (Halbfass 1988: 36–37; Pearson 1987: 116–117), but their discovery and resurrection could contribute to the restoration of the spiritual unity of the world. Thus, instead of exploring the religious context which they aimed to establish themselves through their missions and subsequently even to take control of, the Portuguese built bases for the expected future Christianization of India in the small port enclaves on the west coast that they had managed to conquer. To them it was as if they had merely relocated their cultural and religious customs from their native Portugal. From these bases, they also subsequently made attempts to penetrate deep into the subcontinent, in the first period, quite logically, especially into the areas where until then only the peaceful and non-aggressive community of the Saint Thomas Christians had existed. It was this very community which the Catholic missionaries threw into doctrinal confusion with their uncompromising requirement of absolute obedience to the Church and their exclusive interpretation of Christian teaching and uniform ritual practice. The growing tension finally culminated in the middle of the 17th century with the first of a series of the schisms that Christianity in India has undergone during its intricate history (for the development of the conflicting relationship between the Church representatives of *Estado da Índia* and the Saint Thomas Christians, see Frykenberg 2008: 130–136). The social and religious status of the missionaries declined alarmingly in the eyes of the local population because their way of life completely contradicted the habits that were expected and demanded from the religious elite in the Indian, in particular Hindu, environment. Seeming trivialities concerned imperfections in personal hygiene, consumption of alcohol and eating meat, but also the apparent rivalry among the Church orders and their squabbles for power therefore affected for a long time the prestige of the whole religion that the missionaries represented.[3]

The relationship of European missionaries to the religious environment of India in the first decades after direct and intensive contacts had been established is symbolized to a great extent by the person of Francis Xavier and the methods of his missionary work (Henn 2014: 40–41). When he finally reached India at the head of the first Jesuit mission in 1542, he focused his hectic and considerably aggressive missionary activities on the groups that were socially ostracized or completely excluded from Hindu society. Those, however, had virtually nothing to lose by being converted or in regular and thus ritually polluting contact with missionaries.[4] Moreover, in these new Christian communities that emerged, for example, among the Tamil and Malayam Paravars and Mukkavars, the motivation for conversion was definitely not only religious or spiritual but much more political. Through their active consent to the controlling influence of the Portuguese, which was formally confirmed by the regular mass conversion of the inhabitants of whole villages, the converts hoped to find a strong protector of their interests (Frykenberg 2008: 137–138). Many such established communities were, however, left to fend for themselves after having converted to Christianity. The Catholic orders active in India did not have enough spiritual shepherds, and at that time, the Church proceeded with the utmost caution or even distrust in matters relating to the ordination of local converts as well as the place where priesthood services could be performed afterwards. These communities thus remained distinctly Hindu or rather local in their everyday religious life despite the newly proclaimed Christian identity. This is clearly evident in particular from the manner of celebrating significant religious holidays and the life-cycle rites of passage (Ibid.). The reasons for this remarkable fact lie, on the one hand, in the quantitative evangelizing that had become a trend in the missionary activities of the 16th century. Its success or otherwise was thus assessed depending exclusively on the number of new indigenous converts. On the other hand, it was, however, also the lack of interest on the side of missionaries in understanding the cultural and religious world in which they appeared after their arrival from the bigoted environment of Catholic Portugal.

The need for understanding, its causes and consequences

A new type of approach to Indian religious reality had already began to form in the second and third generation of the representatives of the Jesuit order operating in India, which means roughly from the 1570s. In its full strength and originality, it then found its expression in the missionary experiment of the renowned Italian Jesuit, Roberto de Nobili, who was rightly identified by W. Halbfass as one of the crucial milestones on the road of intellectual encounters of Europe and India (Halbfass 1988: 38). The initial period of Portuguese disregard (Neill 1984: 237) was thus slowly replaced by an informed insight into Indian culture, customs and religion. This insight resulted from the extensive activities of Jesuits, including, for example, three famous, although finally unsuccessful, missions to the court of the Mughal Emperor Akbar. Year after year, the Jesuits sent numerous letters from different corners of India to Rome, where they were copied as well as printed later on and then read not only by their brothers but also by the interested European public. These letters "from the missionary terrain" passed on a huge mass of information of all kinds about India and the Orient in general. Some of them caused a sensation in Europe of that time, arousing a growing interest in the Orient countries and motivating other missionaries who then came to India better prepared in terms of information than their predecessors (Correia-Afonso 1969: 14). The writers of the letters were rarely able to duly appreciate the achievements of Indian civilization, and when they evaluated Indian culture from a religious point of view, they often saw it as a mere obstacle to missionary work. Nevertheless, with their descriptions, albeit quite superficial and not as well informed as they might be, for example, of the Hindu mythology or some ritual practices, they pursued clearly practical objectives. The information they passed on was to equip their fellow order brothers and potential future missionaries with such knowledge of the Hindu environment that would allow them to subsequently combat it efficiently (Ibid., 20–21).

More efficient evangelization, which continued pursuing religious conversions, was the grounds for the pressing need to understand the environment and the people it targeted. Missionaries strived to understand the context in which they operated precisely in order to be properly understood themselves (Halbfass 1988: 53) and thus be able to bring the Gospel message into this context meaningfully. This is exactly how the attempts, connected mainly with the activities of the Jesuit order, to produce the first language manuals need to be interpreted. The key to mutual understanding lay in the knowledge of local languages. Mastering these was a precondition for establishing communication about theological and, also in a more general sense, intellectual topics (Ibid., 37). According to the generally accepted opinion of Neill, the British Jesuit, Thomas Stephens, who had worked in Goa from 1579, was one of the very first Europeans who perfectly mastered an Indian language (Neill 1984: 240). He left behind a catechetic manual in Konkani and the first printed grammar of the language. He gained a permanent place among the missionary greats and in the literary canon of one of the finest of the modern Indian languages with his famous Marathi "Christian Purana", or the Purana about Biblical History (for a modern analysis of the text, see Falcao 2003). Through the classical form of the Hindu Puranas, this extensive poetic composition attempts to present the biblical concept of time as the general history of salvation. This history clearly develops towards the coming of the Christian saviour, in whom historical time and the existence of the world acquire their sense. Similarly pioneering language studies were undertaken at the same time but in the south of India, that is, in the Tamil cultural and linguistic circle, by the Portuguese Jesuit Henrique Henriques. From his pen came the first grammar of the Tamil language written by a European, as well as original works of a catechetical nature or concerning the life of prominent saints (Neill 1984: 242–244). In their efforts to meaningfully present the principles of Christian teachings to an Indian audience, both missionaries found themselves facing the hermeneutic problem of selecting adequate theological terminology. They had to necessarily decide how deeply into the local religious and cultural environment they should and could immerse themselves in translating or transculturally interpreting the key conceptual terms of Christianity. The works by both authors were intended to be a practical tool of evangelization, and so no genuine interest in the Hindu world of ideas is obvious in them (Halbfass 1988: 38).

The previously mentioned hermeneutical problem cannot be solved without knowing the content of the environment which the new religious message is entering through the missionaries, not its mere form. This was the very task that two Italian Jesuits, Roberto de Nobili and Constanzo Giuseppe Beschi, tried to tackle. In Madurai in South India, where de Nobili lived and worked in the first half of the 17th century and Beschi in the first half of the 18th century, they focused their efforts on the members of high Hindu castes as yet untouched by Christianity (Županov 2001: 26, 104). De Nobili argued in favour of his principled openness to the intellectual world of the foreign religion by referring to the positive attitude of the early Church Fathers to conflict-free elements of the ancient culture (Halbfass 1988: 43). He thus tried to separate the religious core of Hinduism and its external expressions as he considered the latter, in agreement with Beschi, to be mere secular customs or folklore clad in a religious robe (Ibid., 41; Županov 2001: 100). Thanks to their life at the interface of two religious worlds, both Jesuits had gained an insight into the indigenous philosophical and religious tradition. Their command of classical Indian languages (Sanskrit and Tamil) was also masterful, and they even adapted, to some degree, their lifestyle to the customs of the Hindu elite. This, however, aroused resentment among conservative high-ranking clergymen in Goa, who viewed their activities with suspicion. Through their new strategy, both had achieved extraordinary success in the form of numerous Brahmanic converts and, in the case of Beschi, also a not-insignificant influence of power in the place where he developed his activities (Frykenberg 2008: 139–140). Both of them also had to face charges of doctrinal heresies. Despite the tolerance they showed towards indigenous Indian culture, the main objective of their missionary revolution continued to be religious conversions (Pearson 1987: 123). Both of them used Sanskrit and Tamil terminology as a medium through which they newly formulated the theological and philosophical principles that the construction of Christian teachings had been built on. However, by their very nature, these principles were still firmly anchored in the traditional Thomist concept (Barnes 2004: 146–147). De Nobili presented Christianity to the Brahmanic elite from Madurai as the fifth "lost Veda" and himself as its qualified harbinger, a Brahman coming from Rome (Županov 2001: 74). This ingenious strategy reveals his firm belief that the Gospel can be transplanted into any cultural and consequently also religious context when all possible means are deployed, and for that reason, it is a universal religion or indeed the only religion in the strict sense of the word. De Nobili's authorship of the lost "Christian Veda", the so-called *Ezourvedam* (Rocher 1984), has already been refuted fairly convincingly (for a summary of all previous arguments against de Nobili's authorship, see ibid., 30–42). The famous forgery originated most probably in the French Jesuit circles of Puttuchery, with an obvious plan to convert the Hindu elite, and caused a considerable intellectual sensation in the Europe of the Enlightenment at the end of the 18th century. Despite that, de Nobili's overall relation to the religious tradition of Hinduism and the applied missionary method of his attitude to this tradition correspond, to some extent, with the reasons this forgery had been created and the enthusiasm, which stemmed from the contemporaneous pre-understanding of India, it aroused in Europe. After all, the fact that the authorship of this forgery had been ascribed to de Nobili for a long time or was at least seriously considered in this connection seems to be sufficiently revealing.

In their interest in the Indian culture and religion, the Jesuits were followed by the missionaries of the Calvinist, Lutheran and also other non-Catholic churches. They were already active in India in the 17th century, but only from the first decades of the 18th century did their activities become extraordinarily intensive. Thanks to them, Christianity in India received new impulses that influenced and gradually totally changed its form on the subcontinent. However, the complicatedly developing relations, often of a confrontational or even conflicting character, among the churches in Europe were concurrently transposed to it from outside. With his revolutionary approach, de Nobili targeted the Hindu elite. The spirit of Pietism, which had dominated religious discourse in the non-Catholic countries of Europe from the middle of the 17th century, by contrast set out the requirement for the general availability of the word of God (Hedlund 2017: 31–32). Indissolubly connected with it was the need to educate, at the maximum possible scope, the underdeveloped and illiterate masses of population in the areas penetrated by Protestant missionaries so that truly everybody could obtain their personal share in the salvation coming through the Gospel (Frykenberg 2008: 144–145). The systematic studying of Indian languages became the first task in this plan. It was precisely being able to command them perfectly that was seen as a necessary tool for addressing the Indian environment religiously. Therefore, the major figures of Evangelical churches compiled grammar books and dictionaries of Indian languages over that period. Subsequently, they translated selected passages of the Gospel and later the whole Scripture into them, as opposed to the translations of the catechisms, which were always given preference by the missionaries of the Catholic Church (Amaladoss 2005: 21).

In parallel, the understanding of the religious traditions of India was deepening. The Dutch Calvinistic missionary, Abraham Rogerius, summed up his knowledge of the Brahman concept of Hinduism and Indian society, which he had obtained through a reliable informant, in his famous book *De Open-Deure tot het verborgen Heydendom*. Thanks to its translation into German and French in the second half of the 17th century, the book considerably contributed to the creation of the European image of India and its religious world (Neill 1984: 379–380). Extraordinarily influential and active in this respect, for several generations, was the Lutheran mission in the Danish village of Tranquebar. Its founder of German origin, Bartholomäus Ziegenbalg, was the first to translate the whole New Testament into Tamil, which he perfectly mastered in an incredibly short period of time, in the first two decades of the 18th century (Neill 1985: 34). Fully in the spirit of the Pietist approach to evangelization and its emphasis on general availability, he also deserves credit for having built modern educational institutions with teachers and pastors of indigenous origin. Furthermore, he had collected and passed on to contemporary Europe a huge amount of precious informational materials concerning various aspects of the Tamil culture and Hinduism in South India (Frykenberg 2008: 148–150). Last but not least, he established extensive contacts with Brahmanical scholars. By means of detailed reports, he acquainted the intellectual centre of his Church based at the University in Halle, Germany, with their views on Christianity. On the basis of the information obtained from these pioneering interreligious dialogues and, to the same extent, extensive studies of the resources, Ziegenbalg wrote his most celebrated work, *Genealogie der malabarischen Götterin*, in 1713 (Jeyaraj 2004). However, because it was misunderstood and strictly refused by the representatives of the Lutheran Church in Europe, it was not allowed to be published in its original version before the second half of the 19th century. In his comprehensive assessment of the current state and form of the world of Hinduism, Ziegenbalg adhered to a considerably conservative approach. It is therefore no surprise that he decidedly rejected it as pagan or blinded by the practised idolatry (Neill 1985: 32–33). Nevertheless, he remarkably further developed the idea of the primordial monotheism that had already been formulated by Jesuit missionaries. According to it, hidden away in Hinduism under the sediments of obscurant superstitions, formal rituals, in principle misguided philosophical views and behind the multitude of various gods, there is the idea of one God, a sort of natural, unrevealed light and religious knowledge. In Ziegenbalg's view, the Hindu environment had already lost its access to this ancient intuitive wisdom centuries ago. It was Christianity, as the revealed religion, that could now help Hinduism to rediscover it (Halbfass 1988: 47–48).

It would certainly be premature to consider the trend of relative openness to the indigenous religious tradition set by Ziegenbalg to be a manifestation of religious tolerance. It was a mere willingness to listen to the opinions that the tradition puts forth to bear witness about itself (Neill 1985: 32). However, the marked-out route was followed also by other representatives of the mission in Tranquebar. They took over the role of mediators of communication between the cultural worlds of Christianity and Hinduism and their conversant interpreters. Thanks to their activities, the Christianity of European Protestant churches thus put down roots in South India. The noteworthy, perhaps originally subtle, yet crucial for the indigenization of Christianity in India, influence of the Hindu tradition on Protestant missions can be discovered in the development of the teacher and disciple relationship. In the vast majority of cases, it was always a relationship between a foreign pastor who had been operating in a terrain for a long period of time and a circle of his or her closest indigenous co-operators or disciples. They are those supported by the teacher in their personal spiritual growth and consistently prepared by him or her for the role of his or her successors (*guru-shishya-parampara*). This formative approach was most efficiently used by the German Lutheran Christian Friedrich Schwartz. In the second half of the 18th century, he developed his activities in politically tumultuous South India, and his disciples subsequently enriched the heritage of the Western character that had been entrusted to them with indigenous cultural impulses (Frykenberg 2008: 153, 159). Thanks to them, the later spontaneous and often lay currents, calling for the deeper integration of Christianity into the Indian environment, turned the religious communities in Tamil Nadu and the neighbouring Kerala into the most active Christian communities across the whole of India. If we therefore evaluate the consequences of the growing need to understand Indian religious reality, as it was expressed by Jesuit missionaries headed by de Nobili and their Protestant fellows, it seems that a more permanent and viable product in the form of an activated lay community of the indigenous origin was left behind by the latter.

Christianity in India in the period of European Enlightenment and the British Raj

The intensive contacts of missionaries with the Indian environment began reaching quite a new level, both in terms of form and content, at the turn of the 18th century. At that time, a large part of the Indian subcontinent had already been permanently pulled into the developments taking place in far-distant Europe. Initially, this happened in the form of the struggle of European powers for political domination in India so that India would subsequently turn into the most significant British colony then emerging. Also, the translation efforts of missionaries continued, to finally reach their undoubted peak in the form of "a Bible factory with many different linguistic departments" (Boyd 1994: 15). It was already established in Shrirampur (Serampore) in Bengal near the end of the 18th century, and its founder, the English Baptist William Carey, had been active as a professor of Sanskrit and Bengali in the newly established Fort William College in Calcutta, also known as "a University of the East" for many years (Frykenberg 2008: 307). Under Carey's leadership, it took just a few years before Shrirampur became the intellectual centre of Christianity in northern India and also an intricately structured educational and awareness-raising institution (Neill 1985: 199–200). By turning towards Sanskrit, Carey significantly contributed to the interest of missionaries in Indian languages, which was then partially motivated by the ideals of the Enlightenment but, to a considerable extent, also by the continuing desire to spread Christianity. Thanks to Carey, the whole Bible was gradually translated into the classic language of Hindu India (under the title *Dharmapustaka*). According to his considerations, the linguistic form of Sanskrit, which is in itself an object of religious veneration of Hindus, could be used for communicating completely new religious content (Young 1981: 35; Oddie 2006: 99). Carey's successors who carried forward his ideas, in particular William Hodge Mill and John Muir (Halbfass 1988: 50), further developed possible solutions for the hermeneutic problems associated with the so-called Church Sanskrit (Young 1981: 48). These were in particular the issues arising from the theological terminology of Christian Dogmatics. Their religious and philosophical tracts written in Sanskrit subsequently truly attracted the attention of Hindu apologists. The latter, however, responded to the raised objections quite unsurprisingly by opening Christian dogmas to similarly relentless criticism. Standing at the forefront in this sense is Muir's renowned and controversial *Matapariksha* (Neill 1985: 373–374), in which he tried to refute the ideological pillars of Hinduism through the Christian perspective. From the point of view of mutual relations between Christianity and Hinduism, the turning of missionaries to Sanskrit provoked, for the very first time in their long common history, the interest of the Hindu intellectual elite. For them, Christianity, that is, a religion allochthonous in India, still remained an inadequate alternative to Hinduism. However, they first started to seriously count on it as an integral part of the Indian religious plurality (Young 1981: 142). On the side of Christian missionaries, this turning then marked the beginning of two parallel processes of Sanskritization of Christianity and Christianization of Sanskrit (Ibid., 48). It was these processes that Brahmabandhav Upadhyay at the end of the 19th century and the Christian Ashram Movement in the 20th century followed up on. No less crucial, however, was the change that took place in missionary methods and sub-objectives. Instead of instant and mass conversions, the most suitable means for meaningful communication with the Hindu environment were looked for using the Church Sanskrit as a medium. The mass character of the missionary efforts was thus replaced with qualitative evangelism.

The turn of the 18th century also saw other significant changes in how Europe viewed India and its religious world. The original, quite narrowly profiled religious identity of Europe was relativized to a certain extent by the effect of the growing number of contacts with other world cultures and also thanks to the ideals of the French Revolution that had been spreading fast across the old continent. The dogmatic, intolerant rejection of everything foreign in the sphere of religion, which was so typical for previous centuries, was slowly replaced with an emphasis placed on rationality and religious tolerance. The pre-understanding that Enlightenment Europe had of non-European cultures was additionally complemented with the Romantic interest in seeking the roots of the human spirit and the beginnings of its expression in religions, including beyond the borders of the ancient civilization circle. In the case of India, fuel was added to this interest by the first translations of the original religious sources, which Europe was becoming familiar with, no longer just by mere hoaxing forgery like *Ezourvedam*. In particular, the translation of the Upanishads into Latin became exceptionally influential. It was made by the French scholar Anquetil Duperron and published under the mangled title *Oupnek'hat* in the first years of the 19th century from the Persian translation titled *Sirr-e-Akbar*, effected by the Mughal Prince Dara Shikoh. Halbfass deservedly describes this work as an anachronism (Halbfass 1988: 64), in particular in the context of the developing Oriental studies as a science built on respectable pillars of knowledge and having direct, not only mediated, access to the source information base. Nevertheless, *Oupnek'hat* played an indisputable role in forming the European perspective on India at the turn of the 18th century. The Upanishads and subsequently also *Advaita Vedanta*, no matter how relatively late Europe became familiar with them, began to be seen as the highest stages in the development of Indian thinking, which had de facto ushered in the advent of Christianity (Ibid., 51). The romanticizing admiration of the famous past of India ("a golden age theory", Županov 2001: 97) and its ancient wisdom was concurrently put into direct contrast with its existing condition, with the degeneration of its original traditions, values and moral ideals, as well as the overall social and religious decline (Oddie 2006: 104). In the imagination of many European philosophers, missionaries and also the first Indologists, whose interest was often motivated by the cause of evangelization, it was Christianity that could become a bridge. As such, it was supposed to help India and its inhabitants to get over the medieval period of religious darkness, to clear Hinduism and in particular to rid it of its idolatrous Puranic ballast.

The protagonists of this quite new interest in India, the first Orientalists and Indologists, even received not insignificant support from major representatives of the British East India Company (EIC) for a certain period of time (Metcalf 1995: 10). However, a response of refusal soon appeared in British missionary and political circles. For a long period, the EIC had tried to impede the activities of missionaries in the territory that was under its direct control because any external interference in the religious matters of India was perceived as a potential risk to its wide-ranging business interests, which were the primary goal of the EIC (Jones 1989: 27). As a result of the pressure exerted by the Protestant lobby in the British Parliament, the strategic approach to religious matters was changed in 1813 when the foundation deeds of the EIC were undergoing their regular twenty-year review (Frykenberg 2008: 205). The EIC was not supposed to bear direct responsibility for the work of missionaries; nevertheless, it was forced to allow them access to their territory. The function of the Anglican Bishop was also established, and missionary activities were even to be supported by the officials of the civil administration (for a selection of individual points of the reviewed Charter of the EIC, see Kuriakose 2006: 88–90). In the upcoming decades, the relation of the EIC officers, and later of the British colonial administration, to missionary activities was not always unambiguously positive (Frykenberg 2008: 282). Despite that, in the understanding of the majority population of India, the political power of the foreign usurper was nevertheless directly linked to the usurper's no less foreign religious and cultural identity. On top of that, the usurping power used its missionaries and conversions to try to force this identity on the Indian environment (Hedlund 2017: 74).

As part of this newly set agenda, the missionaries who would come to India viewed Indian culture and religion through the lenses of their own cultural and religious supremacy (Gravend-Tirole 2014: 115). They brought with them from Europe the belief that European culture represented the only civilization in the true sense of the word (Metcalf 1995: 34). Christian Western culture started to be presented to India as a creator and bearer of civilization progress, in particular in the form of technological achievements that were so much admired by educated Indians at that time. At the same time, it held a mirror up to Indian society, with its archaic rituals and deeply rooted superstitions which it seemed the modern, industrial era had no room for. Although the increased interest in the religious and cultural traditions of Hinduism did not start fading away as a result, its centre of gravity in the form of developing Indology studies was, however, moved to Europe. On the contrary, in the environment of British India itself, its academic cultivation was paradoxically considered useless or even inappropriate for its civilization's progress (Halbfass 1988: 68). In this sense, the statements made by the British historian and politician Thomas Babington Macaulaye are in particular quite famous (Metcalf 1995: 39–41). Along with the Scottish Presbyterian missionary Alexander Duff (Frykenberg 2008: 324–325), he significantly contributed to the development of a modern Indian school system of the British type (Copley 1997: 14). The colleges and universities that started to be established in Indian metropolises in the first half of the

19th century were not missionary institutions in the full sense of the word. However, the curricula and teaching methods in them were mostly developed by missionaries with a not very positive relation to indigenous cultural and religious traditions.

The Evangelical missions operating in the context of the 19th century crucially influenced the form of Christianity in India, the position of Christian churches and their extensive activities in the majority Hindu environment and also the mutual relation between Christianity and Hinduism. The criticism of the indigenous religious tradition led to several considerably different consequences. It was formulated both within the premises of universities where future generations of intelligentsia, that should be first of all loyal to the empire, were raised according to British ideas and models and in the environment of missionary stations active in Indian rural areas. On the one hand, the criticism led to acculturation attempts for a deep internal reform of the indigenous religion, culture and society (Jones 1989: 3–4). Its partial results are generally well known from the history of the so-called Bengali Renaissance. Ram Mohan Roy as well as Keshab Chandra Sen, its two significant representatives who were connected with the neo-Hindu reform organization *Brahmo Samaj* in the 19th century, tried to extract from Christianity its moral teachings. Then they made efforts to place these into their own monistic religious belief based on a non-dualistic perception of the Upanishads (Boyd 1994: 19–20). Keshab Chandra Sen moreover extended this attitude to Christianity by relentless criticism of European churches. In his opinion, they had failed to properly understand the message of the Gospel because in its historical origin it came from the Asian and Oriental rather than European environment, and so it was therefore closer to Indians than Europeans (Ibid., 61). His attempt to create a syncretic, purely Indian Christian Church called *New Dispensation* did not achieve any noticeable response outside the close circle of his sympathizers and students. Nevertheless, he represents an important pointer to the path taken by the first Indian theologians developing the theology of fulfilment at the turn of the 19th century. Due to the inclusive character of Hinduism, this process of fulfilment or completion of one religious tradition through another tradition is not one sided. Its outcome thus cannot be just the Christianization of India, but concurrently also the Hinduization of Christianity (Halbfass 1988: 226).

In the second half of the 19th century, the endeavour of missionaries to achieve new religious conversions was becoming intensely aggressive, in particular in the rural areas of southern and north-western India. A response to this came from the Indian environment in the form of numerous Hindu reform movements with a clearly profiled anti-Christian agenda (Sharpe 2001: 230). The French Catholic mission in the Madras Presidency (Bugge 1997: 97) and a number of various British Evangelical missions in Punjab (Jones 1989: 87) proved considerably successful in the last three decades of the 19th century. As part of mass conversion movements, inhabitants of whole villages were converted to Christianity there, hoping both to escape the caste oppression which they were exposed to and to obtain material assistance from missionaries or churches during natural disasters (so-called "rice-Christians", Bugge 1997: 103). It was the mass character of these conversions that became one of the main motives for establishing the reformist Hindu organization *Arya Samaj* in 1875. The attitudes of its initiator, Dayananda Saraswati, to his own as well as foreign traditions were strictly Orthodox and dogmatic (Sharma 2001: 395). The vision of "a purified Hinduism" (Jones 1989: 96) preached by him opposed all the elements within Hinduism that did not have any catechismal anchoring in the holy Vedic corpus. Unsurprisingly, he spurned Christianity as well as Islam, because their degenerated state of religious cognition, according to Dayananda, exactly corresponds to Puranic Hinduism (Halbfass 1988: 245). Through strictly fencing themselves off from Christianity and Islam alike, *Arya Samaj* and other reformist organizations of the end of the 19th century and the beginning of the 20th century tried to newly construct Hinduism as a religion clearly distinguished from the surrounding religious competitors. However, the strict demarcation of the corpus of their own holy scripts and the unequivocal formulation of the catechismal doctrine is nothing other, by its very nature, than an imitation of the manner of creating a religious identity as both large Semitic religions achieve it (Sikand 2003: 100).

The third and quite opposite consequence of the Christian criticism of the Indian civilization space was then the absolute renunciation of one's own religious tradition and the inclination toward imported Christianity, including all its cultural determinateness, emerging during the whole of the 19th century. Similarly radical development quite frequently also occurred among the Hindu social and religious elite. The passive acceptance of the foreign in the first half of the 19th century, which was so typical in the intellectual urban classes, both from traditional Christian families and also in the cases of recent converts, however started changing in its second half and at the beginning of the 20th century. Of course, the key role was played by the political context of that period and the Indian nationalism which was then forming. If we take a look at the environment of Indian Christianity, we come across several exceptional personalities there. In their life and work, there began to appear signs of intellectual and spiritual resistance to the attempts at cultural and religious dominance of European churches in India. The bold theological thoughts of Brahmabandhav Upadhyay (see Chapter 3 of this book), the social revolt of Pandita Ramabai (Frykenberg 2008: 382–410; Hedlund 2017: 53–66), the Indian Christian poetry of Narayan Vaman Tilak (Winslow 1923; Boyd 1994: 114–117) or the Franciscan "Sadhuism" of Sundar Singh (Streeter and Appasamy 1921; Boyd 1994: 92–109; Sharpe 2004; Dobe 2015) germinated the first attempts to separate Christianity from European cultural heritage. However, this time they were not carried out by foreign missionaries within their missionary strategy but by Indian

Christians themselves. They were determined to bring Christianity in the full sense to India, to express its religious practices in purely Indian terminology and develop a separate Indian Christian theology, based and drawing on the wealth of Indian religious traditions.

Reflections on fulfilment – the exclusive is becoming inclusive

Another of the approaches to the different religious and cultural environment where Christianity seeks to work is built on fulfilment theology, which dominated Christianity in India in various forms and manifestations of the theological discourse for the major part of the 20th century. The popularity of this approach is considerably connected with the relative failure of missionary activities (Halbfass 1988: 53; Frykenberg 2008: 339), at least if we compare the efforts exerted on the complete Christianization of India with its specific fruit in the form of religious conversions. The missionary failure and coming to terms with the fact that a considerable part of India refused to give up the old religious ideas and replace them with Christian tidings led to self-critical reflection. Some liberal missionaries and subsequently also theologians thus reached a new formulation of the Christian relation to the surrounding religious reality (Oddie 2006: 306–311, 313–316). In the succinct statement of the Catholic dogmatics, their effort is generally framed with a gradual change, complicatedly evolving over the whole of the 20th century, of the previous exclusivist claim of Christianity to the fullness of truth and religious revelation. While in the past this claim conditioned the possibility of salvation by affiliation to the Church ("extra ecclesiam nulla salus"), now it turned into an inclusivist claim. This tries to include the whole of humanity in God's plan of salvation accomplished through Christ ("extra Christum nulla sallus"). As Christian theologians believed, archaic religious concepts and their conveying were inherently intuitive and natural, not revealed and supernatural through the action of God's grace. However, the same now began to be seen as preparation for the acceptance of perfection and for its historical completion in Christianity – "praeparatio evangelica" (Dupuis 2001: 132). The attributing of unquestionable positive values to foreign religious traditions instead of their unequivocal repudiation was based on deeper understanding of the content of their teachings, the symbolism present in rituals, the specifics of the mythological language and also on informed awareness of the mystical dimensions of the given tradition. At the same time, direct and personal contacts between authoritative representatives of various religions were also intensified, which added an experiential plane to mutual intellectual discovery (Ibid., 131).

The very idea of fulfilment was, however, not brand new either in the history of Christianity or in the course of its development in the territory of India. Let us leave aside the Jewish context into which the messianic role of Christ is meaningfully put or, more precisely, is directly based on this context of the Gospel message so that it would subsequently bring it to fruition in line with its beliefs.[5] However, when early Christianity entered the mental space of ancient Greece, it tried to extend its understanding of God's plan of universal salvation to this space as well. The method of comprehending pre-Christian religious cults and cultures in the Mediterranean region and the resulting attitude adopted towards them as to the ideas which had been planted by God's will in fertile soil to bear fruit no sooner than in the light of the Gospel and through its intellectual interpretation (Jenkins 2002: 122) found its model expression in the famous sermon delivered by the Apostle Paul to the Athenians.[6] On the one hand, Christianity was thus opening itself up to impulses from the Greek world, with the wealth of its philosophical and religious traditions. On the other hand, it was absorbing this world into itself, accepting some of its ideological motives and modes of expression, which allowed it to newly formulate its own doctrinal content. This approach was turning Christianity into an attractive religious choice in a philosophically cultivated environment when it, in its new guise, attracted the interest of the Roman aristocracy. At the same time, it also began to understand itself in a whole new way – not just as a mere heterodox stream within the Jewish community but also as an all-encompassing worldview. It is within this that the religious aspirations of all the previous traditions and generations of humankind can find their contentment.

In India, de Nobili, in defending his missionary strategy, also referred to the same passage concerning the "unknown God" and the capacity of Christianity to adapt to a foreign cultural context. Also, the object of his interest became the educated and culturally advanced classes of the distinct religious tradition, in his case the Brahmans of Madurai. He rightly considered his activities analogous to the activities of Paul in Athens (Halbfass 1988: 41–42; Župonov 2001: 3). As already indicated, de Nobili's idea that, hidden away in Hinduism, there is the primeval idea of pure monotheism, present in the conceptually absolutized concept of *brahma* (Halbfass 1988: 40), was further developed by the next generations of Catholic and Protestant missionaries. However, at the turn of the 19th century, the contemplated idea of fulfilment occurred in a new period context, outer and inner, religious and political. The religious concepts of Hinduism were not to be automatically dismissed but rather led through Christianity to purification and the achievement of perfection (Ibid., 51). The advocates of the idea of fulfilment and their motives and aspirations also underwent substantial transformation.

An important historical milestone in self-understanding and self-presentation of Hinduism face to face with the Western (Ibid., 228), and to a large extent still Christian, world was undoubtedly the World's Parliament of Religions, which was held in Chicago in 1893 (Boyd 1994: 86). At the same time, it was the beginning of a new phase in creating the Western image of India or the notion of it. Representatives of traditional as well as thoroughly modern

Hindu schools and religious movements made their assertive appearance on the same intellectual platform there as authoritative representatives of various Christian churches and also other major world religions. Thus, the direction was set for the future debate about religious pluralism. There were some common principles of spirituality and religious experience formulated across denominations, which were not necessarily seen as competing with one another. As a result, the process of the end of the cultural and eventually also political hegemony of Western Christian civilization began (Collins 2006: 40–41). The emancipated cultures of the third world countries were gradually abandoning the imposed role of non-independent, parented nations that had received abundant favours by obediently adopting the cultural traits of Christian Europe. On the contrary, they increasingly began to turn to their own traditions, which sometimes even successfully penetrated beyond the borders of their original civilization circuits. This was attracting the interest of the Western public, thus shaping the understanding of India in contemporaneous Europe and the United States, such as, for example, in the case of various spiritual currents arising within Neo-Hinduism. In the 20th century, in particular from its second half, the relationship of subordination and dependence was rapidly changing into a partnership but subsequently also into a new competition. However, the power positions of the opponents were completely newly defined because the seeking of one's own cultural roots easily becomes a welcomed cause of intolerant nationalistic passions.

For the future activities of Christian non-Catholic churches and missionaries in India, the World's Missionary Conference held in Edinburgh in 1910 was as important as the interfaith meeting in Chicago (Frykenberg 2008: 340). On the one hand the Indian delegates, who represented the young churches of their homeland, contributed to the ecumenical spirit of the Conference (Collins 2006: 42). They presented themselves there as the sovereign voice of the new missionary movement which was to be carried forward by indigenous, not European, missionaries (Boyd 1994: 88). On the other hand, they also clearly formulated their new attitude to the autochthonous religious traditions of India. As part of the fulfilment theology, which became the supporting idea of the whole conference, the Christian relation to Hinduism had changed from a generally rejecting standpoint to a sympathizing effort at understanding. This effort seeks and finds noble motives in a foreign religious tradition, which are recognized as "the work of the Holy Spirit" (Commission on the Missionary Message: Hinduism; cit. according to Ariarajah 1991: 27) and its preparation for accepting Christianity.

The famous book by the Scottish missionary of the London Missionary Society, John Nicol Farquhar (1913), became a classical rendering of the fulfilment theology. Its author developed in it the older ideas of an evolutionary religious theory according to which all lower religions had been inevitably heading towards their fulfilment in the higher religion (Boyd 1994: 89). According to this theory, Christianity had been understood as the only religion in the true sense of the word. By fulfilment Farquhar means, on the one hand, the achievement of all spiritual goals and religious aspirations that Hinduism pursues. Furthermore, he also expects the transformation of its religious knowledge and experience into the higher form offered and represented by Christianity. Last but not least, albeit from a long-term perspective, he also supposes replacing Hinduism as such with Christianity, which is inevitable from the logic of the process of this fulfilment (Sharpe 1965: 339). However, the semantic content of fulfilment theology would vary in the course of the upcoming decade and de facto the whole of the 20th century (Hedges 2001: 26). In particular, Catholic theologians of the second half of the century (J. Daniélou, H. de Lubac, K. Rahner, R. Panikkar etc.) significantly contributed to its further differentiation. Along with this, the consequences of this theological view of religious otherness in the form of a newly sought and established relation and the missionary attitude to Hinduism were also changing.

The fulfilment theology, as it expressed itself in India at the turn of the 19th century, responded to the religious streams originating within Neo-Hinduism and profiled in an inclusivist manner (Halbfass 1988: 52). No less, however, did it respond also to the growing nationalist sentiments in Indian society and, last but not least, to the Church and religious mobilization of indigenous Christian laity. Those most distinct of them (Nehemiah Goreh, Krishna Mohan Banerjee, Brahmabandhav Upadhyay etc.), however, did not come from the backward, economically and socially disadvantaged segments of Indian society that the Evangelical missions targeted so hard in the 19th century. On the contrary, their home environment was the traditional, educated Brahmanic circles that began demanding the rehabilitation of their original cultural and religious world in close connection with national emancipation. Under their influence, the religious concepts from the Brahmanic perspective of Hinduism were thus becoming the focus of attention of fulfilment theology. Its prioritization as a representative religious class was also supported by the continuing interest of European Orientalists and Indologists in this Sanskritized form of Indian religion. Through their mediation, the significantly orientalized, romanticizing, exotic-mystical notion of Hinduism, or rather the whole world of ideas of India, was then construed in Europe. It subsequently became an object of the spiritual fascination that Europe experienced with respect to India for the major part of the 20th century and also the projection screen for theological reflections on fulfilment.

The broadly conceived topic of fulfilment theology will appear in this book many times. It is from its concepts of the relation of Christianity to religious otherness, no matter how varying they were in the course of the 20th century, that the theoretical ideas of inculturation of Christianity in India are based on. The same holds true regarding the so far perhaps most substantial attempt at their implementation in practice in the form of the Christian Ashram Movement.

The struggle of Christian Dalits for liberation and religions in conflict

By no means can all missionaries and theologians active in 20th-century India be considered proponents of fulfilment theology. Frykenberg even describes this new liberal theological stream as elitist from the very outset. It was carried forward by European missionaries coming from the higher social classes, and so, in Frykenberg's opinion, it was relevant only for Indian social classes with a similar status (2008: 339). In the 1980s, the hopes placed on the attempted inculturation of Christianity in India were called into question, specifically as to what stream of Indian culture should actually be chosen for the intended process. The interest of missionaries in the religious thinking of Hinduism, which ushered in the development of fulfilment theology, was always focused exclusively on the Sanskrit tradition. The world of ideas of Vedas, the Upanishads, *Bhagavadgita* or classical philosophical *darshanas* was thus gradually discovered. Several remarkable attempts were also made to express the Christian idea of the Holy Trinity by means of the monistic terminology of *Advaita Vedanta*. The bravest and the most radical representatives of fulfilment theology even entered into active dialogue with authentic bearers of Hindu tradition. As common *sadhakas*, they would sit at the feet of Hindu gurus, become disciples of errant holy men or practise some of the meditation techniques in the seclusion of Himalayan hermitages. However, this stream of Indian religion is inherently linked to the so-called high, Brahmanic culture. It was Brahmans who fostered it over centuries. For a long time, they were also its exclusive proponents and guardians, in actual fact having a monopoly on it. But nearly three-quarters of Indian Christians come from the other end of the social spectrum, from very low castes or from the social layers of Dalits, who on the contrary stand entirely outside the caste system, according to the Brahmanical concepts of traditional social codes. Therefore, the tradition of high culture can hardly offer them any appropriate and rewarding stimuli in the form of compelling religious answers or help them to consolidate their own unique religious identity (Evers 2005: 474). Indeed, this culture actually marginalized them for a long time, and the constitutive rules of this culture even exposed them to permanent social, economic and religious oppression. It was only in the 20th century that they sought and found possible escape routes from it.

The political emancipation of Dalits in India inevitably left its marks on the development of Christianity in India (Webster 2009: 204–205). It started unnoticeably as early as with India gaining independence in 1947. However, it thundered and literally shook the political scene with a vengeance in some Indian states in the 1990s, and also Indian society as such. It was from among the proponents of Dalit rights that the criticism of fulfilment theology and the inculturation concept arising from it emerged at the end of the 1970s. They warned against the threat of the Hinduization or more precisely

Brahmanization of Christianity and the danger of religious syncretism. At the same time, they pointed to the scant knowledge of the social conditions in which Dalits were forced to live in India and the need for adequate reflection of the situation on the part of the Church (Frykenberg 2008: 340–341). The initiative was, however, taken over by Dalits themselves or the theologians who emerged in their ranks (for example, Arvind P. Nirmal, perhaps the most distinctive of them so far) from the second half of the 1980s. They found inspiration for expressing their needs in liberation theology as it had developed in Latin America in the middle of the century but freed from its Marxist political overtones.

The Dalit theology as it thus started to be formed gained complete control of the theological thinking of Indian Christianity at the turn of the millennium (Webster 2009: 311). It turned its attention to social topics such as the effort to achieve the cultural and religious emancipation of those who were expelled from Hindu temples only to be frequently automatically assigned an inferior position in Christian churches, where they sought refuge (Ibid., 222–223). This has created for the time being the most recent attitude of Christianity to the Indian religious context. A typical characteristic of this is defiance and resistance to the dominant culture of India as well as to the church structures that have largely adjusted themselves to the social rules of this culture. This time, however, the defiance comes from the grassroots and from within the Christian community, not as an epiphenomena of external religious-power intervention. This approach is quite understandably mostly expressed in an activist, combative manner, fighting against the culture of oppression and for the liberation of Dalits. Over the last two decades of the 20th century, fuel has been abundantly added to their confrontational nature face to face with the majority caste religion as the intolerant communalistic sentiments have been culminating in Indian society. To no lesser extent, however, the violence targeting Christians has also rapidly increased. It has been occurring since the second half of the 1990s, in particular in areas inhabited by indigenous tribes, among whom a variety of charismatic churches today develop their activities with the greatest intensity (Bauman 2015: 52). It is the missionaries of the Pentecostal churches who represent a very important element of the political-social context in which the current Dalit theology of liberation takes place. Due to their proselyte activities with an intensely aggressive emphasis placed on further religious conversions, they are seen by Hindu nationalists as a direct threat to the traditional social organization of Indian society (Ibid., 55). The violent conflicts, whether in Gujarat in 1998 (Kanungo 2002: 250–252) or in Odisha in 2007 (Bauman 2010: 263–290), virtually always have a tragic ending for the Christian minority, regardless of their trigger. The role of the victim, in which Christianity in India currently finds itself on a regular basis, thus strengthens the fear of losing their own fragile religious identity. As a result, it however encloses Christians into the relative safety of social and cultural ghettos. On a more subtle theological plane, the aspects that Dalit theologians then emphasize in Christian tidings are helplessness and suffering. In the role of the suffering Saviour, they see a perfect model of their own life situation, not only a parable of the existential determinateness of human life inevitably ending in death but understandable transcultural expression of the fate of the oppressed. It is exactly for them that the cross and following resurrection represent the hope of freedom achievable through the resurrection while still on earth (Webster 2009: 299).

To be able to understand the Dalit theology of liberation, the development of which has been unusually progressive over the last two decades, but also the more general relation of Indian Christianity to Hinduism today, it is necessary to put the relation into the religious and political context of post-colonial India. With the achievement of Indian independence in 1947, Christianity unquestionably lost a major political supporter of its numerous activities. This happened regardless of how problematic the links which some churches or missionary personalities often had to the British colonial administration were in the previous period. Representatives of religious minorities successfully asserted their right to freedom of religion, its practice and also further spreading in the wording of the Constitution of India (article 25). Nevertheless, the heated debates in the Constituent Assembly associated with the issue of religious conversions (Kim 2003: 42–55; Kashyap 1988: 131–167) clearly signalled the future developments of relations between the religious majority and minority in the secular state. Christians of many different denominations have been actively engaged in the struggle for political freedom since the 1920s. However, they perceived their concern about their existence in the independent state, the political course of which was supposed to be set by the Hindu majority, to be well founded after India won its independence. After all, religious conversions and missionary activities had already been regulated by law and restricted in many areas of North India, primarily in the territory of the Princely States, since the second half of the 1930s (Kim 2003: 38–39). A negative attitude to proselyte activities was also expressed by leading personalities in the struggle for national freedom, including M. K. Gandhi.[7] In their view, the activities of missionaries among the backward segments of Indian society, that is, specifically Dalits, could lead to weakening national political unity and further differentiation of an all-too-fragile common cultural identity.

Already in the first decade of the existence of the independent Indian state, attempts at state control and regulation of activities carried out by churches emerged along with the regulation of missionary operations. A precedent in this respect was set by the report of the commission of inquiry into the missionary activities in the territory of the Indian state of Madhya Pradesh, the so-called *Niyogi Report*.[8] On the basis of the commission's recommendation, anti-conversion laws were passed in the territories of the Indian states of Madhya Pradesh and Odisha in the second half of the 1960s. The legislation outlawed religious conversions of persons under the age of eighteen years and conversions motivated by material gain or aggressive rhetoric targeting other religions (Kim 2003: 207–210). In the following decades, the governments of other states of the Indian Union (Arunachal Pradesh in 1978, here moreover with a considerably disputed definition of the category of local, that is, state-protected, religions) resorted to similar legislative measures (Ibid., 211–212). As a result, these anti-conversion laws contributed to the deepening of the antagonistic relations between Christianity and Hinduism because they sharpened the focus on different religious identities as perceived by members of both communities. This is inevitably reflected in all aspects of their individual and collective life and is therefore naturally subject to the enforcing of one's own interests at the expense of the others in the contradictory categories *us* versus *them*.

The numerous organizational branches spreading from the common ideological platform of contemporary Hindu nationalism as represented by the National Volunteer Organization (*Rashtriya Swayamsevak Sangh*, RSS) contributed to the conflicting tension between Hindus and Christians. The ideological direction of RSS and its relation to Indian religious minorities was set by the historic second leader of this organization, the so-called *sarsanghchalak*, Madhav Sadashiv Golwalkar. In his influential book *Bunch of Thoughts*, he elaborated upon the concept of the common national identity of the inhabitants of India, so-called *Hindutva*, which had already been proposed by Vinayak Damodar Savarkar in the 1930s. This concept is built on demands for the active adoption of the indigenous, that is, Hindu, culture, personal identification with the country and its inhabitants and the demand for a religious relation to India as the Holy Land – "punyabhumi" (Savarkar 2005: 84). The members of the extraneous religious minorities that could not fit into this concept for historical reasons or on the principle of their religious teaching, these being Islam and Christianity, were declared "Internal Threats" to the Indian nation by Golwalkar, following on from his predecessor (Golwalkar 1996: 233). In his opinion, primarily Christian missionaries operating in underdeveloped areas with a significant proportion of the indigenous population threaten the common cultural heritage and thus the unity of the country. It is their proselyte activities that one of the most active branches of RSS, the World Hindu Council (*Vishva Hindu Parishad*, VHP) opposes (Jaffrelot 1996: 193 et seq.). VHP was established in 1964 and in connection with the increase in communalistic passions in Indian society became the most vocal campaigner against the ongoing religious conversions in the 1980s (Sarkar 1999: 1697). Through a number of its affiliated organizations, for example, *Vanavasi Kalyan Ashram*, VHP has attempted to implement its complex ideological programme. Its goal is not only to create a counterbalance to the activities of Christian churches in indigenous areas but concurrently also to liberate Christian converts from the influence of churches and bring them back to the Hinduism fold through the cleansing rites of reconversion.[9] The violent clashes between Christian missionaries and Hindu activists in the underdeveloped regions of the states of Madhya Pradesh, Odisha, Gujarat, Rajasthan, Karnataka and others that have occurred quite regularly since the second half of the 1990s are a sad testimony to the intense conflict situation in which both religions currently find themselves.

Characteristic features of Christianity in India

The brief overview of the various approaches of Christianity to the Indian environment has hopefully provided a sufficiently true picture of the key moments in its history. At the same time, it has also drawn attention to how, alongside the changing relations to religious and cultural reality, the form of Christianity itself also changed. The aim of this review was not to once again retell the history that has already been rendered many times. After all, it would not be relevant for the topic of the book. The intention was only to highlight the trends in developments and suggest their possible causes. What is, on the other hand, absolutely crucial for the subject of the Christian Ashram Movement are the general characteristic features of Christianity in India. As a matter of fact, they may well be the consequences or side effects of its historical development that Christianity and Christians carry today as a burden of their heritage. The significance of these features for the subject of the Christian Ashram Movement lies in the fact that its leaders perceive many of them in a critical manner. They struggle to eliminate them, to limit their scope of influence or at least to somehow respond to them. Many of these traits can even be described as immediate causes and motives underpinning the origination of the idea of Christian ashrams itself.

Foreignness as a programme?

Despite the long history of Christianity in India, this religion is still perceived as a foreign import. It is an extraordinary historical paradox if we compare the community of Saint Thomas Christians, which by its own tradition dates as far back as the first century, and, for example, the medieval *bhakti* movement that started to dominate in Hinduism many centuries later. Christianity has never managed to put down roots in Indian soil so deep as to allow the actual crown of its tree to transform through them. When we proceed from the first impressions that every visitor takes away with him or her on the basis of a simple empirical observation, the following picture will reveal itself to us: the architecture of Christian churches and cathedrals in India is European, most often neo-classical; the casual, everyday apparel of priests, monks and nuns completely ignores indigenous habits and customs – it does not even reflect the demanding climatic conditions in India; the rituals taking place in temples or prayer rooms mostly exactly correspond to European models, including the symbolical gestures with religious meaning, ceremonial robes of participating celebrants, the objects of worship or music accompanying the rituals (with the honourable exception of a portable harmonium that is always present in Indian Christianity, being occasionally accompanied by rhythmical tabla); the Catholic believers earnestly worship saints born and active outside India; the kitsch holy images that Christians decorate their homes with and that therefore significantly shape their identity because they are an integral part of their daily lives look as if they came straight from a market of religious objects in any of the pilgrimage sites in Europe; Christian festivals and the religious festivities that individual churches organize with much fanfare somewhat take place outside the context of the local environment, outside the line of the agricultural year in India, which significantly differs from the agricultural year line in Europe; the official form of the life cycle transition rituals seems to be unsatisfactory, and believers therefore complement or replace them in privacy with customary rituals of the respective caste community, the continuity of which has not been disrupted even by conversion to Christianity; the major language of the church service in an urban environment remains English, but also, where indigenous languages are used, the foreignness in the forms of expression is quite striking in that idioms and metaphors do not have any links to the world of India; English completely dominates all of the Christian educational institutions and is also the only language medium of training centres and seminars where Indian priests are moulded and whose cultural knowledge of other Indian religions is moreover considerably limited, mostly based on deep-rooted prejudices; these future spiritual shepherds undergo many years studying the classical European languages that the culture of Europe was weaned on but come into contact with the classical language of their own country, Sanskrit, only exceptionally, thanks only to their personal motivation and self-studying; the most gifted Indian theologians are sent by their churches to further study at the respective European, and today increasingly also American, church centres, where some impulses leading to a deeper interest in their own culture can hardly be expected;[10] the church structures and hierarchical relations between their individual levels slavishly imitate the system that has developed in Europe under completely different historical conditions; the top representatives of individual churches are virtually always selected or approved by authorities in the centres located outside India, often too distant to be able to adequately reflect the needs and interests of Indian Christians; the Christian theological discourse and also intellectual life as such happens in isolation, without relations and enriching contacts with a non-Christian environment, despite repeated invitations for interreligious dialogue, and so many educational centres or institutions established with this motivation turned into libraries or rather mere book-collecting facilities or into university departments with an obvious Christian orientation; because a considerable number of Indian Christians belong to poorer social classes, huge financial means keep flowing into India from abroad, being designated for the construction of churches, maintenance and further development of Christian hospitals, institutional care facilities, schools of various levels and types, hectic missionary activities in the areas inhabited by indigenous tribes, where Christianity clashes with Hinduism on a real or imaginary battlefield and last but not least for the operation itself of the complex bureaucratic machinery of churches.[11] Christians are still considered a foreign element in India. They themselves often actually feel like that, and the sense of having a different cultural identity is seemingly even programmatically fostered in them. As a result, they therefore remain strangers in their own country (Amaladoss 2005: 3).

The expressions of the foreignness of Christianity in India constitute a convoluted complexity with many mutually conditioning factors, and it is the same with the causes of this foreign character. Its essence arises from the historical fact that Christianity, like Islam, came to India with religious answers that had already been definitely resolved (Puthanangady 1997: 183). However, the answers were formulated in a different language, with all its semantic connotations. They were originating outside the cultural and religious context of India, unconnected to it and its previous development. Christianity was bringing to India in particular an institutionalized religion, not a new religious experience. Its will to share the content of its own faith was scant, let alone to reformulate it under the influence of the local environment or enrich it with yet-unknown stimuli. Even the oldest community of Saint Thomas Christians, which had perfectly integrated itself into the Indian pluralistic society at the social and cultural level, did not further develop its tradition in India from the point of view of its internal theological development. During its more than thousand-year-long isolation from the Christian world, it had remained unchanged regarding both the official liturgical language and doctrine as well as the system of the ecclesiastic structure. Similarly orthodox guardians of the tradition subsequently became Portuguese and other Catholic missionaries. These were firmly doctrinally rooted in the theological system that had been finally refined in Europe. During their activities in India, it was as if they were intensively preventing any attempts at the contextualization of the Gospel message in India (Jathanna 1986: 61), let alone the development of indigenous theological thinking. It is no surprise, then, that when such efforts appeared in the 19th century, they met with categorical rejection, which was moreover often aggressively worded, or rather reprobation by ecclesiastical authorities or even common missionaries. No matter whether these efforts came from Indian converts like Brahmabandhav Upadhyay or reformers of Hinduism such as, for example, Ram Mohan Roy, who drew his inspiration from Christian ethics, played little part in it. Daring independent thinking, which an original theology of Indian Christianity could have germinated from, was not supported even at formative educational institutions and sacerdotal seminaries. These produced zealous evangelists, preachers and pastors but not theologians (Tenneth 2005: 4–5).

The main cause and concurrently also manifestation of the continuing foreignness of Christianity in India was and up to now often still is the negative attitude of Christians towards other Indian religions, primarily the majority Hinduism. Since the arrival of the Portuguese, the Christian relation to the surrounding religious environment had been defining itself for many centuries virtually only through missiology and denunciatory theology (John 1997: 134). Within its context, not only the religion but also the majority of its cultural expressions were deplored. This position was further boosted during the 19th century in connection with British colonial rule and in harmony with it the sense of the cultural superiority of Western civilization, from which and with the legacy of which missionaries were arriving. The flaunted foreignness thus became an external distinguishing feature of affiliation to the seemingly more advanced civilization circuit. Accordingly, it also became a means for defining a new religious identity of converts towards their original religious environment, which they were struggling to leave by their conversion (Kuttiyanikkal 2014: 60).

The unfulfilled ideal of unity in diversity

Another of the general characteristic features has accompanied Christianity in India since the middle of the 17th century. In 1653, in a negative response to the increasing push for ecclesiastical and power dominance of the Portuguese clergy, a part of the community of Saint Thomas Christians from Kerala decided to return to the archaic Syrian rite. Instead of being obedient to the Roman Pope, whose representative in India was the Archbishop of Goa, the Saint Thomas Christians wished to accept the jurisdiction of the Jacobite Patriarch of Antioch (Frykenberg 2008: 136). This led to the first but far from last Christian schism in the territory of India. After all, it is the disunity of individual churches that is typical for India. Since the 19th century, many churches have been active there, and their numbers grow as the popularity of various Pentecostal movements and charismatic communities continues to increase. However, each of them seemingly brings to India a whole complex of mutual antagonisms, which can often be found at the root of their origin and differentiation in far distant Europe and in modern times in the United States. Christian missions then quite rightly seem to be "an export of divisions" (Evers 2005: 516). However, this does not have any historical justification in India and as a result leads to weakening the common Christian identity. Attempts at unification had already been made in the block of Protestant churches since the beginning of the 20th century. However, they were initially motivated by the effort to achieve a common missionary strategy, later to be initiated by the political and social pressure that the churches felt exposed to after an independent India was established. As mentioned before, over the last decades, Christians have increasingly become a target of chauvinistically manifested Hindu nationalism. Today's efforts to create a common organizational platform for a minority religion are therefore motivated by concerns for its own safety and existence. It is then always unity that is sought in order to secure common protection.

Virtually all the churches active in India are "transplanted churches", which have failed to become a firm, integrated part of Indian culture. Strictly speaking, they are not Indian churches but only "churches in India" (Kunnumpuram 1997: 156). At the same time, Christianity failed in fulfilling the ideal of universality, proclaimed Catholicism or, as expressed by the favourite Indian cultural idiom, unity in diversity. What remains today from the many years of missionary activities is only diverse multiplicity. Each of its components keeps the rigid purity of its belief and distance from the others or in extreme cases even shows intolerance towards them. If some day any churches are successfully developed that are Indian in the fullest sense, their necessary and natural feature would be contrarily their interconnected diversity. Seen as a religious complex, they would have to show a reciprocal relationship in diversity – although the individual parts would preserve their own specifics, whether regional, linguistic or ritual, together they would create a community of plurality.

Desire for conversions

The issues related to religious conversions are a permanent stigma for Christianity in India. Not even the already mentioned foreignness instigates such negative reactions from the majority society as does clinging to the right to promote and spread their religious belief, which Christian churches refuse to renounce. The religious conversions issue can arouse hidden passions and change seeming tolerance into violence even among Indian citizens who are secular minded or religiously indifferent and have rid themselves of personally experienced religiousness. Christians, on the contrary, understand any attempt of the Indian state to prevent conversions, or at least regulate them, as a direct attack against the very essence of their religion. They respond to them with a mobilizing hysteria in their own community much like that of the Indian Muslims who have steadfastly resisted the efforts to create a unified civil code since an independent India was constituted.

No other religious system attaches such supreme importance to conversion in the life of an individual and society as Christianity. The existence and historical development of Christianity are perhaps hardly imaginable without the theological justification of conversion and its fixed doctrinal anchoring in religious teachings. The absolute exclusivist claim, which Christianity identifies with the person of Jesus Christ and his good tidings (the Gospel), is to be a once-and-for-all valid atemporal appeal addressed to mankind. It is only through a positive response to this call that time itself and man in it achieve sense. No other religious system presents an individual with such a categorical, and by its consequences, definitive choice. According to the Christian conception, this choice can transform not only an individual himself or herself but the whole world. Despite the religious conflicts taking place across denominations, which relate to the essential theological aspects of religious teachings, all of the Christian churches express themselves in unison on this issue – Christ's Gospel can be either accepted or rejected; there is no middle way: "Go into all the world and proclaim the good news to the whole creation. The one who believes and is baptized will be saved; but the one who does not believe will be condemned" (Mark 16, 15–16).

Such a decided attitude to the surrounding environment and its religious difference does not, in effect, open up much space for interfaith dialogue. At the same time, it also places considerable demands on Christians themselves, all the more so if they represent a religious minority in a certain society. Furthermore, the evaluation of the quality of Christian life and success of Christian activities in a given country or historical period is usually, in accordance with the logic of the cited Gospel passage, derived from the success or failure of missions.[12] In countries where missionary activities did not bring any of the desired results in the form of majority Christianization, churches are subsequently denied a greater degree of autonomy. Authorities in respective church centres view them as not being mature enough to be able to decide independently about their own direction in all seriousness. On the contrary, they are often considered to be exposed to permanent danger lurking in the adverse effect of the religious context in which these churches must exist. The complex of the excruciated Messiah that Christianity has developed in India in this way will manifest itself after every communalistic clash with majority Hinduism. Its victims, as previously stated, are always Christians, regardless of the causes of the conflict. Not even in the face of the tragic consequences of violence would Indian churches back away from their claim for conversions, although it is often their missionary activities that provoke aggression. Quite the opposite, victims within their own ranks seemingly only entrench the churches in the roles of martyrs. Many missionary organizations of charismatic churches, which are the most active in seeking further religious conversions today, then depict contemporary India as a real battlefield. In their minds, modern martyrs of the Christian mission wage uneven battles every day, at the risk of their own lives, with fanatical Hindus. Such an attitude may perhaps contribute to the deeper integration of Indian Christians themselves, to strengthen them at the moments when they are exposed to religious persecution and to secure them material and spiritual support from abroad. However, in other religious communities of India, it will hardly raise a sense of trust and willingness to develop mutual relations.

Many ecclesiastical professions and the spirituality of service

One of the most remarkable features of Christianity in India, which will come to the fore in the fullest sense in particular after the previously mentioned critical remarks, is the exceptionally high number of ecclesiastical professions. If the essential criterion of the inner strength of a religion in a territory were the number of its ecclesiastical professionals, India would be a Christian superpower. Priests, pastors and nuns, active in both missionary organizations and educational and social institutions nowadays, leave in particular the South Indian states of Kerala and Tamil Nadu for other regions of India and currently also for territories far beyond the borders of the country. The reasons for this plenteous harvest have not been convincingly analyzed as yet. No study has appeared based on a reliable sociological survey that would reveal why the choice of an ecclesiastical profession is so attractive to Indian Christians and what exactly makes it such. This attractiveness possibly results to some extent from the economic and social status of the large majority of Christians. As mentioned previously, Christians in India come more from underdeveloped and disadvantaged segments of society, both materially and in terms of their chance to access education. Therefore, the choice of an ecclesiastical career may be a way of improving their own status for many of them. Thanks to this choice made by one of their members, poor families are often relieved of a heavy economic burden and, at the same time, their prestige in the respective community grows as a result. The figure of a clergyman, in particular of a parish priest, much less, however, if he belongs to a church congregation, not to mention monks and nuns, still maintains a sacred aura of uniqueness. In the rural environment in particular, a priest remains someone whose opinion regarding both mundane and everyday problems is always reflected and has considerable weight in collective decision-making. However, this at the same time deepens the gap between the clergy and the Christian laity, who seem to live in two completely separate worlds. It is no coincidence that greater mobilization of the laity and their participation in religious life is considered one of the major challenges that the churches in India face today. The leaders of reform movements and also, as we will see, Christian ashrams have already been calling for it for several decades.

Insurmountable differences between the laity and the clergy stand out all the more if we look at the composition of the elites of the respective churches, whether in terms of the Episcopal congregations in the Catholic Church or representative authorities of the Protestant churches. The top-level posts of the complicated ecclesiastical hierarchy are almost always dominated by clergy coming from South Indian states and higher socio-economic classes. Hand in hand with this, they derive their origin, even though unofficially, yet still evidently, from the upper castes. And vice versa, representatives from the ranks of Dalits or the indigenous population (*adivasis*), whom the missionary activities primarily target today, are virtually missing in the top but also middle positions of the ecclesiastical structures.

One field where the numerous activities of Christians in India have been distinctive since the 19th century is education. While free state education is in a precarious condition, the schools enjoying the highest social prestige are operated by Christian churches. Through scholarships and grants, those who belong to the lowest segments can study there side by side with members of the highest and middle social classes and, it should be noted, regardless of their religious persuasion. After all, a number of prominent figures of Indian cultural and political life obtained their education exactly in this way. However, they are far from being just elite facilities. Christian churches indeed operate schools of all types and levels in India. In particular, the instruction in English or at least the increased emphasis placed on it attracts the interest of a broad population. Today, good knowledge of English is considered, to the detriment and exclusion of Indian languages, a necessary condition of good employment and a successful professional career.

With regard to the dominant role in mediating education, the utterly minimal political engagement of Christians in the life of the Indian state will be surprising. With the exception of the tense moments of the previously mentioned communal violence or the cases when the interests of the entire Christian community become imminently endangered by the political steps of the ruling party, as, for example, towards the end of the 1950s in Kerala, Christians do not engage en masse in socio-political protest movements. It is as if they would always prefer to stand outside it deliberately, in the safety of their parallel world. None of the national political parties of India therefore feel any need to systematically build their electoral base among Christians. Even in those Indian states where Christians make up a sizeable minority, their political preferences often change every single electoral period.

On the contrary, as in other countries of the world, the energetic activity of Christians is highly visible whenever a natural catastrophe strikes India. Charitable religious organizations convey humanitarian aid and run refugee camps. After all, it is the involvement in the social sector in the broadest sense that is somewhat of a generally comprehensible byword for Christianity. This fact harbours in itself far-reaching consequences. The identity of Christianity in India has more of an institutional than religious character. It is through religious institutions of various types and focus that Christianity interacts with its surroundings. The Indian environment recognizes and respects Christianity through education, charity, hospitals, shelters for the disabled and abandoned and so on. However, it is de facto identified with these generally beneficial activities. Outside of them or above them it is as if there was nothing in it. After all, many Indian Christians have no idea at all that there is a spiritual plane in their own religion and that Christianity can offer it to them. It seems they do not even expect any thought-provoking impulses to their spiritual quest and personal growth from it. Christianity in India always abounded in enthusiastic missionaries, reformers of education, effective church organizers and also completely extraordinary personalities developing the spirituality of the service. However, we find only very few traces of great spiritual leaders or mystics in it. The increased emphasis placed on experimental religious experience, which seems to be typical for the Indian environment across the history of its religious thinking and which greatly contributed, for example, to the development of medieval Islamic mysticism, seemingly left virtually no mark on the form of Christianity in India.

Notes

1. According to the data from the census of 2011; see Office of the Registrar General & Census Commissioner, India, 2001 [online]. Retrieved from: www.censusindia.gov.in/2011census/Religion_PCA.html.
2. Frykenberg, however, relativizes this older version of Forrester when he considers it historically unprovable (Frykenberg 2008: 115).
3. The widespread prejudices that the Hindus held against missionaries and, through them, against the whole of Christianity are aptly described by the German Lutheran C. F. Schwartz, operating in India in the middle of the 18th century (Pearson 1835: 89–94).
4. The activities of Francis Xavier in India are associated mainly with mass conversions or rather mass conversion movements that are most probably unparalleled throughout the history of Christianity in India in their scope, in particular the numbers of new converts acquired during a relatively short period of time (Pearson 1987: 118, 121, 128). The missionary himself gives an apt description of his relation to the foreign religious context in his regular letters to the fellow brothers in his order, for example: "When all are baptized I order the temples of their false gods to be destroyed and all the idols to be broken to pieces" (Kuriakose 2006: 33).
5. "Do not think that I have come to abolish the law or the prophets; I have come not to abolish but to fulfil" Matthew 5, 17.
6. "Athenians, I see how extremely religious you are in every way. For as I went through the city and looked carefully at the objects of your worship, I found among them an altar with the inscription, 'To an unknown god'. What therefore you worship as unknown, this I proclaim to you" Acts 17, 22–23.
7. Gandhi's objections to conversions are aptly summarized by (Kim 2003: 24).
8. *Report of the Christian Missionary Activities Enquiry Committee (Madhya Pradesh)*. New Delhi: All India (Hindu) Dharma Sewa Sangha, 1954.
9. The older concept of reconversion, *shuddhi*, as it was understood and presented by neo-Hindu *Arya Samaj*, is in the vocabulary of VHP mostly replaced with ideologically more explicit terms of *paravartan* (literally turning around, returning back) or *ghar vapasi* (literally returning home) (Bauman 2015: 49).
10. With a few honourable exceptions, among whom D. S. Amalorpavadass, who will be repeatedly mentioned in this book, noticeably stands out from the other Indian theologians studying abroad.
11. The previously mentioned enumeration is a criticism through a foreigner's eyes; however, similar observations are also made by many Indian authors (e.g. John 1997: 128).
12. For example, Pope John Paul II in *Redemptoris Missio*, the papal encyclical, in which he responds to the changed missionary conditions in the globalized world: "For in the Church's history, missionary drive has always been a sign of vitality, just as its lessening is a sign of a crisis of faith. [. . .] For missionary activity renews the Church, revitalizes faith and Christian identity, and offers fresh enthusiasm and new incentive. Faith is strengthened when it is given to others!" (*Redemptoris Missio* 1990: par. 71).

References

Amaladas, Anand. 1993. "Dialogue between Hindus and the St. Thomas Christians." In *Hindu Christian Dialogue, Perspective and Encounters*. Edited by Harold Coward. New Delhi: Motilal Banarsidas Publishers, pp. 13–27.

Amaladoss, Michael. 2005. *Beyond Inculturation: Can the Many Be One?* New Delhi: Vidyajyoti Education & Welfare Society/ISPCK.

Ariarajah, Wesley. 1991. *Hindus and Christians: A Century of Protestant Ecumenical Thought*. Amsterdam: Editions Rodopi.

Barnes, Michael. 2004. *Theology and the Dialogue of Religions*. Cambridge: Cambridge University Press.

Bauman, Chad M. 2010. "Identity, Conversion and Violence: Dalits, Adivasis and the 2007–08 Riots in Orissa." In *Margins of Faith: Dalit and Tribal Christianity in India*. Edited by Rowena Robinson and Joseph Marianus Kujur. New Delhi: Sage, pp. 263–290.

Bauman, Chad M. 2015. *Pentecostals, Proselyzation, and Anti-Christian Violence in Contemporary India*. Oxford: Oxford University Press.

Bauman, Chad M. and Richard Fox Young, editors. 2014. *Constructing Indian Christianities: Culture, Conversion and Caste*. New Delhi: Routledge.

Bayly, Susan. 1989. *Saints, Goddesses and Kings: Muslims and Christians in South India Society 1700–1900*. Cambridge: Cambridge University Press.

Boyd, Robin. 1994. *An Introduction to Indian Christian Theology*. New Delhi: ISPCK.

Brown, L. W. 1956. *The Indian Christians of St Thomas: An Account of the Ancient Syrian Church of Malabar*. Cambridge: Cambridge University Press.

Bugge, Henriette. 1997. "The French Mission and the Mass Movements." In *Religious Conversion Movements in South Asia: Continuities and Change, 1800–1900*. Edited by Geoffrey A. Oddie. London: Routledge, pp. 97–108.

Collins, Paul. 2006. *Context, Culture and Worship: The Quest for "Indian/ness"*. New Delhi: ISPCK.

Copley, Antony. 1997. *Religions in Conflict: Ideology, Cultural Contact and Conversion in Late-Colonial India*. New Delhi: Oxford University Press.

Correia-Afonso, John. 1969. *Jesuit Letters and India History, 1542–1773*. Bombay: Oxford University Press.

Dobe, Timothy S. 2015. *Hindu Christian Faqir: Modern Monks, Global Christianity, and Indian Sainthood*. Oxford: Oxford University Press.

Dupuis, Jacques. 2001. *Toward a Christian Theology of Religious Pluralism*. Anand: Gujarat Sahitya Prakash.

Evers, Georg. 2005. *The Churches in Asia*. New Delhi: ISPCK.

Falcao, Nelson M. 2003. *Kristapurana: A Christian-Hindu Encounter: A Study of Inculturation in the Kristapurana of Thomas Stephens, S.J. (1549–1619)*. Gujarat/Pune: Gujarat Sahitya Prakash/Snehsadan Studies.

Farquhar, John Nicola. 1913. *The Crown of Hinduism*. Oxford: Oxford University Press.

Fernando, Leonard and George Gispert-Sauch. 2004. *Christianity in India: Two Thousand Years of Faith*. New Delhi: Viking.

Forrester, Duncan B. 1979. *Caste and Christianity: Attitudes and Policies on Caste of Anglo-Saxon Protestant Missions in India*. London: Curzon Press.

Frykenberg, Robert Eric. 2008. *Christianity in India: From Beginnings to the Present*. Oxford: Oxford University Press.

Golwalkar, Madhav Sadashiv. 1996. *Bunch of Thoughts*. Bangalore: Sahitya Sindhu Prakashana.
Gravend-Tirole, Xavier. 2014. "From Christian Ashrams to Dalit Theology: Or beyond." In *Constructing Indian Christianities: Culture, Conversion and Caste*. Edited by Chad M. Bauman and Richard Fox Young. New Delhi: Routledge, pp. 110–137.
Halbfass, Wilhelm. 1988. *India and Europe: An Essay in Understanding*. Albany: SUNY Press.
Hedges, Paul. 2001. *Preparation and Fulfilment: A History and Study of Fulfilment Theology in Modern Britain Thought in the Indian Context*. Frankfurt am Main: Verlag Peter Lang.
Hedlund, Roger E. 2017. *Christianity Made in India: From Apostle Thomas to Mother Teresa*. Minneapolis: Fortress Press.
Henn, Alexander. 2014. *Hindu-Catholic Encounters in Goa: Religion, Colonialism, and Modernity*. Bloomington/Indianapolis: Indiana University Press.
Hough, James. 1839. *The History of Christianity in India from the Commencement of the Christian Era*. London: R. B. Sealy/W. Burnside.
Jaffrelot, Christophe. 1996. *The Hindu Nationalist Movement and Indian Politics 1925 to the 1990s: Strategies of Identity-Building, Implantation and Mobilisation*. New Delhi: Penguin Books.
Jathanna, O. V. 1986. "Indian Christian Theology: Methodological Reflections." *Bangalore Theological Forum* 18 (2–3): 59–74.
Jenkins, Philip. 2002. *The Next Christendom: The Coming of Global Christianity*. Oxford: Oxford University Press.
Jeyaraj, Daniel, translator and editor. 2004. *Genealogy of the South Indian Deities: An English Translation of Bartholomäus Ziegenbalg's Original German Manuscript, with Textual Analysis and Glossary*. London: RoutledgeCourzon.
John, T. K. 1997. "Image of the Christian Presented in India Today." In *The Church in India in Search of a New Identity*. Edited by Kurien Kunnumpuram, Errol D'Lima and Jacob Parappally. Bangalore: NBCLC, pp. 125–154.
Jones, Kenneth W. 1989. *The New Cambridge History of India III/1: Socio-Religious Movements in British India*. Cambridge: Cambridge University Press.
Kanungo, Pralay. 2002. *RSS's Tryst with Politics: From Hedgewar to Sudarshan*. New Delhi: Manohar.
Kashyap, Anirban. 1988. *Communalism and Constitution*. New Delhi: Lancers Books.
Kim, Sebastian C. H. 2003. *In Search of Identity: Debates on Religious Conversion in India*. New Delhi: Oxford University Press.
Küng, Hans and Heinrich von Stietencron. 1987. *Christentum und Weltreligionen II. Hinduismus*. Güter: Güetersloher Verlagshaus.
Kunnumpuram, Kurien. 1997. "The Autonomy of the Indian Church." In *The Church in India in Search of a New Identity*. Edited by Kurien Kunnumpuram, Errol D'Lima and Jacob Parappally. Bangalore: NBCLC, pp. 155–176.
Kuriakose, M. K., editor. 2006. *History of Christianity in India: Source Materials*. New Delhi: ISPCK.
Kuttiyanikkal, Ciril J. 2014. *Khrist Bhakta Movement: A Model for an Indian Church? Inculturation in the Area of Community Building*. Zürich: Lit Verlag.
Metcalf, Thomas R. 1995. *The New Cambridge History of India III/4: Ideologies of the Raj*. Cambridge: Cambridge University Press.

Neill, Stephen. 1984, 1985. *A History of Christianity in India: The Beginnings to A.D. 1707* (vol. 1), *1707–1858* (vol. 2). Cambridge: Cambridge University Press.

Oddie, Geoffrey A. 2006. *Imagined Hinduism: British Protestant Missionary Constructions of Hinduism, 1793–1900*. New Delhi: Sage.

On the Permanent Validity of the Church's Missionary Mandate, *Redemptoris Missio*, 1990.

Pearson, Hugh Nicholas. 1835. *Memoir of the Life and Correspondence of the Reverend Christian Frederick Swartz, to Which Is Prefixed, a Sketch of the History of Christianity in India*. London: J. Hatchard and Son.

Pearson, M. N. 1987. *The New Cambridge History of India I/1: The Portuguese in India*. Cambridge: Cambridge University Press.

Puthanangady, Paul. 1997. "Christian Community as a Multi-Cultural Reality." In *The Church in India in Search of a New Identity*. Edited by Kurien Kunnumpuram, Errol D'Lima and Jacob Parappally. Bangalore: NBCLC, pp. 173–192.

Raj, Selva J. and Corinne C. Dempsey, editors. 2002. *Popular Christianity in India: Riting between the Lines*. Albany: State University of New York Press.

Robinson, Rowena. 2003. "Sixteenth Century Conversions to Christianity in Goa." In *Religious Conversion in India, Modes, Motivations, and Meaning*. Edited by Rowena Robinson and Sathianathan Clarke. New Delhi: Oxford University Press, pp. 291–322.

Rocher, Ludo, editor. 1984. *Ezourvedam: A French Veda of the Eighteenth Century*. Amsterdam/Philadelphia: John Benjamins Publishing Company.

Sarkar, Sumit. 1999. "Conversion and Politics of Hindu Right." *Economic and Political Weekly* 34 (26): 1691–1700.

Savarkar, Vinayak Damodar. 2005. *Hindutva: Who Is a Hindu?* New Delhi: Hindi Sahitya Sadan.

Sharma, Arvind. 2001. "Swami Dayananda Sarasvati." In *Religion in Modern India*. Edited by Robert D. Baird. New Delhi: Manohar, pp. 388–409.

Sharpe, Eric J. 1965. *Not to Destroy but to Fulfil: The Contribution of J. N. Farquhar to Protestant Missionary Thought in India before 1914*. Uppsala: Gleerup.

Sharpe, Eric J. 2001. "Christianity in India." In *Religion in Modern India*. Edited by Robert D. Baird. New Delhi: Manohar, pp. 224–240.

Sharpe, Eric J. 2004. *The Riddle of Sadhu Sundar Singh*. New Delhi: Intercultural Publications.

Sikand, Yoginder. 2003. "Arya Shuddhi and Muslim Tabligh: Muslim Reactions to Arya Samaj Proselyzation (1923–30)." In *Religious Conversion in India, Modes, Motivations, and Meaning*. Edited by Rowena Robinson and Sathianathan Clarke. New Delhi: Oxford University Press, pp. 98–118.

Streeter, Burnett Hillman and Aiyadurai Jesudasen Appasamy. 1921. *The Sadhu: A Study in Mysticism and Practical Religion*. London: Macmillan.

Tenneth, Timothy C. 2005. *Building Christianity on Indian Foundations: The Legacy of Brahmabandhav Upadhyay*. New Delhi: ISPCK.

Tiliander, Bror. 1974. *Christian and Hindu Terminology: A Study in Their Mutual Relations with Special Reference to the Tamil Area*. Uppsala: Almqvist and Wiksell.

Visvanathan, Susan. 1993. *The Christians of Kerala: History, Belief and Ritual among the Yakoba*. New Delhi: Oxford University Press.

Webster, John C. B. 2009. *The Dalit Christians: A History*. New Delhi: ISPCK.

Winslow, Jack. 1923. *Narayan Vaman Tilak: The Christian Poet of Maharashtra*. Calcutta: Association Press.

Young, Richard Fox. 1981. *Resistant Hinduism: Sanskrit Sources on Anti-Christian Apologetics in Early Nineteenth-Century India*. Vienna: De Nobili Research Library.

Županov, Ines G. 2001. *Disputed Mission: Jesuit Experiments and Brahmanical Knowledge in Seventeenth-Century India*. New Delhi: Oxford University Press.

2
INCULTURATION OF CHRISTIANITY

During the 20th century, in particular from its second half, the churches in Asia and Africa were confronted with extraordinary challenges. These challenges truly had the potential to transform the face of Christianity in these parts of the world. They could trigger extraordinary responses of the churches to the radical changes taking place in a broad cultural, social and political context. In the earlier period, which began after the end of the process of the Christianization of Europe, cultural uniformity was also spread from the Old Continent alongside the Christian doctrine. The reason was the cultural-centric belief of that time that Christianity is a European phenomenon and as such is firmly linked to European cultural idioms. Therefore, it must be not only expressed but also passed on by means of them. In particular, the Catholic Church, after its bitter experience with the Reformation, made efforts to create obedient and "exact replicas of itself" (Saldanha 1997: 42) from young churches in non-European countries, where it sent its missionaries. This trend is related to its claim of being the universal Church and its self-understanding as such, as well as to the need to ensure its internal unity in terms of the purity of the faith and external unity in terms of a unified liturgy. However, uniformity is not a condition for unity (Mattam 2002: 137). Moreover, usually it is only barely creative and prevents further development in the long run. On the contrary, openness to stimuli from outside, which may impede all sorts of things, just as it may enrich and transform them, is always a manifestation of continued growth as well as internal freedom. It was no coincidence that Christianity started its winning journey throughout European history after it had left the cultural and religious context of the Jewish world and boldly entered the environment of ancient Greece in formulating its message.

The principles of the process of Hellenization of early Christianity could be imitated to some extent in the 20th century as part of the Christian inculturation efforts. This inculturation was called for by many Christians from the countries where Christianity spread through missionary activities along with colonial rule. The same was true of some theologians, who themselves were firmly rooted in the cultural determinateness of Europe. Of course, the conditions for such a hypothetical process were considerably different compared to the beginnings of the turn of the Common Era. Christianity was already a firmly established system with abundant religious symbolism based on a thousand-year tradition. Attempts to replace or enrich albeit just one part of it in a certain region of the world could easily be considered a direct assault on the very essence of this tradition. Moreover, according to opponents of the modern efforts to transform Christianity, the current situation is absolutely incommensurable with entry to the world of ancient wisdom. The reason is that Greek thought is not just one of many possible means of expressing the Christian tidings; it is a totally exclusive medium, indispensable to its formulation and subsequent understanding (Painadath and Parappally 2008: 67). As a matter of fact, such an approach fundamentally calls into question the relevance and impact of any inculturation attempts, including those already occurring spontaneously and on the periphery of the Church's interest in the course of the previous centuries. In modern times, the relationship between Christianity and other religious cultures also differs substantially. The former categories that considered this relationship through the dichotomy of the terms of the absence and presence of the revelation, or sometimes later the partialness of the revelation as found in some elements of other religions and its fullness in Christianity, seem to be completely insufficient today (Amaladoss 2005: 26). A pluralist perspective of modern times constantly threatens to relativize the values of one's own tradition. These may suddenly be revealed as historically contingent or too circumscribed by Christian European culture. On the contrary, in other traditions, which were previously ignored or underestimated, this perspective may reveal a deep religious experience that Christianity has not yet seen. Through its recognition, the Christian claim to the fullness of truth and revelation is fundamentally challenged. An important feature of the situation of Christianity in the 20th century is also the fact that the calls for inculturation or specific attempts at it were a reaction to changing conditions in a postcolonial, globalized, liberalized and pluralist world. They were not an assertive action motivated by an inner need for further growth. Therefore, the decision to seek new forms and contents of religious responses and expressions in modern times is not taken on the basis of freedom. On the contrary, it is the result of external pressure. It is then an imposed need, at least if Christianity and its tidings want to be relevant in non-European cultures.

The aim of this part of the book is to outline the contours as well as key issues of the theological discourse under which the Christian Ashram Movement underwent its peak development period. India can also be largely understood as a space where inculturation of various religions happened spontaneously and naturally throughout its history (Michael 2010: 77). However, in its newly articulated religious otherness and in setting up the principal features of the new forms of evangelization in non-European countries, the development of the Christian theological thought in the second half of the 20th century deliberately drew upon the ideas of inculturation to a considerable extent. Over the last sixty years, the broadly approached topic of inculturation appears in the official documents of the Catholic Church repeatedly, although under different, constantly changing designations. However, a comparative analysis of certain statements in those documents, by which the Church expresses its current attitude towards other religions and cultures, at the same time reveals a series of ideological contradictions. These often deny the logical rules of interreligious dialogue that necessarily accompany or are even required in inculturation in any shape or form. Since the late 1980s, more conservative critical voices have been heard alongside the current liberal school of thought in Catholic theology. They warn of the danger of uncontrolled or boundless inculturation, undermining its partial benefits and its very sense. Thus, while the introductory part of our book indirectly defined the historical context of the formation, development and decline of the Christian concept of the ashram, this part will regard its idea from a theological point of view. We will attempt to subject it to critical reflection through the evolving relationship of the Catholic Church with the content, possibilities and limiting boundaries of inculturation of Christianity.

The vagueness of concepts and their contents

The term "inculturation" began appearing in the deliberations of Christian thinkers irregularly in the 1960s (Shorter 1988: 10).[1] Until now, however, it has been set out so vaguely that it is rightly considered a not very precisely defined neologism (Painadath and Parappally 2008: 68). The problems related to it arise mainly from its unclarified relation to earlier concepts. Those also denoted the complex process through which specific Christian churches came to terms with the fact that they had been penetrating the countries with a firmly established religious and cultural tradition, which had moreover undergone a longer historical development than is the case with Christianity. A variety of these concepts seem to be extremely broad. Their clear and mutually differentiating meanings are at the same time confused by the semantic connotations that they may elicit, including in a rather different way, in different cultural contexts and as approached by individual churches or authors. Anscar Chupungco (1992: 14–28) offers a more or less exhaustive list of them (adaptation, acculturation, indigenization, incarnation, inculturation, contextualization and revision), but the arguments he uses in defining and subsequently assessing them also, as with all the others, lack a systematic character and remain very vague. An interesting observation regarding the differences between these two concepts is made by Jyoti Sahi, a pioneer in the field of inculturation of Christian art in India. He considers inculturation a thought concept that received the most extensive elaboration and popularity in the deliberations of Catholic authors, while the earlier contextualization became the domain of Protestants (Sahi 1993:

127). His remark corresponds with historical development, at least in the Indian environment. Here, in the process of coming to terms with the cultural reality that constantly defies accepting Christianity in its European form, no matter how this process is termed, the Protestant churches have outstripped the Catholic Church by a whole half century. The very popular concept of indigenization, which still keeps its position, in particular in pastoral texts, is remarkably explained by Paul Collins, the author of the groundbreaking work on the history of inculturation in India. In his view, the aim of indigenization is to create such a church in a given country that will be financially independent of its church centre and autonomous regarding its decision-making and further proliferation in the region (Collins 2006: 102). In defining their terminology, Chad M. Bauman and Richard Fox Young draw attention to the missionary motivation of those who seek to naturalize Christianity in a particular territory. Therefore, they consider inculturation a conscious, targeted act, while the term "acculturation", according to them, indicates a spontaneous, unintended and unplanned process that often takes place despite the intentions and will of the official church leaders, who may even try to prevent it (Bauman and Young 2014: xii).

Some of the previously specified terms can be seen as the designation of the different stages of development of the relationship of Christianity with different cultural and religious realities. The aforementioned indirectly follows from the defining observations made by Julian Saldanha, a precise theorist of inculturation in India, who seeks to apply his findings also in the pastoral and modern concepts of missiology. Saldanha considers that shifting the meaning from the adaptation that was enforced in an authoritarian manner earlier is absolutely crucial for the development of Christianity in India. It was within this framework that the Christian tradition as formed in Europe was brought into the local context. Only external, even though numerous, adjustments were allowed, primarily in the form of minor concessions to the cultural environment, which were not in irreconcilable contradiction with church teaching or its European cultural manifestations, as they were performed, for example, by Roberto de Nobili. Indeed, in such a case, adaptation would really have been more of a strategy or tactic with a missionary objective (religious conversions) than anything else. Through the adaptations, the Catholic Church neither expressed nor felt the need to be enriched by external stimuli; it was "one-way traffic, in which the Church was the giver" (Saldanha 1997: 14). Inculturation, contrarily, draws a specific church or, more precisely, the whole of Christianity directly to the heart and mind of a local environment. It seeks to get through to the emotional and intellectual expressions of faith, as they are common in a given culture. The result but also the very intention of inculturation is to provide mutual enrichment. New ways of understanding the Christian faith and its own religious identity in the context of the local culture are to bring new stimuli to Christianity. Thus, they will contribute to its religious universality, as it is claimed by Christianity (Ibid.). Faith does not grow stronger by being passed on, which was endeavoured for by adaptation and still remains the main motive of the major stream of missionary activities, but through the variety of its manifestations.

The courage shown in defining the content of the concept of inculturation varies considerably in individual authors who have attempted to do so. Logically, they arrive at various conclusions that quite faithfully correspond to the degree of their radicalism and willingness to go against the norms of the missionary tradition. Since 1622, the watchful guardian in the case of the Catholic Church has been the Sacred Congregation for the Propagation of the Faith (*Sacra Congregatio de Propaganda Fide*), today under its modern name of the Congregation for the Evangelization of Peoples (*Congregatio pro Gentium Evangelizatione*). At the same time, the degree of this radicalism is always closely related to the imaginary, but also real, geographic distance of the place of operation of specific persons from the respective church centre and, concurrently, to their position in the structures of the church hierarchy. Not without reason, the most courageous inculturation attempts, which took place in the later phases of the development of the Ashram Movement, occurred in some kind of church gloom. The rightful doubts whether they can still be described as expressions of Christianity at all can be put aside at the moment. The implementers of the ideas of radical inculturation either voluntarily chose such a shadowy place themselves as their refuge or had it assigned to them by their church as a strictly delimited field where they were allowed to safely experiment.

The attraction of the issues related to inculturation was growing in theological and ecclesiastical circles throughout the 1970s and 80s. In this context, the attitude of the Catholic Church is particularly noteworthy, because it is this church where the permanent tension between hasty radicalism and protectionist caution is the most obvious and the most prolific. The year 1979 was apparently the first time the term "inculturation" was used in an official document by John Paul II, in the apostolic exhortation about the catechesis in the Church, *Catechesi Tradendae*, by virtue of his papal authority. He called it an apposite representation of one of the key elements of the mystery of the incarnation of Christ, through which the Gospel shall enter into many different cultures (*Catechesi Tradendae* 1979: art. 53). The Extraordinary Synod of Bishops, which dealt with a number of topical issues that the Church had to cope with two decades after the Second Vatican Council in 1985, recognized the importance of inculturation. They defined it as "the intimate transformation of authentic cultural values through their integration in Christianity in the various human cultures" (The Final Report of the 1985 Extraordinary Synod, II., D. 4). This definition clearly builds on the ideas of the earlier Council documents of *Ad Gentes*, *Gaudium et Spes*, *Nostra Aetate*, *Lumen Gentium* and *Sacrosanctum Concilium*, where the notion of inculturation did not yet appear, but the Church repeatedly proclaimed the change in its attitude of refusing other religious traditions. Strictly speaking, it was only after the Second Vatican Council when these traditions were officially recognized as true religions (Kunnumpuram 1993: 21). They ceased to be regarded as a mere complex set of cultural expressions coming to existence in the course of history as some non-Christians sought to find their road to God by taking intuitive and, in the view of the Church, mostly misguided paths. A very general statement, calling for the free adoption of anything from every culture that brings a positive value in itself, is contained in both the Council's edicts and the previously cited definition of inculturation. It has, however, never been officially determined how exactly the mentioned processes of transformation and integration should take place. Therefore, it is no surprise that it was the vague attitude of the Church towards the implementation of the programme of inculturation that in many cases became fatal for the interesting experiments, primarily in the field of liturgy. Nevertheless, it is worth repeating in conclusion that through inculturation, although not sufficiently defined, Christianity approaches other cultures and religions as something positive, containing in themselves many valuable elements which may merit a relationship being established with them (Wilfred 2005: 29).

Inculturation as a theological inevitability

For some advocates of inculturation, its ideals represent something much deeper and more compelling than a mere response of Christianity to the changing conditions in the modern world. In their view, inculturation, in its principles, is based directly on the essence of the Christian tidings and the person of their herald, Christ. He was no exception in taking bodily form during a certain time and space, which was in a specific era and religious culture (Gravend-Tirole 2014: 114). Thus, he made his universally valid annunciation tangible and applicable in a clear context. He outlined it to people at a particular historical time by becoming one of them, to the extreme, with all the existential determinateness of humanity (Amalorpavadass 2009: 264).[2] The very fact of Christ's incarnation seemingly appealed in itself as something to be imitated and followed because he himself had not come to destroy Jewish culture. On the contrary, he became its part by his very birth. Subsequently, he tried to transform it through the Gospel, completing it and guiding it to its fulfilment via the paschal mystery, which also made sense in the Jewish religious context, though a sense radically different from what was expected from the arrival of the Saviour. Through its theological justification, revealing that it is not an option but rather a necessity, inculturation can even unfold as a constitutive feature of Christianity, making Christianity fundamentally different from other religions (Saldanha 1997: 48).[3] The theologians of inculturation thus take the view that Christianity loses nothing of its character and values even if it actively accepts and integrates foreign religious cultures, including their ritual elements, religious symbols and sacred texts. Quite possibly the reverse is the case as Christianity matures, grows in historic time and faithfully fulfils the task given to it by Christ himself, setting an example for it. The Indian theologian Amalorpavadass considers that this is not about stealing, borrowing or imitation. In his opinion, everything that is good and holy in other religions already inevitably belongs to Christ. Yet the followers of these religions, and Christians along with them, have not been aware of it so far. Christianity (in Amalor's concept, the Catholic Church as the universal Church) has merely been rediscovering these meaningful elements of Hinduism, and also other religions and cultures, through the inculturation process. By accepting, purifying and integrating them into the system of their religious tradition, it subsequently consecrates them to God (Amalorpavadass 1976: 209).

It is quite obvious that these thoughts of inculturation are based to a large extent on the theology of fulfilment. Its idea is aptly expressed in *The Crown of Hinduism*, the earlier work by John Nicola Farquhar, set in the Indian environment, as well as the concept of anonymous Christians developed by Karl Rahner. It was his theological considerations that substantially influenced the entire Second Vatican Council and on that account also the entry of the Catholic Church into the modern world. However, a certain difference between the theology of fulfilment and radical inculturation does exist. This time, the reason why and the manner of how Christianity accepts elements of foreign religions lies in discovering their until then un-manifested value and the religious meaning they already had or have been newly attaining in the context of Christianity. However, it is not for the members of these foreign religions but for itself in constituting its new, inculturated identity.[4]

The subject and stages of the inculturation process

As mentioned before, official representatives of the Catholic Church sanctified the general programme of inculturation with their approval because it largely corresponded to the ideals of the Second Vatican Council and the trend established by the Church through the Council and post-Council edicts. In India, for several years, the declared approval went hand in hand with the direct support of inculturation by the Congregation of Bishops, or at least some of them. However, the Church authorities failed to clearly define its exact content, methods and individual partial steps that are the specific agenda of inculturation. Therefore, its determination was based solely on the ideas of those who truly wished to attempt inculturation. This fact, the conflict between the idealized promise of a change and the lack of subsequent activities leading to the change, is where one of the major causes of the failure of inculturation, including its genuine fruit in India, that is, Christian ashrams, stems from.

The first systematic reflections arising in the environment of the Indian Catholic Church at the time coincident with the Second Vatican Council still speak about acculturation and adaptation. However, they also preemptively set out the specific areas of Church life where inculturation must take place (Amalorpavadass 2009: 220–222). The primary task should be to form domestic clergy. This will occur not according to the European Catholic model but will adequately reflect the conditions of the local environment and thus will grow from it spiritually and theologically (for the doctrinal support of this claim, see the conciliar decree titled *Ad Gentes II 16*). It was at this point where the Catholic Church somewhat built on the most important task of the older Protestant concept of contextualization. This became unexpectedly but potently apparent during the two missionary conferences held in Jerusalem (1928) and especially in Tambaram, Tamil Nadu (1938) (Collins 2006: 53–56). But in the case of Protestant churches, the sustained enforcement of this requirement more often than not finally led to growing demands for a greater degree of autonomy or even to dissensions and the formation of totally new ecclesial communities. Besides the naturalized clergy, the lay community, which had been passive to that point, was further targeted to be motivated through the inculturation process, once again in accordance with the contextualization plans, because the conclusions of the Second Vatican Council turned their attention also to the laity, inviting laymen to contribute more to the life of the Church (see *Ad Gentes III 21*). The remaining points of this first Indian demarcation of the subject of inculturation relate to the areas where a deep breakthrough into the culture and religion of the local environment should happen and its numerous elements should be subsequently integrated into Christian practice. It is catechesis and liturgy (see *Ad Gentes III 19* and *Sacrosanctum Concilium 37*), art in its broadest sense (see *Ad Gentes III 22*), philosophy and theology (see *Ad Gentes III 22*) or the methods of personal spiritual growth stemming from domestic ascetic, contemplative and mystical traditions (see *Ad Gentes II 18*).[5]

The same author, but in a later period, after replacing the concept of adaptation with indigenization somewhat inconsistently for several years, leading to him finally and definitively switching to the concept of inculturation very soon afterwards, conceived the description of a complex process with intensifying, interrelated stages. Unlike many of his predecessors and contemporaries, who limited themselves to abstract general considerations and definitions of inculturation, Amalorpavadass presents considerably specific drafts of individual stages of the planned development. It does not matter at all that the field concerned in this concept of his is more or less just Indian Christian liturgy (Amalorpavadass 1976: 214). According to him, the first manifestation of actively entering into a foreign religious and cultural environment should be external changes in rituals. By this he means the ways in which the faithful, together and individually, refer to God – the overall atmosphere in which the service or personal prayer is taking place, symbolic gestures during it, the used language phrasing with religious symbolism, liturgical objects, the apparel of the celebrants and their behaviour towards the believers and vice versa the behaviour of the faithful towards them. Indeed, at this stage of the liturgical inculturation of the Indian Catholic Church, fairly significant changes were achieved, as we will see in the main part of this book dealing with the history of the Movement, permanently, at least in small experimental communities, and officially by approving the so-called list of the Twelve points of adaptation. The second stage of inculturation should add individual creative activity to the adoption of external features. It should continue in the already significantly developed translation tradition, which, however, would be additionally enriched with the moderate and prudent adjustment of the internal conditions of a foreign religious context. Gradually, it would even lead to original compositions of liturgical texts. Here, too, there were a few brave attempts, mainly in the form of the so-called Indian mass. Amalorpavadass practised it in the environment of his ashram, and his disciples still continue in it there. Worthy of increased attention to that effect is in particular the so-called *Bharatiya puja*, which has already been the subject of experimentation in the *Kurisumala* for several decades. The composition and publication of an Indian anaphora most probably represents the peak of this second phase. At the same time, however, the controversial anaphora became a neuralgic point of conflict between the proponents of inculturation and the official Church circles. The latter rejected it in a very heated atmosphere, banning any efforts to introduce it gradually, if only on an experimental basis. They even called it a serious danger to the unity of the Catholic rite and purity of the Christian faith, since they saw in it attempts, though unintentional, at the Hinduization of Christianity in India. Therefore, it is no surprise that the third and last stage of inculturation in Amalorpavadass's concept had not reached, and, as a matter of course, truthfully could not reach, fruition. The reason was that it had planned to integrate the Sacred Scriptures of other religions directly into Christian liturgy. The Scriptures would be used not only as a source of spiritual inspiration during contemplative reading but would be placed at a similar level of religious stature as the Christian Scripture during a service. Amalorpavadass himself was clearly aware that the implementation of this stage was improbable and considered it more of a distant goal which should be worked towards slowly and carefully.

Ideological antinomies and the conceptual problems of the demand for inculturation

However, there are many unresolved issues present in the considered process of inculturation, both in the theological plane of its general design and justification and in the partial steps towards its accomplishment. Some of them stem from intellectual inconsistencies in the official and doctrinal documents of the Catholic Church; others result from vaguely defined anthropological categories. It is the latter that expose the whole concept of inculturation or the partial steps towards its accomplishment as inadequate religious, ecclesiastical and social realities of the country concerned, into the cultural environment of which Christianity seeks to permeate and become integrated. The critical analysis of the most important of these issues highlights the ideological weaknesses of inculturation, at least in the form it was considered in the environment of the Catholic Church of the 1970s and 1980s.

Interfaith dialogue

The history of the Catholic Church is not composed of approved documents of the Church because, contrarily, these are the result of its life (D'Sa 1993: 66–67), and they only show the condition of the Church in a certain historical period. Nevertheless, authoritative documents set out the future conditions under which the further historical development of the Church may occur. Reflections on inculturation emerged in the Catholic Church as one of the practical implications of the general calls for dialogue with other world religions, as they were revolutionarily formulated in the *Nostra Aetate* conciliar decree: "The Church, therefore, exhorts its sons, that through dialogue and collaboration with the followers of other religions, carried out with prudence and love and in witness to the Christian faith and life, they recognize, preserve and promote the good things, spiritual and moral, as well as the socio-cultural values found among these men". At the same time, the same decree, however, claims that the Church "proclaims, and ever must proclaim Christ 'the way, the truth, and the life' (John 14:6), in whom men may find the fullness of religious life, in whom God has reconciled all things to Himself" (*Nostra Aetate* 1965: art. 2). Within the rules of the interfaith dialogue laid down in this manner, there is not much space left for active participation of believers from other religions. Despite its proclaimed openness, the Church maintains a haughty stance on them (Gravend-Tirole 2014: 127), stemming from the attitude of the theology of fulfilment. The prerequisite for any dialogue is that both partners are, as a matter of principle, ready to be persuaded by the other party. Such willingness, however, seems to be incompatible with the enduring missionary task of the Church, which remains evangelization and its fruits in the form of new religious conversions. But here, quite contrarily, the partner inviting the dialogue determines the conditions and roles of those involved before the dialogue even starts. The spiritual worlds of both actors are assessed beforehand, giving one of them a monopoly on the "fullness of religious life" (*Nostra Aetate* 1965: art. 2), while the religious rules and doctrines of the other merely "reflect a ray of that Truth which enlightens all men" (Ibid.). From the perspective of the representatives of other religions, such a dialogue necessarily appears to be unreliable and suspect, if it is additionally understood by one of the participants as complex, although a specific part of their own missionary policies and strategies:

> From the Christian point of view, interreligious dialogue is more than a way of fostering mutual knowledge and enrichment; it is a

part of the Church's evangelizing mission, an expression of the mission ad gentes. Christians bring to interreligious dialogue the firm belief that the fullness of salvation comes from Christ alone and that the Church community to which they belong is the ordinary means of salvation.

(Ecclesia in Asia 1999: chap. V, art. 31;
Redemptoris Missio 1990: art. 55)

Christianity is resolved to enter the spiritual world of other religions with open arms and the motivation not only to embrace them in a brotherly manner but also to be mutually enriched. If, however, behind the lofty ideals there lies an envisaged approach to the foreign other, what sense do the attempts at inculturation have when it is well known before the dialogue, that is, long before the inculturation itself, that "our religion effectively establishes with God an authentic and living relationship which other religions do not succeed in doing, even though they have, as it were, their arms stretched out towards heaven" (*Evangelii Nuntiandi* 1975: art. 53)? Thus, the question has been left open as to why one religion, which is, in its own words, the bearer of fullness, should and actually would wish for anything to extend this fullness by what is necessarily only partial. The fundamental incapacity of Christian theology to acknowledge other religious traditions as equal to Christianity and assign them religious autonomy in the full sense of the word condemns every attempt at dialogue to misunderstanding and, paradoxically, leads to the strengthening of the conflicting roles in which the two religions stand against each other (Gravend-Tirole 2014: 128).

The spontaneity of inculturation

The critical issues emerging in connection with the presented concept of interfaith dialogue, however, take on yet another aspect, having an inevitable impact on the planned process of inculturation. The dialogue, if it is to be genuine and sincere, should be first of all spontaneous. Only through such spontaneity, which is an essential prerequisite on both sides, can a true, inner desire motivated by an interest in getting to know and understand the religious world of the other reveal itself. Doubt is, however, cast on such spontaneity by the fact that at the moment when it is introducing the topic of dialogue into the theological discourse, the Catholic Church had already created a special office[6] for such dialogue with the aim "to coordinate and, of course to control" the whole process (Prasad 1993: 102). This unresolved problem of the tense relationship between spontaneity and institutionalization ties down those who make attempts at dialogue. Likewise, it provokes a priori distrust of potential partners in this dialogue because the rules of their particular religious world often do not even know such clear-cut obedience to superior authorities. Members of other religions may then fear, and quite rightly so, that in this case the dialogue is just a vehicle for mapping the chances of new methods of evangelization to be subsequently implemented through inculturation with the aim of further religious conversions:

> The Church respects and admires these non-Christian religions because they are the living expression of the soul of vast groups of people. They carry within them the echo of thousands of years of searching for God, a quest which is incomplete but often made with great sincerity and righteousness of heart. They possess an impressive patrimony of deeply religious texts. They have taught generations of people how to pray. They are all impregnated with innumerable "seeds of the Word" and can constitute a true "preparation for the Gospel" [...] Such a situation certainly raises complex and delicate questions that must be studied in the light of Christian Tradition and the Church's magisterium, in order to offer to the missionaries of today and of tomorrow new horizons in their contacts with non-Christian religions.
> (*Evangelii Nuntiandi* 1975: art. 53)

The specific attempts at inculturation of Christianity that could arise from dialogue as a process of mutual learning about each other are then doomed to failure because they originate in an environment of institutionalized churches where freedom is often lacking. The Indian Christians involved in the Ashram Movement repeatedly encountered this problem. As a result, some even had to choose between their membership in the church and their desire to fulfil their spiritual callings in the ashram environment.

The right to inculturation

Religious ideas and their manifestations always turn a respective religion into a very intricately arranged, complex system with interdependent and integrally linked rules. Tearing out any element from such a construction can lead to its serious endangerment on the one hand, and also to its destruction or at least its substantial alternation with a profound meaning on the other. This may happen because such a meaning is contained in a given element and, concurrently, in the relationship of this element to the whole. It is not possible just to pick the religious symbols of one religious teaching, isolate them and replant them into a completely different religious context where they can be reinterpreted so that they would acquire a new meaning. The reason for this is that symbols continue carrying their old semantic meaning, or at least a part of it. Therefore, they may transform, expand or even question the tradition into which they are transplanted (Cornille 1991: 2). In the process of inculturation, virtually all of its theoreticians anticipate a phase called purification so that everything adopted from a foreign religion would be purified of negative connotations, "raised up and perfected unto the glory of God, the confusion of the devil and the happiness of man" (*Lumen Gentium* 1964: chap. II, art. 17). With the exception of their own, and therefore very controversial, self-arguments, through this adoption, the agents of inculturation, whether Christianity as such, the church or the individual in question, do, however, arbitrarily enter quite a distinctive religious system. They pick the wealth out of it that "a generous God has distributed among the nations of the earth" so that they would take it to perfection according to their own perceptions, when they claim through inculturation "to furbish these treasures, set them free, and bring them under the dominion of God their Saviour" (*Ad Gentes* 1965: chap. II, art. 11). An inculturation approached in this way, however, inevitably represents the opposite of the respect that is appealed for with the same urgency in the same place and also elsewhere many times: "Let them be joined to those men by esteem and love [. . .] let them be familiar with their national and religious traditions; let them gladly and reverently lay bare the seeds of the Word which lie hidden among their fellows" (Ibid.). From this point of view, the right to picking particulars as well as meaningful units from the profound religious wealth of one tradition and implementing them into another tradition, and therefore the right to inculturation as such, is bound to prove very problematic.

Arbitrariness vs. authority of interpretation

From the previously described theoretical grasp of inculturation, it also does not seem to be clear whether there are any boundaries in its approach to religious otherness and, if so, by whom and exactly how they were determined. Thus, we are faced with a fairly major problem of a tense relationship between the authoritative interpretation of a religious tradition or its certain elements as is made within the tradition by its bearers and the interpretational arbitrariness of those who approach it from the outside, understanding its elements as potential objects of the inculturation process. Undoubtedly, the freedom in choosing what can and cannot be inculturated must undoubtedly have fixed limits. The agent of inculturation will understand many religious concepts, for example, those associated with the mythological tale in which the characters of gods representing goodness clash with the forces of evil, as metaphors of general facts. But for the authorities and common believers of the religion from which these concepts originate, they may on the contrary be the subject of their deep personal faith that fundamentally shapes their religious identity and expression. The careless handling of key motivations of a foreign religion will readily lead to grossly insulting its believers. At the same time, it can arouse considerable resentment or doctrinal confusion among the Christians who disagree with the principles and reasons of inculturation or are not familiar with the concept at all (Amaladoss 2008: 140–141).

The boundaries of culture and religion

It is extremely difficult to demarcate a field in a foreign religion where Christian inculturation could happen without seriously affecting the religious feelings of its worshipers because the boundaries between culture and religion are also not fixed. More precisely, there is no consensus among theologians, anthropologists and certainly not the members of individual religions on where the borderline should be drawn. Culture can be understood as a mere tool of religion, a space in which religion manifests itself and therefore, from the Christian point of view, as good soil in which "the Gospel seed" (Gravend-Tirole 2014: 125) can be sown. According to another concept, the reverse is the case and both categories cannot be separated at all. They are "also inherently bound together" (Collins 2006: 29), as Catholic and Protestant missionaries were still assuming in accord well into the 19th century. In the environment of India, it seems as if numerous and varied contemporary attempts at attaining some sort of synthesis of the two religions as well as Christian inculturation have led to a significantly disputed assumption that Hinduism is not a religion at all but merely a culture. In it, there is plenty of space for any religious doctrine, while Christianity, on the contrary, can be applied to any cultural context: "The Hindu culture is the world's most magnificent endeavour to reach perfect self-awareness; it makes man actually aware of being destined for union with God. Jesus Christ offers himself as the way that leads to union with God. Thus, Christianity and Hinduism complete each other as the seed and the soil" (Staffner 1987: 121). It was already sufficiently mentioned in the introductory part of this book that it is a radical about-face in the approach to religious and cultural otherness, and its causes were briefly named. However, the assertion which denies Hinduism its religious nature can hardly be accepted by the Hindus themselves. Even if a truly sincere effort at combining the two separate worlds into one meaningful complementary whole were behind that, in its impact it may well cause a chauvinistically intolerant Hindu belief that "Christianity has never been a religion; it has always been predatory imperialism par excellence" (Goel 1996: v).

Which culture?

Another unresolved, yet very serious, issue remains the dispute about the layers of the respective culture on which Christian inculturation should be built. The culture of a specific country or a religion is never a homogeneous unit. On the contrary, it is an intricately ordered system with many layers that have been formed in its architecture during its historical development and which still continue evolving dynamically. These may even carry different values and stand in stark contrast to each other. In addition, there may be considerable tension between individual levels of the cultural system that leads to open disputes, including from time to time shows of violence. The theological understanding of inculturation, however, has never resolved the question of whether Christianity should penetrate through inculturation into the cultural layer which is dominant in the country concerned, to the highest layer or rather into the layer that is relevant for local Christians because, for most of them, it is the background they come from in terms of their origin. This question takes on importance especially in India because a great number of religious teachings and hierarchized social groups have been mingling and clashing with one another there for centuries, and each of them has somewhat created its own specific culture. However, in the imagination of the theorists of inculturation in India and those who actually experimented with it, the Indian culture was automatically considered identical to the culture of Hinduism. In addition, the Indian culture was related only with its highest, Sanskritized layer, the tradition of which is borne by a sparse religious elite and has always been the sovereign domain of this elite. The cultures of other Indian religions nor cultural manifestations of folk Hinduism, which represents the major religious current in contemporary India, were more or less not taken into account, not to mention the cultural features of the lowest social groups. The decision of a group of Christian intellectuals, though probably more intuitive than deeply thoughtful, to inculturate Christianity in India exclusively through the Brahmanical tradition provides significant evidence about their relationship to the cultural environment and the status of the Dalits. It is, however, from their ranks, as has been said several times, where, paradoxically, a large amount of Indian Christians come.

Inner or outer inculturation?

It seems undeniable that a religious community will not have its new and distinctive cultural identity established until this identity finds its expression in rituals (Amaladoss 2005: 82). It is through meaningful rituals that the life of a given community takes place. Rituals connect a community when its members identify with them actively and satisfy their need for religious expression through them. In Indian Christianity, however, the vast majority of attempts at inculturation and often very bold experiments focused exclusively on the transformation of the Christian liturgy and the mere adoption of external religious elements from a foreign cultural and religious environment. The inculturated Christian identity created for the needs of the church service and identifiable only at the time when the service is taking place, however, fails to change the status of Indian Christians as foreigners in their own country. This is because liturgy accurately reflects the spiritual life and religious beliefs of the whole community. It corresponds with spiritual needs and the values of its members, however, not only during a ritual but always in close connection with everyday life. The real needs and interests of the local Christian community, however, have not been adequately reflected. The selection of new religious symbols and their integration into the Christian rite were not a result of a free decision made by the members of this community and of their own initiative. On the contrary, they were the work of the church experts who sought to formulate a new religious identity of Indian Christians in accordance with their own ideas of how inculturated Christianity should look (Kuttiyanikkal 2014: 89). The process of inculturation of Christianity in India, with its emphasis on new forms of liturgical expression, which finds its inspiration in the local religious environment, was thus exactly the opposite. The inculturation of Christianity in the form of radical changes in the spiritual and secular life of Indian Christians did not happen and so could not be reflected in natural changes in liturgy (Amalorpavadass 1976: 216).

The failure of inculturation and the search for its new form

Towards the end of the 1980s, the Catholic Church started changing course with respect to inculturation, its function, possibilities and goals and alongside it also with respect to the horizon of interfaith dialogue. Both at the level of national churches and from the point of view of the Church authorities in the Vatican, inculturation attempts often caused controversies and differences of opinion inside the Church, among its official representatives as well as the laity. Legitimate concerns were raised in particular by the danger of the relativization of the exclusivity of the Gospel message and the misguided theological opinions that all religions are the same in their deepest essence (*Redemptoris Missio* 1990: art. 36). Last but not least, there was also the questioning of the missionary nature of the Church as a permanent, universal community, which all people all over the world at all times are invited to participate in because "all the laity are missionaries by baptism" (Ibid., art. 71). It was exactly this relativization that the urgent appeal for the permanent validity of the missionary function as formulated by John Paul II in *Redemptoris Missio*, the papal encyclical published in 1990, was aimed at. In the words of this encyclical, in the history of the Church, "missionary drive has always been a sign of vitality, just as its lessening is a sign of a crisis of faith [. . .] For missionary activity renews the Church, revitalizes faith and Christian identity, and offers fresh enthusiasm and new incentive. Faith is strengthened when it is given to others!" (Ibid., art. 2) However, through the inculturation of Christianity, in particular regarding Asian cultures with their own highly developed religious traditions, the exclusive identity of local Christians was paradoxically weakened (Pattathu 1997: 376–377).

As a result of the attempts at interreligious dialogue and inculturation experiments, the theology of religious pluralism germinated from the environment of these countries in the 1990s. It was inventively formulated by the Belgian Jesuit Jacques Dupuis, who was active for more than thirty years entirely in India, in his magnum opus *Toward a Christian Theology of Religious Pluralism*. Nowhere in his book does Dupuis put all major world religions on an equal footing with Christianity because this would clearly deny the meaning of his missionary claim. Nevertheless, he holds the opinion that the same God who revealed himself in the human form of Jesus Christ is also somewhat active in other religions. Their members thus can claim their share of the salvation by being faithful to the methods and spiritual values of their own religious tradition (Dupuis 2001: 305–329). The inclusivistic, christologically oriented theology of fulfilment, dominating the theological fermentation of the Second Vatican Council, thus turned, through inculturation, interreligious dialogue[7] and exploring the otherness of others (Barnes 2004: 6–8) into the theology of religious pluralism. Its access to other religious traditions is theocentric (Gravend-Tirole 2014: 128). Such a radical shift in the understanding of the means of salvation was, however, unacceptable for the authorities of the Catholic Church. Dupuis's work was placed under the microscope by the Vatican Congregation for the Doctrine of the Faith, headed by the then Cardinal-Prefect, Josef Ratzinger. In 2000, Dupuis finally recanted some of his theological opinions presented in the controversial book when he signed the document that has been published in further editions of his book since then, confirming that

> it is contrary to the Catholic faith to consider the different religions of the world as ways of salvation complementary to the Church. [...] According to the Catholic doctrine, the followers of other religions are oriented to the Church and are all called to become part of it.
> (*Notification on the Book Toward a Christian Theology of Religious Pluralism by Father Jacquis Dupuis, S. J.* 2001: IV, 6–7)

In the last year of the millennium, the Sacred Congregation for the Propagation of the Faith also expressed its opinion on the issue of religious pluralism in its *Dominus Iesus* declaration, which confirms by the concise words of its subtitle the uniqueness and salvific universality of Jesus Christ and the Church. Like many others, it also echoes an unaddressed, yet clearly targeted complaint against the boundless inculturation, which uses relativistic theories to attempt to justify religious pluralism, thus threatening the missionary goal of the Church (*Dominus Iesus* 2000: art. 4). The declaration also repeatedly mentions other religious traditions, admitting that they "contain and offer religious elements which come from God . . . some prayers and rituals of the other religions may assume a role of preparation for the Gospel". However, it concurrently passes judgement on them by saying "one cannot attribute to these, however, a divine origin or an ex opere operato salvific efficacy, which is proper to the Christian sacraments" (Ibid., art. 21). By making this unequivocal doctrinal statement, Church leaders officially ended their support for all existing inculturation experiments, especially in the field of Christian liturgy and the program of inculturation as such, at least in the form it had been understood and implemented in India during the previous forty years.

However, even today, the Indian theologians and scholars dealing with Christianity in contemporary India do not lose sight of the idea of the process through which Christianity has been naturalized in the Indian cultural and religious environment and has become an Indian religion in its fullest sense (Painadath and Parappally 2008: 66), despite the apparent let-down that inculturation suffered. In full accord with the social agenda of churches, to which the Dalit theology of liberation turned its attention, attempts appear to develop a new form or method of inculturation or a whole new conceptual plan of it. Thus approached, inculturation is to be critical of the previously admired mystical values of Hinduism. It should focus its attention on the social reality of India and the everyday environment of Indian Christians, which is characterized by poverty, social oppression and fundamental inequality among people. It is exactly the oppressive cultural values that are the cause of this disparity that inculturation should try to transform (Michael 2010: 81). Its role should be to mediate the interaction between the Gospel and the many different cultures of India, which will be enriched by this process, while the Gospel itself reaches a comprehensible expression of its own values within them and therefore also within the Indian reality (Ibid., 82). Of course, it is impossible to predict for now whether the terms of interculturation or contextualization (Gravend-Tirole 2014: 111) will take root among theologians and scholars for this "new" trend in the process of finding and expressing relevant forms of Indian Christianity or whether the process will result in success.

Notes

1 For detailed analysis of the term "genesis", see (Gravend-Tirole 2014: 112–114).
2 Amalorpavadass is one of the most important figures of the Movement and the most active promoter of inculturation in India. He was one of the founders of the "inculturation laboratory" of the Catholic Church, the NBCLC in Bangalore (National Biblical, Catechetical and Liturgical Centre; see Chap. 3 of this book) and subsequently also took the lead of it for many years. In this essay of his, written in France in the first half of the 1960s and published in India almost half a century later, he still uses the old and not very suitable concept of adaptation. At the same time, he does not feel any need to differentiate himself from its meaning and negative connotations. Because this text was created amid the upheavals of the theological ferment of the Second Vatican Council, the concept of inculturation had not yet been introduced. The ideas presented by Amalor, however, correspond exactly to its concept.
3 See also the conciliar decree of the Catholic Church titled the Pastoral Constitution on the Church in the Modern World, *Gaudium et Spes* 1965: art. 58: "The Church, sent to all peoples of every time and place, is not bound exclusively and indissolubly to any race or nation, any particular way of life or any customary

way of life recent or ancient. Faithful to its own tradition and at the same time conscious of its universal mission, it can enter into communion with various civilizations, for their enrichment and the enrichment of the Church herself."

4 In this context, it is definitely worth mentioning the revealing book by R. Panikkar, *The Unknown Christ of Hinduism* (1964). Its title alone could be understood from the typical point of view of the theology of fulfilment and as a clear allusion to the already cited passage from the Acts of the Apostles in the New Testament, in which Paul explains to the inhabitants of Athens that they are already de facto the devotees of Christ. However, Panikkar appears to have in mind something quite different, namely to discover the unknown Christ present in Hinduism for Christians themselves, not for Hindus.

5 Amalorpavadass, who is the author of this first draft of the content of inculturation, worked it out and put it into concrete terms in the following years (e.g. Amalorpavadass 1978: 27–28). But he also persistently tried to implement the ideals of inculturation in the life of the Indian Catholic Church already during his pastoral and organizational period when he was at the head of the NBCLC and during the last ten years of his life when he turned into a real Christian guru, in the full meaning that this term implies in the tradition of Hinduism, in the *Anjali ashram*.

6 In 1964, Pope Paul VI established the Pontifical Council for Interreligious Dialogue.

7 Surely worth mentioning in this context is the fact that Dupuis himself was a member of the Pontifical Council for Interreligious Dialogue in the early 1990s.

References

Amaladoss, Michael. 2005. *Beyond Inculturation: Can the Many Be One?* New Delhi: Vidyajyoti Education & Welfare Society/ISPCK.

Amaladoss, Michael. 2008. *Beyond Dialogue: Pilgrims to the Absolute*. Bangalore: Asian Trading Corporation.

Amalorpavadass, D. S. (undated, probably 1976). "Indigenous Liturgy: Indian Christian Worship." In *Praying Seminar*. Edited by D. S. Amalorpavadass. Bangalore: NBCLC, pp. 207–216.

Amalorpavadass, D. S. 1978. *Gospel and Culture, Evangelization and Inculturation*. Bangalore: NBCLC.

Amalorpavadass, D. S. 2009. *The Destiny of the Church in the India of Today*. Mysore: Anjali Ashram.

Apostolic Exhortation, *Evangelii Nuntiandi*, 1975.

Barnes, Michael. 2004. *Theology and the Dialogue of Religions*. Cambridge: Cambridge University Press.

Bauman, Chad M. and Richard Fox Young, editors. 2014. *Constructing Indian Christianities: Culture, Conversion and Caste*. New Delhi: Routledge.

Chupungco, Anscar. 1992. *Liturgical Inculturation: Sacramentals, Religiosity, and Catechesis*. Collegeville: The Liturgical Press.

Collins, Paul. 2006. *Context, Culture and Worship: The Quest for "Indian/ness"*. New Delhi: ISPCK.

Constitution on the Sacred Liturgy, *Sacrosanctum Concilium*, 1963.

Cornille, Catherine. 1991. *The Guru in Indian Catholicism: Ambiguity or Opportunity of Inculturation?* Leuven: Peeters Press Louvain.

Declaration on the Relation of the Church to Non-Christian Religions, *Nostra Aetate*, 1965.

Declaration on the Unity and Salvific Universality of Jesus Christ and the Church, *Dominus Iesus*, 2000.
Decree on the Mission Activity of the Church, *Ad Gentes*, 1965.
Dogmatic Constitution on the Church, *Lumen Gentium*, 1964.
D'Sa, Francis X. 1993. "The Dharma of Religion: Towards an Indian Theology of Religion." In *Quest for an Indian Church*. Edited by Kurien Kunnumpuram and Lorenzo Fernando. Anand: Gujarat Sahitya Prakash, pp. 66–96.
Dupuis, Jacques. 2001. *Toward a Christian Theology of Religious Pluralism*. Anand: Gujarat Sahitya Prakash.
The Final Report of the 1985 Extraordinary Synod.
Goel, Sita Ram. 1996. *History of Hindu-Christian Encounters (AD 304 to 1996)*. New Delhi: Voice of India.
Gravend-Tirole, Xavier. 2014. "From Christian Ashrams to Dalit Theology: Or beyond: An Examination of the Indigenisation/Inculturation Trend within the Indian Catholic Church." In *Constructing Indian Christianities: Culture, Conversion and Caste*. Edited by Chad M. Bauman and Richard Fox Young. New Delhi: Routledge, pp. 110–137.
Kunnumpuram, Kurien. 1993. "Towards a New Ecclesiology in the Light of Vatican II." In *Quest for an Indian Church*. Edited by Kurien Kunnumpuram and Lorenzo Fernando. Anand: Gujarat Sahitya Prakash, pp. 1–30.
Kuttiyanikkal, Ciril J. 2014. *Khrist Bhakta Movement: A Model for an Indian Church? Inculturation in the Area of Community Building*. Zürich: Lit Verlag.
Mattam, Joseph. 2002. "Monchanin: The Christianization of India, and *Ecclesia in Asia*." In *Saccidanandaya Namah: A Commemorative Volume*. Thanirpalli: Saccidananda Ashram, pp. 134–147.
Michael, S. M. 2010. "Cultural Diversity and Inculturation in India." *Sedos* 42 (3/4): 77–84.
Notification on the Book toward a Christian Theology of Religious Pluralism by Father Jacquis Dupuis, S.J. Rome: Offices of the Congregation of the Faith, 2001.
On the Permanent Validity of the Church's Missionary Mandate, *Redemptoris Missio*, 1990.
Painadath, Sebastian and Jacob Parappally, editors. 2008. *A Hindu-Catholic Brahmabandhab Upadhyay's Significance for Indian Christian Theology*. Bangalore: Asian Trading Corporation.
Panikkar, Raimundo. 1964. *The Unknown Christ of Hinduism*. London: Darton, Longman & Todd Ltd.
Pastoral Constitution on the Church in the Modern World, *Gaudium et Spes*, 1965.
Pattathu, Paul. 1997. *Ashram Spirituality*. Indore: Satprakashan.
Post-Synodal Apostolic Exhortation, *Catechesi Tradendae*, 1979.
Post-Synodal Apostolic Exhortation, *Ecclesia in Asia*, 1999.
Prasad, Swami Iswar. 1993. "Preparation for Inter-Faith Dialogue." In *Christians Ashrams: A Movement with a Future?* Edited by Vandana. New Delhi: ISPCK, pp. 102–106.
Sahi, Jyoti. 1993. "The Ashram as a Place for Spiritual Wholeness." In *Christians Ashrams: A Movement with a Future?* Edited by Vandana. New Delhi: ISPCK, pp. 126–140.
Saldanha, Julian. 1997. *Inculturation*. Mumbai: St Pauls.

Shorter, Aylward. 1988. *Toward a Theology of Inculturation*. London: Geoffrey Chapman.

Staffner, Hans. 1987. *Jesus Christ and the Hindu Community: Is a Synthesis of Hinduism and Christianity Possible?* Anand: Gujarat Sahitya Prakash.

Wilfred, Felix. 2005. *On the Banks of Ganges, Doing Contextual Theology*. New Delhi: ISPCK.

3
HISTORY OF THE CHRISTIAN ASHRAM MOVEMENT

The previous chapter described the Christian Ashram Movement as the most prominent attempt to implement theological reflections and ideas of inculturation of Christianity in India. The actual beginnings of the history of Christian ashrams, however, date back several decades before the churches in Asia and Africa discovered the opportunities that the inculturation process offered them. Therefore, they overlap with the development of the Movement only partially. However, the Movement undeniably owes its gradually gained strength and even attraction, albeit transient, to this very process, because it brought the Movement into the spotlight of church authorities and also some Indian Christians for a certain period of time.

Except for some notable exceptions (in particular Ralston 1987; Pulsfort 1989), primarily, those who have systematically dealt with the Christian Ashram Movement to date, regardless of whether their motivation was apologetic or moderately critical, have also been personally involved in it. Therefore, their observations and conclusions inevitably reflect the ideological assumption that the ashram phenomenon really has the potential to transform Christianity in India, making it more Indian. How deep and momentous in terms of its content the transformation should be, when it started in the past, which historic events belong to its framework and which do not, whether the Christian ashram vision is a clearly defined and graspable concept or, conversely, if it has been transformed into something completely different in the course of its development are all questions left unanswered. Very little clarity is thus provided in the present works dealing with the history of the Movement. As a matter of fact, the same applies to the broadly conceived conceptual plan of inculturation. In an effort to find the beginnings of the Movement and its historical inspirational models, individual authors take their own excursuses into the history of Christianity in India. They look for parallels of thought where they find only partial external similarities. Inevitably, they arrive at simplifications and hasty conclusions as they relate to something that was created in considerably different historical contexts, perhaps even with a motivation completely opposite to that which motivated the founders of Christian ashrams.

Therefore, the aim of the present part of our book is to draw a complex picture of the history of the Christian Ashram Movement. We strive to aptly depict the key motives underlying the origin and development of the idea of Christian ashrams. We seek to follow the transformations of the idea throughout the 20th century as it was conceived by various churches and personalities involved in the Movement. We thus hope to stake out individual phases of the complex process that the ashram idea has undergone. Within the existing literature dealing with the Movement, this is the very first attempt at describing its entire history. We aspire to achieve this goal both in terms of the extent of the chosen coverage, where no truly significant personality or event is missing, as well as by putting the Movement in the context of Christianity in India in the 20th century.

Beginnings – the pioneer myth

The Jesuit Mission in the South Indian city of Madurai was founded in 1600, but its true development began six years later with the arrival of the Italian missionary Roberto de Nobili. The aim of the mission was to weaken the Portuguese influence on the emerging Christian communities and to change the object of missionary efforts, namely to shift conversions from low castes and untouchable segments of society to the Brahman castes. There is probably no other missionary in the history of Indian Christianity whose achievements in spreading the Gospel are more positive, albeit limited in time. Although evaluations of de Nobili's conception vary (Barnes 2004: 146–148), he was undoubtedly centuries ahead of his time. Like Alessandro Valignano and his disciple Matteo Ricci, both coenobites of the same order, a few decades earlier in Japan and China, de Nobili also refused to yield to the stereotyped approach of missionaries of his time (Županov 2005: 16). As a true pioneer, he made use of external adaptation to draw attention to the difference between the Christian doctrine and the European cultural customs that missionaries until then had brought with them to India together with the Word of God. Embracing the customs was an epiphenomenon accompanying every conversion; for converts, it was probably even more important than their inward spiritual conversion. In addition to his extraordinary intellectual achievements that put him on an equal footing with the Brahman elite in debates, de Nobili also adapted his own lifestyle to the Hindu environment. He adopted local eating habits, learned certain spiritual practices, dressed himself in the manner of Hindu saints, which also included the controversial wearing of the sacred thread of the twice-born and the Brahmanical braid on the top of the head. He decided to become a Christian *sannyasin* (Cronin 1959: 70–71), so he would be able "to preach the message of Christ more effectively and to reach the Hindu mind" in the Indian environment (Rajan 1989: 71).

These experiments, as well as their relative success regarding conversions achieved among the Brahmanical classes, which of course sparked envy among less successful missionaries, did not always meet with a positive response from de Nobili's Church superiors. Eventually, he had to face a charge of abandoning the Christian faith and becoming a Hindu and was therefore called by the Inquisition to Goa to confess his acts. He eventually lost his case in the Conciliar Court proceedings held in 1619, but immediately appealed to the Pope. In the remarkable letter that he sent in his defence to the then Pope Paul V in the same year, which is truly deserving of a longer quote, he explained the motives behind his actions. Only thanks to them, he managed to attract the interest of some Brahmans from Madurai and later won them over for baptism:

> When I noticed that certain Brahmins were highly praised because they led lives of great hardship and austerity and were looked upon as if they had dropped from the sky, I thought that, if to win popularity among the pagans, and raise themselves in their esteem, they contrived to keep perpetual chastity and weaken their bodies by watching, fasting and meditation, I could, to win them to Christ, conform myself to their mode of life in all such things which were not repugnant to the holiness of Christian doctrine, for it seemed to me that with divine help I could do for God's sake, what they did with wicked cunning to win vain applause and worldly honours.
> (Kuriakose 2006: 50–51)

The overwhelming majority of the representatives and advocates of the Movement usually automatically consider de Nobili's missionary centre in Madurai the first Christian ashram in India (e.g. Amaladoss 2008: 157; Pattathu 1997: 168). The description of the centre and the activities taking place there, as it was drawn up at that time, is, however, too vague. Therefore, when evaluating them, we have to rely on the insights of later biographers of de Nobili (in addition to the aforementioned Cronin, see also Sauliere 1995; Rajamanickam 1972) and other authors, who, however, a priori longed to find the ideals of inculturation in his bold experiments with adaptation. If being a place where personal experience with God is sought after intensively and over a long period of time (Amaladoss 2008: 161) is assumed to be at least one fundamental characteristic that varied definitions of the Christian ashram have in common, then de Nobili's centre was scarcely in accord with it. Being a leading missionary figure, he could in principle live up to the demands imposed on a guru as somebody who had already achieved such experience and so a circle of disciples gathered around him. Nevertheless, the available information does not suggest that de Nobili then led these disciples in his "ashram" systematically and individually and accompanied them on the journey of their spiritual growth. Neither do we find here any traces indicative of an increased emphasis being placed on spiritual contemplation, which is, to the contrary, pivotal for later Christian ashrams and their search for personal experience of God's existence. De Nobili replaced the process of seeking God with a missionary presentation of evangelization, although in a revolutionary manner of *accommodatio* (Županov 2001: 22–23) because it took place in the setting of the Tamil cultural environment.

It is not only misleading to describe de Nobili as a promoter of inculturation (Hedlund 2000: 183) but also primarily methodologically incorrect. In fact, the concept arising from the modern evolution of Christianity is thus translated and applied to completely different historical conditions. By contrast, identification of the Indian cultural tradition with expressions and acts of its elite representatives and creating thus a pan-Indian religion (Županov 2001: 90) is where de Nobili's conception of the Christian mission in India notably coincides with later missionaries' efforts at adaptation, indigenization or inculturation. It is not so important to find the exact term in this context, because de Nobili really approached the world of Brahmans' religious ideas as "the only voice of India" (Arun 2007: 8). And like many theorists of inculturation as well as those who tried to turn the defined ideas into a living practice in Christian ashrams, de Nobili either did not see or intentionally refused to see the deeply dynamic relation between cultural and religious symbols (the saffron robe as the traditional clothing of Hindu ascetics, the sacred thread of the twice-born, the tuft of hair, the sectarian sign made with sandalwood paste on the forehead etc.) and religious teachings that constitute the actual meaning of the symbols to a fundamental extent (Ibid., 31).

Hand in hand with his pioneering merits of creating the concept of Christian ashrams, de Nobili is also credited with the role "of the father of Christian *sannyasa*" (Teasdale 1987: 23; Rajan 1989: 71). The belief that it is just and solely Christian *sannyasin* that can efficiently address India because he will offer it the Gospel using the expressive means that are understandable and meaningful within the context of the local religious traditions connects de Nobili with Brahmabandhav Upadhyay from the end of the 19th century. He can be truly considered the actual founder of the first ashram, not only a mythologized pioneer. This connection, stretching over several centuries, is crucial for the history of the Movement regarding the emphasis it puts on the role of an ascetic missionary. It even extends to the many ashrams, in particular Catholic, from the middle of the 20th century, when a real movement emerged from what had until then constituted only a peripheral, unique phenomenon. However, regarding the understanding of *sannyasa*, de Nobili, unlike Upadhyay, seems to stick to the outward impression, because he simply "chose elements that suited his purpose and discarded the rest" (Županov 2001: 208). According to his own words, de Nobili accepted the lifestyle of self-denial and the attributes that are characteristic for Hindu ascetics out of strategic necessity because "if these people did not see me do such penance, they would not receive me as one who can teach them the way to heaven" (Cronin 1959: 74). Despite all of his revolutionary adaptation performances, de Nobili only used his knowledge of Tamil and Sanskrit religious texts to make Christian doctrines and Catholic Church dogmas more accessible to the educated Brahmanical classes (Barnes 2004: 144), and thus he "mimed Hindu culture in order to transform it" (Županov 2001: 208). His extraordinary activities in India continued to be dominated by the usual missionary agenda with the simple motive of converting the locals to Christianity. If the members of Christian ashrams profess him as their predecessor who boldly charted the way forward for them, by doing so, they ignore the fundamental difference between the means and ends. For de Nobili, the adopted Indian lifestyle and the whole complex of assumed "inculturation" elements, no matter how daring they were in his time, were only a means to an end, "a weapon to win over the enemies" (Arun 2007: 32), while religious conversions remained the clear goal. By contrast, the aim of the Christian Ashram Movement, or at least of its strongest and most notable stream, is inculturation itself. The further spreading of the Gospel message among non-Christians and the possibility of their conversion stand aside the interest in ashrams. It is essential for their members to express their religious beliefs and language in ways that emanate from the cultural and religious traditions of India and are thus inherent in this tradition. It seems that the relating of ashramites to de Nobili arises from the unresolved theological question concerning the still valid or already overcome missionary claims of Christianity in a postcolonial, globalized world. Its urgency may be ignored temporarily; however, the question itself will not automatically disappear of its own accord.

Beginnings – a less well-known myth

The second attempt to establish an "ashram" is also shrouded in the mist of conjectures and conflicting interpretations. As opposed to de Nobili, whose followers virtually the whole Movement profess to be, the ashram created in the middle of the 19th century in Kerala is mentioned by only a few of the authors dealing with the Movement. Moreover, their opinions differ markedly; while Amaladoss (2008: 157) claimed it was an ashram community, without basing his claim on any convincing evidence, J. Rajan (1989: 176) says precisely the opposite (see also Vineeth 2003: 205). Three Indian priests of the Syro-Malabar Church, Thomas Palackal, Thomas Porukara and Kuriakos Chavara, founded the first monastery of the newly established order of Carmelites of Mary Immaculate (CMI) in Mannanam, Kerala, in 1831.[1] Their desire was to create an indigenized contemplative community drawing inspiration from the ascetic way of life of Hindu *sannyasins*. However, from the time of de Nobili, Church authorities had viewed with utmost caution any efforts to express Christian religious content and the spiritual message of the Gospel through Indian means of expression, even more so if they arose from the local clergy. The founders were therefore discouraged from their originally extreme concept of ascetic hermitage. As a result, the congregation finally set off for their journey following a sort of middle course – the life of a religious order divided between contemplation and active service to help needy persons (Teasdale 1987: 23). The centre of their community was called "Darshana Veedu" ("the house where you 'see' God") (Rajan 1989: 175). It was dedicated to prayers and spiritual contemplation, and, since its very beginning, it was also very much open to local laymen who could receive personal spiritual leadership from the order priests there. In particular, K. Chavara, the first prior general of the order, and also the vicar general of the Syro-Malabar Catholic Church from 1861, who was beatified by Pope John Paul II in 1986, was remarkable for the extraordinary charisma he possessed for a spiritual leader and his good organizational abilities.[2] Under his leadership, the activities of the order expanded. However, the regular contemplative encounters organized in many parishes throughout Kerala were soon supplemented with educational and generally socially beneficial activities. Subsequently, the original idea of a community of Christian *sannyasins* living in seclusion and seeking the mystical experience of God's existence in the manner of Hindu holy men vanished very quickly. The uncertainty and hesitation in assessing this early "ashram" are also caused by the fact that, despite the proclaimed inspiration by the Indian religious and cultural environment, the community retained all the external features typical for the tradition of Western monasticism, including the way the monks and priests of the order dressed (Teasdale 1987: 24). Any direct Indian influences on the form or identity of the community thus remained obscure. Hence, this attempt at establishing an ashram also seems more like a myth in the history of the Movement.

Beginnings – the "Hindu-Catholic" ashram

The 19th-century reformist religious and social ferment bore ample fruit for majority Hinduism and, somewhat later, also for Islam and Christianity in India. The unprecedented rise in Christian missionary activities, however, had already begun in the second decade of the 19th century. It came as an immediate result of a change in the religious policies as they had been implemented after 1813 in connection with the revision of the founding charter of the British East India Company in the territories under the Company's administration. Missionaries were no longer to be denied entry to these territories or the right to perform their activities in them. On the contrary, officials responsible for civilian administration were supposed to support their activities because, in the long run, the emerging colonial power was not able to staff its existence in India in sufficient numbers solely from its own, necessarily limited, resources. The efficient operation of such a complex bureaucratic apparatus required with increasing urgency that the local educated population be involved. If they were Christians, their loyalty would understandably be more credible and durable. The approach to the Hindu cultural and religious tradition characterized by the considerable verbal aggressiveness as practised in particular by Protestant field preachers began to bear real fruit no earlier than towards the end of the 19th century. It resulted from mass conversions, but once again mainly among members of the low castes of Hindu society or the socially ostracized classes. In the long run, however, these conversions only contributed to the growing polarization of religious communities present in India.

A more important and interesting role in the inner evolution of Christianity in India seems to have been performed by notable Christian reformers of the educational system in the then centre of power of the British India, Calcutta. It was due to their influence that the Christian doctrine appeared in the spotlight of the urban intellectual classes, firmly and decisively, and de facto for the first time in Indian history, becoming either an appeal for radical reforms of the indigenous traditions or a real religious alternative to them. Those who let themselves be inspired by Christianity (Ram Mohan Roy, Keshab Chandra Sen etc.) or who finally became Christians after many personal trials and tribulations (Nehemiah Goreh, Lalbihari De etc.) refused, however, to only passively accept everything that was brought from the outside and presented to them as an immutable set of allegedly fundamental features of Christianity. In the fast-changing social atmosphere of the second half of the 19th century, the political assertiveness of educated Indians was growing, inevitably finding its expression also on the religious plane. Perhaps nobody else embodied the evidence of the permanent existential tension under which these "new Indian Christians" had to live alongside the reluctant responses of the Churches to the changing conditions in the countries to which they sent their missionaries more convincingly than Bhabani Charan Banerjee. Under his adopted name of Brahmabandhav Upadhyay, the Brahman convert from Bengal became not only the first Indian Christian theologian but also a founder of the first Christian ashram, (roughly) in the sense of how it is perceived by the later Movement.

The testimony of pursuing a quest in life

Although Bhabani Charan Banerjee was born in 1861 into a traditional, religiously conservative Brahman family, belonging to the ritually high-ranking *kulin* caste, the period of the second half of the 19th century induced important changes in these strata as well. The process of the formation of the inquisitive intellect, which, however, never goes beyond personally experienced religiosity, somewhat corresponded in its many aspects to certain patterns of that time prevailing in the environment of the Hindu social elite. Modern English education was combined with traditional schooling based on Sanskrit as its medium and content; reformist religious movements were adopted alongside the culminating efforts to delimit against them;

inspiration was sought in Christianity and the fascination with the figure of Christ was increasing; personal engagement in service to country was considered while ideas were germinating of relieving it from the humiliating yoke of dependency and inferiority that was imposed on the country by the colonial rule of foreigners. Many of Bhabani's peers necessarily underwent individual yet complementary phases of such a process, however, with markedly varied outcomes.

On his remarkable life's journey, Bhabani met many spiritual leaders of that time in the Bengali environment. During his studies, he was significantly influenced by the educator and political leader Surendranath Banerjee. He was bound by personal friendship with Narendranath Dutt, later known as Swami Vivekananda. Having met the founder of the "Indian Church" titled *The Church of the New Dispensation*, Keshab Chandra Sen, Bhabani became an active member of it, just as shortly before his conversion to Christianity, he had been active in the reformist Brahmo Samaj. The field where Bhabani found himself to some extent became education and activities raising public awareness in the broadest sense of the word. After all, it was such activities that led him, in the last years of his life, to a short yet intensive cooperation with Rabindranath Thakur in the building of the ashram training school in Shantiniketan.

The strenuous intellectual and spiritual quest no doubt underpinned Bhabani's fated decision to become a Christian. However, the idea had been slowly germinating in him for a long time. He was baptized by an Anglican pastor at the beginning of 1891 but joined the Catholic Church several months later, being attracted to it by the general universalism which the Catholic Church lays claim to. At his baptism, he chose the name Theophilus (friend of God). Three years later, he started to consistently use its sanskritized version Brahmabandhav, along with the cognomen Upadhyay (Teacher), during all his public activities. At the same time, aged 34, he also became a *sannyasin*. Like de Nobili less than three centuries before, he also adopted the traditional external sign of Hindu ascetics, the saffron robe, to the great displeasure of his ecclesiastical superiors and to undisguised consternation and misunderstanding among many ordinary believers. For the rest of the last decade of the 19th century, Upadhyay de facto devoted himself to a theological elaboration of this symbolic and concurrently also existential act of his. It culminated finally in a daring attempt, probably historically too early and therefore unsuccessful, to establish an ashram community of Christian *sannyasins*. He presented his revolutionary theological ideas, in which he strove to express the essence of Christian teaching not only by means of terminology but, in particular, by means of the principles of the philosophy of *Advaita Vedanta*. He formulated them boldly in the lectures he gave occasionally and in the several periodicals that he had tried to publish until his premature death. Of these publications, *Sophia*, a magazine written in English and published mostly at monthly intervals during

1894–1899 (in the second half of 1900, Upadhyay renewed the magazine as a weekly for a short period of time), rightly deserves the greatest attention. In *Sophia*, he presented not only his theologically erudite discoveries when comparing Christianity and Hinduism but also visions of their integration and mutual enrichment. The most intriguing of these seem to be his considerations relating to the Christian *sannyasa*, Christian *Vedanta* or the theological concept of *Saccidananda* as a representation of the Holy Trinity. Thus, *Sophia* can justly be described as "the first Catholic periodical with a positive approach towards Hinduism, its implied goal was to build up an Indian Christian Theology" (Pattathu 1997: 172–173). *Sophia*, however, soon became a thorn in the side of ecclesiastical authorities. The magazine and its publisher and author in one person were exposed to ever more pointed attacks that reached their peak in 1900 when further publishing was banned. A similar fate also awaited Upadhyay's further journal attempts, *Twentieth Century* (1901) and *Sandhya* (1904–1907). With the onset of the new century and with his typical determination, he became ever more involved in the political struggle of Indian nationalists against the British colonial empire. He fully engaged in the *Swadeshi* movement, which mobilized Indian society on a mass scale for the first time in 1904. Its ever louder attacks against the power structures of the Empire, against the domination of foreigners as such and the open call for Indian self-government, or even independence, finally put him in jail in 1907. A short time later, after a failed hernia operation and subsequent medical complications, Brahmabandhav Upadhyay died at the age of 46.

In this later stage of his life, he seemed to be moving more and more away not only from official Catholic circles but even from his supporters among the ranks of Christians and also from some of his students (among them his later biographer Animananda, who will be mentioned later). He confused and even embarrassed them by his active participation in the major Hindu holidays and, in particular, by publicly undergoing the cleansing Hindu ritual of *prayaschitta*.[3] A separate subchapter will try to explain that this confusion was due to the misunderstanding of the concept of the "Hindu Catholic", whom Upadhyay had considered himself from as early as his conversion. Similarly, we will strive to explicate that the cleansing ritual he underwent did not mean his re-conversion and return to Hinduism but on the contrary was just a summary and explicit expression of Upadhyay's lifelong theological mission.

Brahmabandhav Upadhyay – the source base and literature

The importance of Upadhyay in the development of Christianity in India, in particular the Catholic Church, is evidenced by numerous critical studies dealing with his life and work (for their selective overview, it is best to see Lipner 2001: xix–xxiii; Tennent 2005: 34–38). After almost a century of facing difficulties in accessing the source base, the collected edition of Upadhyay's legacy appeared in two volumes titled *The Writings of Brahmabandhab Upadhyay* (Lipner and Gispert-Sauch 1991, 2002). It can be definitely classified as a crucial contribution, opening up a vast field for further research. Regarding the biographical literature, the first who asked for the floor was Upadhyay's disciple, Revachand Gyanchand. In 1908, he had already published a shorter biography sketch titled *Swami Upadhyay Brahmabandhav: A Story of his Life* under the name of B.[rahmacharin] Animananda and at his own expense. The publication, which is now virtually unavailable, was further reworked by Animananda himself near the end of his life. The resulting work of *The Blade: Life and Work of Brahmabandhab Upadhyay* (Animananda 1946), considered Upadhyay's definitive biography, became so standard and widely quoted in all subsequent critical reflections that this work itself can be classified as a source of its own kind. After all, such an assertion immediately follows from the fact that Animananda converted to Christianity under the influence of Upadhyay. He also participated in all Upadhyay's activities for more than ten years, including the first unsuccessful attempt to establish a Christian ashram. Finally, he grew apart from his teacher in 1904 after the previously mentioned misunderstanding about Upadhyay's alleged re-conversion. Besides the generally summarizing information, the content of which is more or less repeated in the three fundamental works dealing with the beginnings of Indian Christian theology,[4] the monographic study by J. Lipner titled *Brahmabandhab Upadhyay: The Life and Thought of a Revolutionary* (2001) merits special attention. It is an extensive and so far the best biography, approached in a modern way and dealing with its topic in a truly thorough manner. The last major contribution to the topic, *Building Christianity on Indian Foundations* (Tennent 2005), can also be considered an exceptional work. The author puts Upadhyay into the context of the historical space and time in an absolutely innovative manner. In terms of the scope and depth of his work, Tennent is undoubtedly the very first researcher who systematically analyzes Upadhyay's theological contribution to Christianity in the context of the Indian religious and cultural tradition.

The idea of Hindu Catholicism

The connection between Upadhyay's approach and the approach selected by de Nobili seems to be undeniable. At a fleeting, simplifying glance, it is as if Upadhyay only developed the reflections and methods of his famous predecessor, adding weight and significance to them by being firmly anchored in the Brahman tradition, this time without the necessity of the imitative self-presentation that de Nobili resorted to for pragmatic reasons (Barnes 2004: 145). The starting points of both of them may really seem to be similar. Upadhyay, however, abandons de Nobili, leaving him far behind himself somewhere in the middle of his life's theological journey. De Nobili rehabilitated some selected, conflict-free elements of this system (attire, diet, philosophical and theological terminology etc.) to increase the efficiency of evangelization. Upadhyay no more perceives them as mere means leading to conversion. He tries to discover a completely new content, latently present in Christianity, through them. Like de Nobili, he is also committed to converting India, at least in the first years after his own conversion.[5] However, with time, he is increasingly convinced that because such a conversion can only be enabled by throwing away the European garb which Christianity in India has been clothed in so far, adoption and adaptation of the Hindu garb will naturally lead to the enrichment of Christianity itself ("The Clothes of Catholic Faith" in Lipner and Gispert-Sauch 2002: 205–207). As he further ruminated on this initial idea, his demands for conversion seemed to be sidelined, with requirements for inner transformation of the Catholic Church and Christianity in India emerging in their place (Cornille 1991: 131).

The approach adopted by all of the great Indian predecessors of Upadhyay, such as, for example, Nehemiah Goreh, Lalbihari De or his own uncle, also a Christian convert, K. M. Banerjee, to their original philosophical and religious tradition was considerably confrontational (Tennent 2005: 7). They were, as a matter of fact, indigenous Christian apologists, who challenged the Hindu customs and religious practices from the perspective of those having personal experience with this religious system. According to T. C. Tennent, the importance of Upadhyay lies in the fact that it was he who first attempted to newly define the content and essence of the concept of Hinduism (Ibid., 9) in comparison with universal Catholicism and thus separated the firm, easy-to-grasp religious belief from its multiple cultural expressions. He was able to accept the former without necessarily having to reject or stop practising the latter and relate to it as to something that was personally very important and inalienable for him. According to Upadhyay, there is no unified set of generally accepted religious doctrines that could be traced in Hinduism across its historical development. Consequently, Hinduism represents "an orientation in the world" (Lipner 2001: 209) and an inherent and therefore also culture-specific manner of thinking and experiencing rather than a precise religious content.

Upadhyay first came up with the key idea of the Hindu Catholic in 1895[6] in his polemic with the theosophist Annie Besant, whom he himself introduces as "a Brahman by birth and a Christian and Catholic by faith" ("Open Letter to Mrs Annie Besant" in Lipner 2001: 159). This idea creates the real backbone of all of Upadhyay's considerations, theological and, in a later period, also nationalist but also of his specific acts by which he wanted to rehabilitate Christianity in India and further present it as a meaningful religious message. In his cardinal "Are We Hindus?" article, appearing in *Sophia* in July of 1898 (Lipner and Gispert-Sauch 1991: 24–25), he develops the idea with a brief list of constitutive properties of the Hindu experience of life's internal and external reality. Among these he includes the tendency to contemplate, pensiveness and the synthetic way of thinking, which stands in contrast to the activity, practicality and analysis that are in turn typical of Greek thinking. By this, he alludes to the considerations that were presented earlier in *Sophia* concerning the fatal mistake of bringing Christianity to India in its ancient garb, that is, through the language, methods and content themes that served well for the adoption of Christianity across Europe but could not appeal to India. According to Upadhyay's conceptions, *Vedanta* should become the language and principle of Indian Christian thinking,[7] because "a Hindu-Catholic" remains "a Hindu so far as his physical and mental constitution is concerned, but in regard to his immortal soul he is a Catholic" (Lipner and Gispert-Sauch 1991: 25). It is *Vedanta*[8] that Upadhyay perceives as an applicable method of learning about God, man and the world, while understanding Christianity as a universal religious message that is complementary to any cultural tradition and way of thinking. Thus, newly conceived Indian Christianity was supposed to be created by specific means of the *Saccidananda* concept on the theological plane and missionaries-*sannyasins* and Christian *matha*-monastery on the practical and spiritual plane.

God is Saccidananda

In the later Upanishads, the ultimate reality (*brahma*), exclusively possessing the absolute fullness of being, is usually understood as being without qualities (*nirguna*). Every attribute through which we would attempt to capture the fullness thus approached would inevitably define and limit it and therefore deprive it of some part of its indivisible fullness. However, the pure being that is thus viewed most probably represents a reality that is too abstract. The human mind inevitably grasps the world and its own place in it through the word, and so Shankara and many of his disciples appear to somewhat abandon the requirement for undefined absoluteness; otherwise, they would have nothing to say on the matter, describing the experience of the supreme being (*parabrahma anubhoga*) as the fullness of being (*sat*), the fullness of consciousness or intelligence (*cit*) and the fullness of joy or bliss (*ananda*). It is not different qualities that this triad of concepts is to represent but integral features of the unity that are mutually conditioned to such an extent that they cannot even be imagined as separate. The Sanskrit grammar also gives symbolic weight to this requirement of theirs, as the form of individual words in the final compound word – *Saccidananda* – is slightly, yet still substantially changed, due to the sandhi alternations resulting from the phonemic merger.

Upadhyay was not the first who, in this context that we can outline here only in a too-simplified way,[9] recognized that it could be utilized for the presentation of the key Christian tenet, the Trinity mystery, in the Hindu environment. The previously mentioned Neo-Hindu reformer Keshab Chandra Sen, in his famous "That marvellous mystery – the Trinity" lecture, given in 1882, identified the individual features with which the Sanskritic tradition of *Vedanta* describes the supreme being with the respective entities present in the Christian Trinity (Scott 1979: 220–229). Upadhyay, obviously more erudite in the source texts of *Vedanta*[10] and without doubt free from simplifying conclusions that are typical for Neo-Hinduism in its reflections of its own religious tradition, further developed this idea indicated by his early teacher. He enriched it with reflections concerning the relationship dynamics present inside the Trinity as well as a creative interconnection of the Trinity with the world, which he approaches, in agreement with *Vedanta*, as an illusion or rather as an astonishing, inconceivable and powerful creative force (*maya*). Last but not least, he consistently applied the neo-Thomism deductive argumentation to the whole concept of *Saccidananda* so that the resulting ontological vision concerning the nature of God would correspond as closely as possible to the traditional concept of Catholic theology. God the Father (*parabrahma*) represents and concurrently possesses the fullness of being (*sat*). God the Son is the Father's self-consciousness (*cit*). Because consciousness becomes revealed and apparent through the word, the Son becomes the word (*logos* or also *shabdabrahma*). Finally, God the Holy Spirit (*shvasitabrahma*) as the epitome of the eternal and loving relationship between the Father and the Son can be nothing other than joy or absolute bliss (*ananda*).

Upadhyay repeatedly returned to the concept of God who is *Saccidananda* on the pages of his *Sophia* for a large part of the time when the magazine was published. As an original thinker, he sought to express his intellectual theological discoveries but concurrently his personal love for God. His theological language is therefore often full of astonishing poetry, magically clad in Sanskritic attire, hence, as a matter of fact, resembling the most genuine and refined expressions of *bhakti* in terms of language and ideas. In this sense, the prime and internally firmly concise form seems to be his famous Sanskrit hymn celebrating the Divine Trinity, *Vande Saccidanandam*. It appeared together with its English translation in the October issue of *Sophia* in 1898 (Lipner and Gispert-Sauch 1991: 126–127; Tennent 2005: 383–384). The hymn that Upadhyay himself presents as the "canticle" actually meets all of the rhythmic, metaphorical and thematic requirements of the traditional Sanskrit stotra that praises the chosen deity (*ishtadevata*) by piling up one after another praising attributes with mythical, mythological or philosophical meaning and symbolism. Because Upadhyay addresses his hymn to the Trinity, the initial refrain and the first strophe that jointly define the object of adoration are gradually followed by the next three strophes dedicated to the Father, the Son and the Holy Spirit.[11] The importance of this hymn lies in the fact that it was rehabilitated after several decades of oblivion and set to music and spread as the "best example of a deep adaptation of the Christian faith to the cultural patterns of Indian religious thought" (Gispert-Sauch 1972: 60) among Christians throughout India. In connection with the topic of ashrams, it deserves special attention also because the Catholic ashramites quickly adopted it, it found a firm place in their liturgical hymnbooks and, as such, it became an integral and in many cases a truly everyday part of experimental ritual systems that appear in ashrams. The fact that the hymn in its theological anchoring remains consistently conservative, being in fact a Sanskrit expression of the essence of the Catholic catechism, detracts nothing from its importance for the whole Movement. In the aptly summarizing words of Upadhyay's sympathetic critic and biographer, J. Lipner, *Vande Saccidanandam* "straightforwardly presents fulfilment theology at its most brilliant" (Lipner 2001: 201). A similar assessment can, however, also be related not only to the hymn and the *Saccidananda* concept but also to the overall legacy Upadhyay bequeathed to Indian Christianity.

The order of Christian sannyasins

That the still-new convert from a high Brahman caste adopted the saffron robe, the traditional external sign of Hindu ascetics that Upadhyay first put on in December 1894, was not due merely to his eccentricity. Nor was it a subconscious expression of his doubts regarding the conversion itself, as some Church leaders and common believers may have assumed. It was as if Upadhyay had already adumbrated his forthcoming decision through the pages of *Sophia* two month earlier, in his article titled "Conversion of India – An Appeal" (Lipner and Gispert-Sauch 2002: 175–178). The theological message of this contribution is still strictly anti-Vedantic and pro-theistic, directed in particular against the increasingly active *Arya Samaj*. Nevertheless, Upadhyay also outlined the basic contours of his future conceptual plan here and subsequently became fully engaged in its implementation during 1898–1899. Having briefly summarized the principal errors of previous missionary attempts and evangelizing strategies, he came up with the requirement to create the all-India missionary centre. A new class of missionary-preachers would be shaped there and subsequently sent to all the regions of India without being tied to a single parish or diocese, acting as wandering religious teachers – *parivrajakas*, fully in the spirit of the freedom of the Hindu tradition. At this early stage of his concept of Indian Christianity, which means before the fundamental intellectual and spiritual rehabilitation of *Vedanta*, Upadhyay emphasizes in particular the need to present the Christian tidings as something that does not take away the key attributes of the Hindu cultural, or even national, identity. He primarily inveighs against the missionary activities of Protestant Churches.[12] In his own words, contrariwise "the itinerant missionaries should be thoroughly Hindu in their mode of living [...] should be strict vegetarians and teetotallers, and put on the yellow *sannyasi* garb" (Ibid., 177). Just as de Nobili, whom Upadhyay ranks among "the glorious old Fathers of the South", did three centuries before him, Upadhyay also argues that only a preacher who became a *sannyasin* can acquire and enjoy the highest esteem among Hindus, and only a preacher who is well knowledgeable of the Sanskrit tradition is able "to vanquish Hindu preachers" (Ibid.).

Two and a half years later, in the spring of 1897, Upadhyay returned to this briefly outlined idea to further elaborate it in his article titled "The Impending Crisis – An Appeal" (Ibid., 194–196) published in *Sophia*. Here, he presents the proposed missionary brotherhood, or perhaps even a new religious order, the leader of which he quite possibly aspired to become himself, in the opinion of J. Lipner (2001: 206), as "learned and zealous missionaries, holy men, of ascetic habits, and a metaphysical turn of mind issuing from a common centre of operations established in India [...] travelling all over India, giving lectures and holding public disputations with learned Pundits" (Lipner and Gispert-Sauch 2002: 195). It was the possibility of establishing and developing such a community or spiritual centre that Upadhyay was most strongly attracted to. And so May of the next year found him not only in the middle of intensely searching for a suitable location that would accommodate his dreamed-of experiment, and securing the necessary support from the ecclesiastical authorities that would take the entire project under their wings,[13] but also in the full flood of thinking out ideological and purely practical details of the educational formation of future Christian *sannyasins*. An increased emphasis on the monastic way of life, adapted, needless to say, to the cultural and religious traditions of India, is first fully voiced in the article titled "A Catholic Monastery in India" (Ibid., 202–204). *Sannyasins* would have to accept it because it is this very way of life that is compatible with, or even inherent to, the local environment. Only through it can India be won over for Christ and the Catholic Church. Here, Upadhyay also describes his spiritual centre as a monastery (*matha*)[14] for the first time, although his concept would be radically different from the monastic patterns that the religious orders of monks had already been bringing to India for several centuries. On the contrary, Upadhyay expressly mentions the exclusivity of his project compared to the established Church communities. Not "the least trace of Europeanism in the mode of life and living of the Hindu Catholic monks" (Ibid., 203) was expected to exist in the monastery. The clearly formulated, once again for the first time, idea of the two types of ascetic *sannyasins* who would be produced by this monastery – wandering preachers and contemplating monks – also seems to be very interesting. While the first would be engaged in direct evangelization, as Upadhyay considered it four years earlier, the latter would spend their lives praying and meditating, hence presumably permanently established in a monastery or anywhere else away from society. It was perhaps Upadhyay's growing interest in *Advaita Vedanta*, perhaps the kind of his mystical attunement in this phase of his lifelong spiritual searching that contributed to it. In any case, the creation of a place designed for long-term contemplation of Christian *sannyasins* had transformed the whole originally broadly conceived project of a *matha*-monastery from the beginning of 1899. It therefore became a real prototype of later Christian, in particular Catholic, ashrams.

Kasthalik Matha

Of course, Upadhyay did not conceive his idea to build a missionary centre that would prepare new missionaries – Hindu-Catholic monks and Christian *sannyasins* – for accomplishing their mission in the outside world in isolation. In addition to the confessed inspiration gained from de Nobili's long-past experiment, the influences that formed the idea can also be found in the achievements accomplished at that time by two Neo-Hindu religious organizations – the already mentioned *Arya Samaj* and also the *Ramakrishna Mission*. The latter was established by Upadhyay's one-time friend Narendranath Dutt, who had, in the meantime, after his glorious return from the United States, become Swami Vivekananda, a highly regarded religious leader. We can only guess to what extent certain personal rivalries and Upadhyay's hidden, never acknowledged envy in the face of the extraordinary success and acceptance that Vivekananda enjoyed played their role here. Subtle hints on the pages of *Sophia* nevertheless indirectly indicated something of this sort.

In the August issue of *Sophia* from 1898, Upadhyay presents a remarkable Sanskrit neologism, which is, according to him, a perfect expression of the idea of Catholicism, clad, however, in Indian attire. Although the used etymology remains elusively mystical to a large extent, fully in the spirit of the tradition of the Upanishads,[15] the word was created as a title for the intended ashram experiment to serve as its shield. In the key constituting article titled "The Casthalic Matha" (Ibid., 207–209) of January the next year, one could already read about the specific site intended as the monastery location as well as about the relevant ecclesiastical authority having taken over the patronage of the project. This contribution of Upadhyay's as well as the issue of the magazine were the last to be published for a long time, because the events of the first half of that year moved rapidly; Upadhyay left Calcutta to try to realize his dream. The ecstatic ardour is noticeable here in the author's words ("Come then, O ye children of the Catholic Church, children of the soil! Come and rally round the *Kasthalik* banner".) (Ibid., 208); he informs his readers about the geographic location of the site ("The *Kasthalik* or Catholic *Matha* (monastery) will be located on the Narmada [...] just where this ancient stream encounters the Marble Rocks and rushes on to a magnificent fall. The spot is romantically situated in the very heart of India and commands almost equally the three great cities of Calcutta, Bombay and Madras".) (Ibid.) and the religious spirit that will fill in the place and so create a unique environment where Christianity and Hinduism embrace:

Here in the midst of solitude will be reared up true yogis to whom the contemplation of the triune *Sachchidanandam* will be food and drink. Here will grow up ascetics who will [...] do penance for their own sins as well as for the sins of their countrymen by constant dewailing and mortification. [...] They will possess nothing that they may possess all. They will desire to know nothing that they may know all. They will take delight in nothing that they may delight in the All. In this hermitage will the words of the eternal Word be best strung in hymns of eastern melody [...] Catholic devotions be clothed in Hindu garb. [...] Here will the *Vedanta* philosophy be assimilated to universal Truth.

(Ibid.)

With the January issue of *Sophia* from 1899, Upadhyay broke off. Therefore, in keeping track of the fortunes of his ashram, we have to rely on the several letters that he addressed to the bishop of Nagpur, Charles Pelvat, during February. The bishop administered the diocese that the area of the Marble Rocks came under and provided Upadhyay with the ecclesiastical support mentioned previously. Another significant source seems to be several pages from the already presented authoritative biography of Upadhyay, *The Blade*, written by his disciple Animananda. He personally participated in the whole experiment and is even likely to have been in charge of it himself to a large extent, at least regarding everyday practical issues concerning the coexistence of several monks. It is from Animananda that we learn about the three Indian Christian monks (i.e. Upadhyay, Animananda and Shankerjee, originally from Madras) who appeared in the streets of Jabalpur, about 20 km from the Marble Rocks, at the beginning of 1899 (it must have been in February). They were all barefoot with shaven heads, dressed only in the plainest clothes in the manner of Indian ascetics. They made a meagre living by begging, each of them prepared their own meals according to the rules set by their respective caste, they slept on the bare ground in a rented unfurnished house and devoted most of their day to prayers, studying and contemplation (Animananda 1946: 80). However, Upadhyay himself soon retired to meditative seclusion, where he fasted for forty days before Easter. As J. Lipner aptly observes, the question therefore remains as to what role he actually played in the life of the newborn community (Lipner 2001: 220). The care of novices, the circle of whom was soon widened to include two Brahman boys from Calcutta, was taken over in its entirety by his faithful disciple Animananda.

However, the path was not smooth for *Kasthalik Matha*. The first negative responses refusing the whole concept had already emerged even before the monks arrived in Jabalpur, which means before the ashram was formally established. They appeared, as could have been expected, in reaction to Upadhyay's bold innovative thoughts and ideas that he presented on the pages of *Sophia*. The Papal Nuncio Ladislaus-Michael Zaleski, de facto supreme representative of the Catholic Church on the subcontinent, took a totally disapproving stance on the project at the moment when the plan to build an indigenized missionary centre was introduced in the middle of 1898 and also had his standpoint sanctified immediately afterwards by Rome. In an effort to find a way out of the impasse that his obligation of obedience to the Church was prodding him into with increasing intensity, Upadhyay tried to take shelter under the protective wings of the bishop of Nagpur, who decided to defy the Papal envoy. Such a decision was certainly very bold and constituted important support for Upadhyay. Nevertheless, it must have been obvious to Upadhyay himself that the background provided by the ecclesiastical authority was limited in time. Soon after the establishment of the community and with the growing pressure that bishop Pelvat was exposed to, Upadhyay was advised to attempt to reconcile his unilaterally conducted dispute with Zaleski. When the bishop of Nagpur, who was coming under ever greater duress from Nuncio, finally withdrew his support for the ashram, Upadhyay decided, with the bishop's blessing and a letter of recommendation, to settle the whole issue directly with the papal seat, even doing so *in persona* (Animananda 1946: 81). Thanks to the financial support granted by a Catholic patron from South Indian Mysore, Upadhyay came to Mumbai and was actually about to board a ship; however, a sudden severe febrile illness deterred him from his intention to depart. His desperate personal economic situation subsequently forced Upadhyay to work in Karachi in the Province of Sindh for several months as an editor of the political newspaper published by the Congress, and it seemed he had completely lost interest in his dream project. In all probability, he returned to Jabalpur briefly sometime towards the end of 1899, but only to formally terminate the existence of the abandoned ashram. His later biographers are only able to vaguely speculate about the precise reasons that led him to do so.[16] Animananda did not make them much clearer either. Nevertheless, this experience seems to have left a shadow of bitter disappointment in Upadhyay's devoted disciple and marked the beginning of the end of their relationship (Ibid.).

We can only speculate about how long *Kasthalik Matha* existed in fact; however, it is certain that Upadhyay was spiritually and intellectually shattered by the failure. The bond connecting him to Christianity and the Catholic Church less than ten years before was not completely severed; however, his relationship with the Church had undoubtedly cooled off. Also in this regard, in the hardship, lack of understanding and its sad end, it was as if the first Christian ashram in India foreshadowed the fate of many of the later Catholic ashrams established as part of the Movement, as well as numerous personal fortunes of their members. All of them, without exception, profess Upadhyay to be their predecessor. Some even, as we shall see, immediately follow in his ideas by further developing the theology of *Saccidananda* (H.

Le Saux or Swami Abhishiktananda), attempting to acknowledge the Christian testimony in the language of the Hindu religious elites (J. Monchanin) or develop an idea of several types of such testimony. Its bearers would be both monks permanently meditating in the heart and depth of silence, permanently wandering preachers preaching love for God and all creation in the manner of St. Francis and direct evangelists working in parishes and congregations (H. Heras).

Causes giving rise to the Movement at the beginning of the 20th century

At the turn of the 20th century, the Christian Churches in India found themselves in a difficult situation. Although the number of Christians was continuously increasing due to the hectic missionary activity and many cases of mass conversions, they rarely received adequate evangelizing and pastoral attention after the conversion itself.[17] The mainstream of mission strategies in India continued to be dominated by the quantitative aspect, which was measured against the success or failure of the respective Church or an individual missionary. However, dissatisfaction with the attitude that ignored the local cultural and religious context or with ostentatious indifference towards this context was about to manifest itself very soon in the form of many Christian organizations and movements which were set in motion, in particular by local converts.[18]

The surrounding Indian environment, seemingly regardless of its religious affiliation, and yet always inevitably existing and acting in strong connection with it, was also going through a turbulent period. In the second half of the 19th century, the assertive political currents of the emerging Indian nationalism, originally inconspicuous, yet extraordinarily significant in their consequences, were rather seeking a direction to take. During the passing decades, they concurrently gained strength, finally merged at the beginning of the 20th century and manifested themselves on a massive scale for the first time. Official representatives of the Christian churches seemingly watched this fateful process of national self-searching of India and its people only from the position of non-participating spectators for some time. In some cases, in particular among the higher Catholic clergy, who continued to be dominated by foreigners, disbelief and growing concerns can be mentioned contrarily. It seemed to be obvious that the forthcoming and perhaps already inevitable political changes would be necessarily reflected in the attitude of Indians towards Christianity in general and towards individual churches, their organizational structures and activities, missionary ones in the first place, in particular.

Along with the socio-political changes concerning the whole country, serious internal transformations were underway inside the churches themselves. In all of the earlier stages of the development of Christianity in India, the division of roles remained definite and unquestionable for a long time, with the missionary-foreigner coming to bring a religious message, to specify the form of religious expressions and the lifestyle linked to them. Now it was Indian Christians who, in forming their own cultural and religious identity, started asking for the floor with growing vigour. The period when foreign patterns were passively accepted and merely imitated therefore came to a definitive end. Numerous daring attempts to openly express purely domestic ideas on what the life of a Christian in India could or should look like arose instead. Leaving aside the unique and therefore perhaps finally unsuccessful Catholic attempt of Upadhyay, the main activity in the process of searching for a new identity of Indian Christianity was taken over by Protestant churches, in particular their lay representatives, from the beginning of the 20th century. At least until the mid-20th century, this environment seemed to be intellectually and spiritually freer compared with the Catholic Church and thus more open to domestic impulses. It was in this environment where the concept of the ashram, as a distinctive organizational unit from which and through which the new identity may eventually grow up, won significant supporters and implementers. The key role in the process was played by educated lay people from cities. They were aware that the foreign nature of Christianity in the Indian context represented a major barrier to the understanding of Christ's tidings. At the same time, they also realized that the image of the Church as a mere refuge of the oppressed or otherwise disadvantaged social classes could hardly capture the attention of or reach out to mainstream society, not to mention its religious and intellectual elite. But it was the elite that the founders of the first Protestant ashrams and later the whole Movement targeted, letting themselves be inspired by the universe of its religious ideas, just as the previous efforts of de Nobili and Upadhyay had been. This time, however, the hidden major missionary agenda, which motivated de Nobili, that is, the desire for more religious conversions, was to be left out (Chenchiah, undated: 222–223).

However, the new concept of Christianity and the churches in India that was searched for seemed to reflect two conflicting, simultaneously operating tendencies in Protestant circles at the turn of the 20th century. On the one hand, there was the desire here for greater unity of a fragmented Christianity, the growing need to stop mutual antagonism or even open hostility among individual churches, the causes of which were rooted entirely outside of the geographical area and the historical development of India. The reasons for this need were both practical in their nature, namely the efforts to coordinate the missionary activities and thus make them more efficient, and ideological or even theological. Inconsistent Christianity with many factions in the form of sectional churches being on bad terms with one another could hardly constitute an interesting religious alternative for non-Christians and at the same time denied on principle the universal and thus unifying character of Christ's Gospel message. In addition to the desire for unity, the efforts to create a new identity of Christianity and Christians in India, however, began to be accompanied by the belief that it was necessary to assertively break free and become released from the solid organizational structures of the churches as they had been transferred to India by European missionaries. The unsolvable dilemma between the controlled, meticulously cherished unity and spontaneous non-organization, which is in many aspects inherent in Indian religious and cultural space, is a key hallmark of the beginnings of the Ashram Movement. This deep internal conflict, moreover, seems to be constantly present in all other stages of development of the Movement, as well as in the history of individual ashrams and in the life stories of their founders and members.

The roots of the Movement, as it was definitively shaped in the second decade of the 20th century, run deep into the 19th century and were nourished by a slowly changing attitude to Indian religious reality. Thanks to the first generations of Orientalists who managed to understand the rich intellectual and spiritual world of Hinduism (and other non-Christian religions) and mediate it to the interested intellectual environment in Europe, comparative religious studies developed. In the first stage, they were motivated by the search for a better Christian missionary strategy. In the second stage, they were supplemented by the existential need to cope with the sovereignly established religious tradition, which, moreover, shows historically longer continuous development than is the case with Christianity. In the third stage, additional impulses even emerged that relativized the sovereignty of the comparing with the compared that had been a priori assumed until then. In all of the three stages, the relation to religious diversity could no longer be built on the principle of unequivocal rejection and condemnation so typical of earlier centuries. A new relation was inevitably searched for and revised, but, of course, always with a different result. It is from this newly established relation that the idea of the "mission without missions" (Taylor 1979: 281; Collins 2006: 124) arises, being extremely inspirational and influential in Protestant circles in the late 19th and early 20th centuries. It is also where the core lies of the reflections of the slightly later Protestant intellectual stream of "Rethinking Christianity in India".[19] Its apparently most important fruit became the very Christian Ashram Movement.

The influence of Neo-Hinduism and Hindu ashrams

The previously mentioned set of general causes giving rise to the Movement neither appeared nor developed in isolation. On the contrary, as admitted by ashramites themselves, it emerged in a direct response to the changes that Hinduism had been undergoing during the 19th century. The significant reformist religious and social currents, originating in 1828 alongside the constitution of Bengali *Brahmo Sabha*, renamed a little later *Brahmo Samaj*, took on many different forms in later decades, in particular in the second half of the 19th century. As a matter of fact, they emerged both as a direct and indirect Hindu response to the establishment of the political domination of Christian Europe over the subcontinent. Thanks to it, not only the conveniences of modern science and technology reached India, but also the ideals of the Enlightenment sprang up, which, no matter how belated they may have been, represented an absolute novelty in the Indian environment because they were opposed to the medieval social and religious obscurantism. The common denominator of all of the reformist religious organizations that emerged as part of what is called Neo-Hinduism seems to be a return to the sources – the ancient, magnificent, but now rather faded glory of Indian civilization, the main sources of Hindu religious wisdom; no matter whether some considered the abstract philosophical concept of the God of Upanishads such a source and others solely the Vedic literary corpus. As part of this idealization of the Golden Age, which was intended to serve as an inspiration and concurrently as proof of religious maturity, hence the competitiveness of Hinduism in the face of Christianity, the ashram concept was newly grasped or constructed in the second half of the 19th century.

Ashrams may seem to be an integral and fully integrated component of the religious world of India today because they had already sprouted copiously and in extremely diverse forms all over the country during the 20th century. However, the origins of this important, undoubtedly fully autochthonous religious institution are shrouded in a veil of legends. The considerably mythologized idea of a hermitage hidden in the depths of a silent forest, where a wise teacher would dwell in harmony with the surrounding nature, encircled by his devoted disciples whom he would lead on their spiritual path, is based on numerous, yet not completely unambiguous references in the Upanishads, both Epics of *Mahabharata* and *Ramayana* and the Puranas.[20] However, no return to sources can ignore the time ticking away. On the contrary, every such attempt is primarily motivated and influenced by the topical needs of the given period, through the perspective of which the old source is subsequently not only seen but also interpreted. The literary idea of an ancient ashram gives the impression of a mysterious, yet not inaccessible place, situated in an indeterminate historical timelessness. In some cases, it is even completely removed from any clearly identifiable geographical space, thus creating a parallel world, shrouded in meditative immersion, existing by itself and for itself. By contrast, the Hindu ashrams emerging as part of Neo-Hinduism at the end of the 19th century and the first decades of the 20th century can be considered institutions firmly nestled in the specific historical time and location of India. They came into existence in the period of turbulent social, political and religious reforms and changes, because all of these external pressures significantly contributed to the form of a specific ashram, often even being the main cause of its spontaneous origin or deliberately organized foundation. The pioneers of the Christian Ashram Movement, coming from Protestant churches, who proudly acknowledged their link to the idealized legacy of ancient ashrams, also always shrewdly and critically pointed out the significant differences in their own conception of a modern ashram. No longer need it be necessarily "confined to the forest", that is, outside of secular society, "nor is its primary aim the religious attainment of their members" (Forrester-Patton 1952: 2),[21] but ashrams are and should be a rewarding alternative to life, including the life behind the walls of an ashram, "a place from which one could change the world" (Schouten 2008: 164). However, similar assertions at the same time reveal how vaguely defined or on the contrary all-embracing the word "ashram" really is. Clear evidence of this is the diversity of the concepts of Hindu ashrams as they emerged at the period of the height of late Neo-Hinduism. Only some of them became models inspiring Protestant churches in their first serious attempts at Christian indigenization.

Richard W. Taylor, an authoritative historian of the oldest, that is, the Protestant, period of the Movement, considers the first modern Hindu ashram the so-called *Bharat Ashram*. It was established by Keshab Chandra Sen near Calcutta in 1872 for married members of the reformist *Brahmo Samaj* (Taylor 1979: 281, 1986: 3). Although Taylor himself marvels at the ambiguity of the studied concept, he does not dig deeper into the issue of infinite diversity but only enumerates, in the manner of chroniclers, further religious institutions that were either termed as such by their founders themselves or were attributed this function for clearly demonstrable or contrarily less apparent reasons. The next extremely important ashram mentioned by Taylor, in agreement with the other authors mapping the early Hindu ashrams that the Movement took its cue from, is the educational experiment seeking the renewal of the concept of so-called forest academies (Taylor 1979: 281–282; Collins 2006: 122; Pattathu 1997: 133–134; Ralston 1987: 19). It was successfully implemented by Rabindranath Thakur, the later Nobel laureate in literature, in his famous *Shantiniketan* in 1901. He rebuilt the older institution of the same name, which had already been established in 1888 by his father Debendranath, creating de facto an ashram school from it. Thakur's vision of a training school located aside the hectic modern world, in which there was a very informal interaction between teachers and pupils, was undoubtedly significantly influenced by the very idea of the ancient ashram. During the 20th century, *Shantiniketan* became a respected centre of traditional and modern Indian art and learning. However, at the same time, its popularity and the impressive number of prominent personalities of India who studied there for a while inevitably removed a number of features from it that were essential for ashrams. It was inevitably turned into what was still principally a university due to its primary orientation, no matter how open it was, located outside the environments of big cities. In a broader sense and for a broader purpose, Taylor also considers *Gurukul Kangri*, the university offshoot of *Arya Samaj*, which was established in Haridwar (Taylor 1986: 7–8)[22] at the foot of the Himalayas, in 1902, an ashram of a similar type. The conservative *Arya Samaj* was established with a decidedly critical reformist agenda, and its radical concept of Hindu nationalism was directed primarily against the missionary activities of Christians and Muslims. The process of an offensive ideological return to the sources reached its absolute extent within *Arya Samaj* under the imaginary motto "nothing except Vedas". Taylor rightly points to the interpretation difficulties associated with the evaluation of this "ashram". Indeed, it seems unclear whether *Gurukul* was intended to restore the idea of the ancient training school where students lived and studied at the feet of their teacher, which would also tally with the selected name, or rather an institute of the Vedic university modelled after the famous Takshashila (Ibid.). But, at the same time, Taylor neither mentions nor suggests how *Gurukul* should or at least could inspire the Christian concept of the ashram. Therefore, if we even consider both "university ashrams" (*vishvavidyalaya ashrama*) to be ashrams, their influence on the final form of the Movement seems to be totally vague.

An ashram of a significantly different type, which on the contrary had an undeniably direct influence on the later emerging Christian ashrams and the ideology of the Movement, appeared as a result of the activities of the Ramakrishna Mission. After his glorious return from the United States in 1897, its founder, Swami Vivekananda, de facto the first transcontinental Hindu missionary, decided to give his philosophical conception of practical *Vedanta* a specific organizational shape of a newly established religious organization or, more precisely the whole Neo-Hindu movement. Vivekananda, however, did not choose the term "ashram" for his ideological centre located in the Belur, the northern part of Calcutta, in 1899. Similarly, as in Upadhyay's parallel Catholic experiment, it was supposed to be a monastery (*matha*) in the traditional Indian meaning of the word. Since its very beginning, the form of the monkhood of this Hindu monastery had, however, clearly reflected its founder's several years' experience with the Christian cultural and social environment and also Vivekananda's familiarity with the Christian concept of monasticism. The life of monks, who observe celibacy and make hierarchically structured monastic vows, in this monastery is governed by the monastic discipline. It distributes their everyday activities at a reasonably healthy ratio among personally experienced spirituality in the form of contemplation, common prayers, studying and manual work. Since its initial stages, the Ramakrishna Mission has placed increased emphasis on self-sacrificing community service; hence, it operates hospitals and schools of various types and levels and provides humanitarian aid in the event of man-made or natural disasters. All this takes place fully in the spirit of the unifying practical *Vedanta*, and the unification of people takes place regardless of their religious affiliation, social or economic status, nationality, age or gender and so on. The aforementioned combination of personal spirituality, authentically embedded in the Indian cultural and spiritual context, and devotion to the service of the needy became the most important inspirational resource of the Christian Ashram Movement, in particular in its first, Protestant stage of development.

A real revolution in the modern concept of the ashram, the delimiting of its characteristic features, ways of ashram life, philosophical and practical objectives and also in the following historical development of ashrams across Hinduism and Christianity was brought about by Mohandas Karamchand Gandhi after his return from South Africa to India. Gandhi had already established experimental communities, operated as an alternative to modern society with the emphasis placed on an individual's uniqueness, and almost always nestled in a rural environment, be it the Tolstoy Farm or the Phoenix Settlement, during his mission to South Africa. However, he did not call them ashrams at that time. It was only after he returned home to India in 1915 that he resorted to using this term, most likely under the impression of his personal visits to already existing ashrams or thanks to the opinions of his devoted followers who themselves had lived in some of the ashrams for a longer time (Taylor 1979: 282, 1986: 17). Gandhi's groundbreaking ashram idea first crystallized in the form of the famous *Satyagraha Ashram*, located on the banks of the Sabarmati River, in the suburban city district of Ahmadabad. It then, however, had a purely rural character, yet was situated in close proximity to a large city.[23] This first Indian ashram of Gandhi's represents a noteworthy attempt to combine simple, non-contemplative spirituality with social and economic reform and comprehensible political activism. Gandhi's holistic approach to life perceives religion as a vital sign and a need completely inseparable from everyday events in the world and society. In his understanding, the universally valid moral religious order does not apply only to an individual and his or her personal relation to God. It should also substantially guide individuals towards their personal participation in contemporary social topics, starting from the policy up to the protection of the socially oppressed and weak. No more was the ashram intended to be a laboratory of spirituality where traditional values were cultivated in a traditional or modern manner. It was to become a centre of selfless, self-sacrificing service to the homeland, a preparatory for future political and social reformers leaving it for the world where all their activities would permanently remain enshrined in their personal relation to God. If we use the Sanskrit terminology, moderate *bhakti yoga* (piousness) embraces *karma yoga* (unselfish activeness) in Gandhi's ashram with the background of consciously experienced political and the social context of that time. In Gandhi's practical philosophy, the previously mentioned *seva* (service) found its comprehensible symbolic expression in the form of a campaign to support local spinning, the so-called *khadi*. Without making any major sacrifices, virtually anybody could join the campaign. Gandhi promoted *khadi* as a specific means of active meditation, and it was also intended to support local industry and to guide wide public masses to material modesty, raising the awareness of national unity, the sense of belonging and equality regardless of social status, possessions or education. The perception of an ashram as a place where devoted and at the same time pious servants of the needs of the homeland are trained had dominated the ashram ideology for several decades. Ashrams of a similar type started emerging in many sites all over India, significantly, as we will see in the next chapter, influencing the concept at Protestant churches. With a certain degree of exaggeration, it can even be claimed that Gandhi's ashram ideal set the whole Movement in motion in the 1920s. With India gaining its independence in 1947, thus also after one of Gandhi's key goals was achieved, the idea of *khadi* ashrams[24] became depleted to a large extent. However, its continuous development line can be seen in the form of numerous *seva* ashrams, emerging thanks to the activities of Gandhi's followers, whether we seek them among his direct disciples (Vinoba Bhave undoubtedly ranking among the most important of them) or Christian churches.

The goal of this chapter was not to mention all of the contemporaneous inspiration resources of the Christian Ashram Movement but to point out the significantly differentiated development trends inside Hinduism at the turn of the 20th century which the Movement drew upon and was ideologically based upon in its initial stages. The significant Hindu ashrams emerging in particular at a slightly later period of time, from the 1920s, which are more true to the traditional ideal of the ancient ashram (unless we, however, concurrently bear in mind its previously mentioned mythologized form) were thus necessarily put aside. There, the primary goal is still the own spiritual growth of the ashramite coming to the ashram to seek and find his or her personal path to God under the guidance of a guru's authority, which is not called into question and is uncritically accepted, since the guru, de facto God's witness, has already experienced God himself. This type of Hindu ashram is the most widespread in contemporary India and is perceived as the ashram *per se*, although the everyday life in it, the person of the guru and the main spiritual practice (*sadhana*) may differ as much as the types of ashrams do themselves. If we leave aside the sufficiently well-known examples of ashrams popular on a mass scale, often connected with the controversial personalities of their founders, the asserted plurality of the modern concept is well enough proved by mentioning the three ashram projects as distinctive from one another as the Aurobindo Ashram in Pondicherri, Ramana Ashram in Tiruvannamalai and Shivananda Ashram in Rishikesh. The ashrams envisaged in this way, however, influenced the origins of the Movement and its development in the first decades rather insignificantly. They did not become the major source of inspiration until the 1950s, when the concept of the ashram as a meaningful self-expression of Indian Christianity was also embraced by the Catholic Church. The Movement then obtained not only new impulses and an environment where it could continue developing itself intricately, but in particular the persons who started participating in it or sustaining it further had motivations and spiritual and intellectual dispositions significantly different from those in the first, Protestant stage.

All the Hindu ashrams emerging as part of Neo-Hinduism at the end of the 19th and beginning of the 20th century could be put in a highly specific place within a considerably wide scale. This ranged from community service via the emphasis placed on an expression of affectionate piousness, cultivation of intellectual cognition up to personally experienced spirituality (*karma–bhakti–gyana–dhyana*).[25] However, none of the ashrams can probably be considered an extracted, clean type. On the contrary, each of them complements and enriches its main orientation with further elements and methods of this scale. After all, life in any ashram must be approached in a holistic manner on principle, because this is the demand placed on man by the ashram idea. All of the previously mentioned modern Hindu ashrams were influenced concurrently by modernity and tradition. The mutually inspirational or, conversely, distinctively conflicting interaction of Hindu India with Christian Europe significantly contributed to their final form. Every ashram, although it may not so admit, therefore represents an assertive Hindu response to European culture and Christian religious tradition as it was presented in India. So we find ourselves facing a noteworthy paradox concerning mutual, reciprocal influences that have been present in the Movement since its very beginning. However, in the context of historical development, this paradox unfolds as most logical: modern Hindu ashrams emerged in the environment of reformed Hinduism significantly influenced by Christianity, with the subsequent attempts at reformed and completely newly approached Indian Christianity being inspired in the very Hindu ashrams.

The Protestant Ashram Movement

The Christian Ashram Movement has already been described several times as considerably differentiated. This characteristic of the Movement necessarily follows both from its history and the very nature of the formation of individual ashrams. However, the two main development streams, as if exactly, corresponded to the different religious denominations. The double-track nature of the Movement is universally accepted by all of the authors who deal with it, whether they are favourably disposed apologists or moderate or hard-line critics. The same approach can also be identified regarding the stakeholder theorists or ideologues personally participating in the Movement, belonging themselves to one or the other of the development streams and making efforts to implement the concept plan of the Movement in the environment of their home church. The gap between the Catholic Church and non-Catholic churches opened up at the same width and depth in the Indian context as anywhere else in the world. Not even a religious experiment as heterodox and essentially unifying as the Movement was intended to be from its very beginning has ever managed to bridge it, with a few notable exceptions, which will be further discussed in the appropriate places herein.

It is a sad paradox of modern Christianity and its internal development (not only in India) that it strives hard to explore ways towards other religions through its calls for interreligious dialogue, however, without having first built a pathway to mutual understanding between Christians themselves or bridging the gap between Christian churches.

Each of the churches participating in the Movement during its development approached the ashram concept with a significantly distinctive motivation. Such a motivation was always necessarily influenced by contemporary needs and the setting of a particular church in the broader context of sociopolitical discourse, which, however, transformed itself considerably during the 20th century. Each of the churches also sought and found inspiration in different aspects of Indian culture, using its language with the aspiration of expressing its own religious message, and in the spiritual or theological components of the religious world of Hinduism. The founders of Protestant ashrams were influenced by the Neo-Hinduism of the turn of the 20th century, in particular with its emphasis placed on the social reform of Indian society and the nation-unifying nationalist struggle against colonial domination. The Catholic as well as Orthodox Church benefited from the wealth of Indian spirituality, mysticism and the traditions of Indian monasticism (Ralston 1987: 26).[26] Catholic and Orthodox priests or monks then attempted to select themes from them that were not in conflict with their own religious teachings. They tried to connect them with the Christian conception of monasticism and spiritual life in general, to dress Christianity in India in brand-new attire by integrating some elements of Hindu liturgy and symbolism and as a consequence to create a radically new identity of Indian Christians as well. Therefore, the expectations that each of the churches had with respect to the outcomes of the complex process of indigenization, later known as inculturation, was bound to be diverse from the very beginning. The previously mentioned double-track nature of the Christian Ashram Movement therefore de facto creates two considerably different movements. Their mutual contacts are minimal, and the meaningfulness or validity of the existence of the other was often as not even taken into account at all. This is the case in particular with respect to how the Protestant stream views the slightly later Catholic stream, which is quite often virtually ignored on the side of Protestant ashrams and ashramites.

The ashram as a plan and an attempt

The first explicit mention of the ashram as a possible way of expressing Christian testimony that can be found in Protestant circles is probably in the appellate article by S. K. Rudra, an educationalist of the prestigious St. Stephens College in Delhi. He addressed it to the Bengali Christian Conference held in 1910. An open call appears in it for a deeper interest in the spiritual plane of Christianity that would be inextricably linked with the emphasis placed on study and contemplation. New Christians could thus model themselves on Indian saints ("to be like swamis and paramahansas") (Taylor 1986: 19) and become the bearers of a new expression of Christian holiness and Indian Christian spirituality. Rudra suggests that a Christian ashram should be formed to meet these needs. He imagines it as a sort of centre of thought of indigenized Christianity where suitable adepts would receive continuous formative leadership and from which they would later set out to embark on their own spiritual-evangelizing mission (however, we do not learn much about its specific content from his paper). Two years later, in 1912, a similar appeal was heard on the grounds of the National Missionary Society (NMS).[27] It came from the mouth of the co-founder and former secretary general of NMS, K. T. Paul, on the occasion of the NMS meeting in Delhi. Making reference to the main theme of the conference ("The Indigenization Nature of Our Work"), Paul called for a Christian ashram to be built of such a nature that would target in particular young Indian Christians. In the intended ashram, they would receive training for their subsequent independent evangelistic work. The methods and objectives of it would be fully in the spirit of the Indian cultural tradition. However, here they would also deepen their knowledge of providing basic health care and would be led to master some practical manual skills so that not only they themselves but also any future Christian communities emerging under their potential leadership could be economically self sufficient (Taylor 1979: 283). As can already be seen in this first systematically thought-out and presented plan to set up an ashram, the significant representative of a Protestant church sought to unite evangelizing goals with socioeconomic objectives (Ralston 1987: 28). And although NMS had to wait for the actual establishment of the first ashram for almost a decade, the vast majority of the pioneering Protestant ashrams that turned from a mere plan into actually implemented projects, and out of which many even survived for a number of decades, were always in close contact with the Society or arose from the direct activities of its members (Thomas 1969: 281).

Meanwhile, however, an attempt occurred in Protestant circles to set up an ashram of a new kind. The significant Maratha poet, Narayan Vaman Tilak, a Hindu convert to Christianity, established an organization in Satara in 1917 after having worked for the American Marathi Mission for many years. He named it "The Darbar of Jesus Christ" and defined its seat located in his own house as a Christian ashram (Taylor 1990: 20).[28] Both Christians and non-baptized heterodox individuals who related to the person of Jesus Christ as to an incarnation of the supreme teacher (*sadguru* or *paramaguru*) and who sought to express the testimony about this relationship of theirs to God in a purely Indian language were intended to be members of this ashram. Tilak himself became a Christian *sannyasin*, although his approach to the concept of asceticism proclaimed in such a manner was quite free. He saw the sense of his *sannyasa* in particularly in throwing away or abandoning the foreign garb in which the identity of Indian Christians had been clothed (Hedlund 2000: 173). The new expression of this identity was supposed to be firmly anchored in the Maratha cultural and religious tradition. The great medieval bhakti poet Tukaram became the model that Tilak is often compared to by his supporters. After all, it is the emphasis placed on *bhakti* in the form of affectionate poems and songs, in which the Christian poet sang out his boundless love for God, that represents the principal contribution of Tilak to Maratha Christianity as well as to modern Maratha literature (Ibid., 173–174). Various biographers of Tilak state different figures regarding the number of the members of the newly built ashram (e.g. Winslow 1923; Jacob 1979). However, the ashram most likely aroused virtually no interest in non-Christians. Nevertheless, it is the emphasis the founding father placed on creating an open interreligious community that seems to be an absolute novelty in the history of the Movement and perhaps even in the context of the development of Christianity in India. Unfortunately, the roots of the ashram were prematurely cut off by Tilak's death in 1919. It marked the swift end of the remarkable and hopeful experiment on the Christian concept of *bhakti*. Tilak, however, significantly influenced the whole first generation of Protestant ashramites. After a few years, S. Jesudason and E. Forrester-Patton, the founders of the *Christukula* ashram in Tirupattur, Tamil Nadu, retraced his footsteps. A little later, they were followed by J. Winslow, an authoritative biographer of Tilak, translator of his Maratha poems to English and, on top of that, the founder of the *Christa Seva Sangha* ashram in Pune. This very ashram can be considered the rightful successor of Tilak's Jesus Christ Fellowship due to its strong *bhakti* orientation.

Another intended attempt, resembling, in some of its aspects, the previously mentioned "ashram" of the Blessed Chavara from the first half of the 19th century, comes from a completely different part of the wide variety of Christian churches in India. Although the religious affiliation of its creator does not fall within the scope of Protestant churches, we include it in this overview chapter partly because of the early time of its creation but also because it finally turned into one of the typical *seva* ashrams, which were and still are the main domain of the Protestant stream of the Ashram Movement. In 1919, Panickeruveetil Geevarghese, who later became the bishop of the Malankara Orthodox Syrian Church and received the name Mar Ivanios, established the first house of the Order of the Imitation of Christ (OIC) and alongside it also the first ashram of this Church named *Bethany* (Bergen 1978: 182; Taylor 1986: 19). In the initial period of its existence, in particular due to its ascetically profiled location in the middle of the wilderness, life in the ashram inclined to deeper spiritual contemplation of the community of monks. They were ordered by their superior Mar Ivanios to remove their traditional order robes and to dress in the manner of Hindu saints (so-called *kavi* attire). However, an orphanage was added to the ashram very soon, which later even became a kind of pilgrimage site. The original monastic ideal of the community of monks living their quiet Christian testimony in meditative seclusion was thus abandoned sometime after 1930. A huge number of similar institutions, which were set up by various churches under the identical name of Bethany, emerged in the following decades and not only in Kerala. It must be admitted that they had undeniable merits in the field of charitable and socially beneficial work. The careless use, however, and in some cases even the strategic use of the word "ashram" in their names, attractive for a certain period of time, contributes to the misunderstanding and confusion with which the Movement is often viewed.

Christukula – the first Protestant ashram

To draw a clear line between the ashram and the socially beneficial Christian organization is extremely difficult within the whole Protestant stream of the Movement, in particular when we view these ashrams or institutions from the outside as disinterested observers, not participating in the everyday life of the ashram community. *Christukula*, generally accepted as the first-ever Protestant ashram, also seems to provide eloquent proof of this (Pattathu 1997: 202; Ralston 1987: 30; Taylor 1979: 284). Two doctors, the Tamil Christian Savarirayan Jesudason and the Scotsman Ernest Forrester-Patton, had worked at a Christian hospital in Pune from 1915. The hospital was established and operated by the United Free Church Mission of Scotland, of which both men were missionaries. According to their opinion, the personally experienced plane of Christian spirituality and the emphasis placed on selfless mutual love lived in a community circle had been fading from the Church structures (Jesudason 1937: 41).[29] Their long-standing discontent with the overly professionally managed institution finally ripened into their decision to establish an ashram that would function as a genuine family (*kula*) of people fully devoted to Christ (*Christu*) (Ibid., 39). As is astutely noted by J. P. Schouten, a very important aspect of the entire Movement, in particular its theology, is present in the very name of the ashram, and it has not disappeared from it during its whole further historical development. It is the perception of Christ as the only genuine guru (Schouten 2008: 165–166), to whom the founder of an ashram, a mortal guru, just leads the other ashramites or his students and disciples in the long term. This aspect seems to be critical for the foundation and day-to-day functioning of any Christian ashram because, on principle, no Christian spiritual leader can actually dare arrogate to himself the role of the guru in its full, traditional sense that is attributed to it by the Hindu environment. Permanent tension was thus generated between the two authorities even at the very beginning of the existence of ashrams. As we will further see, in individual stages of the Movement, as well as within individual ashrams, various approaches were experimented with to try to answer the crucial question: who the guru is, solely thanks to whom, through whose action and at whose feet, both literally and figuratively, an ashram community can actually come to existence.

The NMS, aiming towards radical indigenization of Christianity in India, the missionaries of which Jesudason and Forrester-Patton hence became, had a significant share in the establishment of *Christukula*.[30] The ashram was officially established in March 1921 in Tirupattur, Tamil Nadu. During its first year, the community, which was fast growing in its numbers of permanent and temporary members, lived and worked in rented premises; however, it subsequently moved to the suburbs of Tirupattur for good in 1922 to build a genuine ashram there (Jesudason 1937: 45). Given the common professional viewpoint of the two founders, the main focus of their self-sacrificing work continued to be on health care, and the ashram hospital quickly became sought after and extremely busy. Because *Christukula* was intended to be the epitome of loving service (*prema seva*) to others, ashramites soon expanded their activities with farming so that they could offer their direct material support to poor villagers from the wide surroundings. From 1925, they also started operating a basic school that was primarily designed for children from socially ostracized layers of Hindu society (Ibid., 46). In later decades, a similar scenario to the gradual expansion of the main activities was followed by the vast majority of Protestant ashrams and also a smaller number of Catholic ones; thus, all of them can be rightly designated as *seva* ashrams.

However, hand in hand with numerous work activities, the inner life of the community had also been developing in a meaningful way. In compliance with the ideas of its founders, the community's external appearance and therefore also the identity of the ashramites themselves was intended to naturally fit into the cultural style of the surrounding Tamil environment. Fully in line with the spirit of that time and as an expression of their liking of the nonviolent form of struggle for freedom in India, members of the ashram strictly dressed themselves in clothes made on home weaving looms (see the aforementioned Gandhi's programme *khadi* and also one of the reasons R. W. Taylor [1979: 284] refers to *Christukula* as "Gandhian in style"). The practice of vegetarianism was observed in the ashram, and all its members were expected to adhere to celibacy, in the case of volunteers always for the time of their stay in the ashram (Jesudason 1937: 42–43).[31] The founders of *Christukula* set clear conditions under which a novice could become a member of the ashram, thus answering positively to God's calling. At the same time, since its very beginning, they understood their community as open to all candidates regardless of the candidates' religious affiliation, theological views and even own religious beliefs. In the words of Jesudason, they both were well aware "that the 'Inner Light' illumines many honest souls who have not named the name of Christ" (Ibid., 44). Unfortunately, it is not possible to ascertain from this heartfelt profession of Jesudason's whether such a tolerant statement is an expression of the classical fulfilment theology or of the prematurely emerging theology of religious pluralism.

Christukula also contributed to the development of indigenized Christian architecture and arts, although both were still in their infancy in India and took place more on the periphery of cultural expressions of individual churches. In 1932, a shrine (*japalayam*) was built on the premises of the ashram, fully in the style of the classic Hindu temples of the Dravidian south, including the richly decorated high entrance gate (*gopura*), water tanks intended for ritual ablutions before prayer, roofed halls with ornate stone pillars (*mahamandapa*) and the most holy shrine (*garbhagriha* or *mulasthana*). Here, the vast spaces of the temple are decorated with symbolic motifs, as if the Hindu environment attempted to express the Christian message in its own artistic language. The ashram community, never comprising more than 20–30 people in the first decades of its long history (Pattathu 1997: 204), meets here to this day for two regular common prayers. These are also adapted to the Hindu religious context with their timing in the rhythm of the day. They are held regularly at dawn and at dusk, in the moments of transition between day and night (*sandhya*), having been perceived by the Hindu tradition for long centuries to be extremely convenient for prayer and meditation. It is the very emphasis placed on personally experienced spirituality that is not afraid to draw its inspiration from the cultural and, to a moderate degree, also spiritual world of Hinduism, which seems to come to the foreground of the ashram ideal as Jesudason and Forrester-Patton tried to implement it, at least in the first decades of the existence of *Christukula*. After all, these were the reasons they chose to term their dreamt-of project the ashram and did not seek to resurrect the ancient concept and replant it unchanged into the modern world. In their opinion, the ashram exactly and comprehensibly for the Indian environment expressed the feeling of oneness with India and its inhabitants experienced by them both, "our oneness with them", as well as the strong belief of both founders that "whatever was beautiful and true in the past heritage of India should find its fulfilment and enrichment in the Kingdom of God" (Jesudason 1937: 44). Here, however, and there is no doubt about it, the fulfilment theology comes into play.

The expression of Christian bhakti in Christa Prema Seva Sangha

It was the fulfilment theology, which was extraordinarily influential in the Protestant and also, a little later, Catholic circles of India throughout the first half of the 20th century, that the number two Protestant ashram sprouted from. Its founder, the Anglican pastor Jack Copley Winslow, was motivated by a similar desire for the indigenization of Christianity in India as were Jesudason and Forrester-Patton. Moreover, all three men were in contact personally and by correspondence, regularly discussing their dreams, ideas and steps that had been gradually leading to the establishment of both ashrams. Winslow was also significantly influenced by Gandhi's concept of the ashram. He considered C. F. Andrews, the Anglican pastor famous and celebrated in India, belonging to the inner circle of Gandhi's friends and associates, his teacher. Gandhi himself visited both the first ashrams in person, although otherwise, as it appears, he rather meticulously shunned Christian institutions due to his principled disagreement with the missionary activities leading to religious conversions (Taylor 1977: 22). Unlike *Christukula*, Winslow saw the role of his ashram in a more extensive and bolder interaction with the elements of Hindu spirituality. He wanted to fully integrate his ashram community into the cultural and religious environment of India. Although the word *seva*, placing the emphasis on social service for the needy, is also heard in the name of his ashram, this social aspect had never been primary in the long and extremely convoluted history of the ashram. It was the testimony to the possibilities and methods of expression of Christian *bhakti* in India that was to become its goal and main expression across decades (Thomas 1977: 211).

By 1922, Winslow had gathered around himself a small group of likeminded Christians of Indian origin who sought to find a suitable location to establish an ashram over the following five years. It was found in 1927, in Shivajinagar, located in the remote suburbs of Pune, where the *Christa Seva Sangha* community, or the Society of the Servants of Christ, which had been joined by several Christians of English origin in the meantime, was subsequently formed. In later years, the word *prema* (love) was most aptly integrated into the title, and the term ashram – *Christa Prema Seva Sangha Ashram (CPSSA)* – would be added to its end not very consistently or even rather randomly. However, as C. Cornille suggests (1991: 139), the fact that Winslow himself perceived his community as an egalitarian fellowship (*sangha*) rather than an ashram principally based on the teacher-student (*guru-shishya*) relationship seems to be quite crucial for the Protestant environment. As a matter of fact, Winslow's original idea was perhaps to create a non-hierarchical and absolutely open community, into which he was also willing to accept married couples without requiring them to observe celibacy. In general, he did not seek to bind ashramites with monastic vows and strict daily discipline, as in traditional Christian monasteries and also, for example, in the partner *Christukula*. The characteristic, de facto one and only, yet fundamental feature of this new type of ashram was intended to be only total devotion (*bhakti*) to Christ: "The object of *Christa Seva Sangha*, the Society of the Servants of Christ, is to build up a body of men and women who, accepting Christ as their Lord and Master, will seek to follow Him in the way of renunciation and sacrifice for the fruitful service and uplift of his brethren in the world" (Vandana 2004: 80). The *bhakti* lived out in this way was, however, intended to be fully adapted to Indian conditions so that the whole ashram could truly live up to Winslow's bold plans "in all things to be truly an Indian community, in its life of devotion it aims at developing forms of worship and methods of prayer congenial to the religious genius of India" (Ibid., 81). It is no coincidence that in the evaluation of the whole history of the Movement, *CPSSA* appears to be the very first and for a long time the only ashram that ascribes an unquestioned value to the religious environment, not only to the culture which Christianity aims to integrate into through the phenomenon of ashrams, as had been the case before. It is not by chance that *CPSSA* had become a source of inspiration for the radical experiments with inculturation that later took place in some Catholic ashrams. And it is no coincidence that Winslow's words from 1928, when he wrote the establishing rules of his ashram, largely herald the ideas of the consequential Church documents arising from the Second Vatican Council, as well as the revolutionary reassessment of the relationship of the Catholic Church with other religions: "In its work and study, it approaches with reverence and sympathy the great non-Christian systems of religion, seeing in Christ the One who came not to destroy the other faiths of mankind, but rather to be the fulfilment of man's spiritual quest" (Ibid.).

The degree of inspiration that Winslow was willing to accept from the Hindu religious tradition and everyday practice seems to be astonishing, even in hindsight. Following in the footsteps of the then already deceased Maratha Christian poet Tilak, he made *bhakti*, which means the desire of a human soul for unification with the personal God, the core of the newly designed liturgy. It had been the subject of experiments from the beginning of *CPSSA*. Thus, he set a completely new direction for the Christian indigenization in India during later decades. It was to be taken by the successor ashramites, coming mainly from the Catholic Church in the second half of the 20th century. Besides the increased emphasis placed on meditation proven in an Indian environment as a means of personal experience of God's existence and closeness, Winslow was probably one of the first Christians who also rehabilitated some sacred religious texts of Hinduism. He drew inspiration from them for his own spiritual growth and search for answers to spiritual questions. He even did not hesitate to integrate them into the liturgical order of the daily church service or prayer gatherings of the ashram community, which were held mainly at dawn and dusk, just as at *Christukula*.

The strong charismatic personality of Winslow apparently failed to prevent the disruption of the originally proclaimed ideal of equality of all ashramites. His role as the founder and the ideologue as well as his ordination had destined him in a sense from the very beginning also to become a guru for members of his ashram, no matter how much he himself would have resisted such a designation and authoritative position. In addition, a serious issue emerged within the community after several years. It had, however, been present at the bottom of it from the moment of its origin, resulting from Winslow's generously conceived idea of a totally open fellowship, regardless of gender, age or life situation. From 1928, several of the new members of the ashram, coming from Britain, began calling for a stricter monastic discipline for all members of the community. Because they themselves had been significantly influenced by the Franciscan movement, which was very popular in the Anglican Church at that time, before they arrived in India, they raised objections to the presence and full-fledged membership of any ashramites not observing celibacy (Schouten 2008: 171). The growing differences of opinion in the ashram finally resulted in its split in 1934. The visionary Winslow disappointedly left India, while the ashram community started forming its new identity according to more stringent, tightly codified rules. They set up a hierarchical structure of membership in quite a rigorous spirit, introduced the taking of graded monastic vows, instituted a consistently observed everyday order of life in the ashram and, last but not least, reorganized the married members of the ashram into the so-called third order, which was, however, denied full membership in the ashram.[32] Although the ashram continued to be operated in the *bhakti* spirit, the space for free, experimental searching in the field of personally experienced spirituality, which is so typical of the Hindu environment, was slowly abandoned. After India became independent, hence in connection with the new political and social issues that churches in independent India were faced with, and also after Winslow's successor, Bill Lash, was appointed Bishop of Bombay in 1947, the ashram way of life at *CPSSA* quickly declined. In 1962, this remarkable and truly unique project was categorically terminated.

CPSSA was revived in 1972, this time as a community of nuns belonging to the Community of St Mary the Virgin (CSMV), an Anglican women's order, and the Catholic Society of the Sacred Heart (RSCJ). The then Bishop of the Anglican Church in Bombay, Christopher Robinson, whose diocese the abandoned premises of the ashram belonged to, agreed that an experimental ecumenical community would be created to enter into direct dialogue with non-Catholic churches as well as the traditions and members of other religions, fully in the spirit of the ideals of the Second Vatican Council. The Parsi convert Sister Vandana (legally named Gool Mary Dhalla) took the lead of the ashram for several years in the role of the first *acharya* (teacher). Under her leadership, *CPSSA* really got its second wind and, moreover, became one of the most important Christian ashrams across the whole of India, of which several dozen had in the meantime emerged there. During the following years, the ashram premises were the setting for everyday life, in which an increased emphasis was once again placed on the meditation plane where fruitful and mutually rewarding dialogue between Hinduism and Christianity could take place. Numerous seminars were also held there to deal with Indian Christian spirituality, theological and pastoral discussions, ideological conferences of ashramites and so on. *CPSSA* also obtained the official confirmation of its exceptional status as an authorized centre for experiments in the field of Catholic liturgy (Vandana 2004: 83). After a few years, however, Vandana had embarked on her own ashram mission, which is still to get its due attention herein, because Vandana undoubtedly belongs among the key figures of the whole Movement. Instead of her, another nun from the Catholic order of RSCJ, coming from England, Sara Grant, a significant theologian and Indologist, came to the lead of the Pune ashram. Her contribution to the Movement, the search for the form and content of Christian spirituality as well as the development of interfaith dialogue in contemporary India, must also be considered absolutely essential. Although in its second period of existence, *CPSSA* officially remained an ecumenical ashram, and so the previously mentioned role of the female *acharya* was always held by two nuns coming from both the Anglican and Protestant Church, the ideological dominance of the Catholic ones seems to be noticeable in the new forming of the ashram (Schouten 2008: 172). Undoubtedly, it is related to the radical changes inside the Catholic Church in India as well as outside of it that had been brewing from the beginning of the 1950s. They reached their peak with the Second Vatican Council and inevitably also marked the Ashram Movement. However, this period belongs to a completely different chapter in its history.

The *CPSSA* ashram in Pune ceased to be an ashram sometime after 2000 when Sara Grant left it, and soon afterwards this world as well. It is difficult to determine the exact date because the orphaned community tried to keep the dying ideal alive with the help of other ashrams and ashramites. Today, its faded glory is evoked only by the dusty books in the once well-equipped library, several devotional objects carelessly scattered all over the haphazardly landscaped garden and sad-looking sacral works of art. Christianity combines with Hinduism in them through the symbolic language of which it strives to express its own religious content.

Reflection of ashrams in the "rethinking Christianity in India" Protestant initiative

The Ashram Movement, which had been gaining momentum from the beginning of the 1930s, received support from the influential group of Protestant theologians and reformers known under the umbrella term of the "Rethinking Group" (Boyd 1994: 144; Gravend-Tirole 2014: 118). The term is based on the most significant collective publication released by these thinkers in 1938 (Chenchiah undated), representing the major contribution to the emerging domestic Christian theology. Following the first, somewhat older theological work by A. J. Appasamy,[33] who also became part of the group, its members attempted to separate the person of Christ from institutionalized churches. But that was not all: they further sought to emancipate or liberate him from Christianity itself because, for them, even Christianity was a product of the European religious and cultural civilization sphere. In their view, Christ should be transferred to the religious environment of India, which had already been constituted with sovereignty, so that he would reveal himself there, proving and purifying what India had already known through its own religious intuition for a long time.

It was the ashram communities that members of this group considered the most appropriate instrument for this radical transformation of churches and Christianity in India. They saw in them not only experimental spiritual centres which may or may not bear the longed-for fruit – the unmistakable, inherent identity of Indian Christians. They understood these communities as an entirely new way of expressing the essence of the Gospel and thus bearing witness to Christ yet one that was agreeable with the Indian environment. Attention should no longer be paid to long, spectacular projects with the widest possible scope, as they are understood by the traditional concept of evangelization and missionary work, but, on the contrary, on meeting the spiritual needs of individuals. In the words of S. Jesudason, who was also a member of the group, "the Indian Church can come to its own only when ashrams rise and flourish" (Chenchiah, undated: 215).

The two key agents of change of the Madras *Rethinking Group* were the laymen Pandipeddi Chenchiah and Vengal Chakkarai, co-authors of the first truly thorough theoretical analysis of the concept of both Hindu and emerging Christian ashrams, in their diachronic and synchronic perspective (Chenchiah, Chakkarai and Sudarisanam 1941). This important contribution to the studied issues seems to be all the more significant since it came into existence twenty years after the establishment of the first Protestant ashram. Therefore, it is possible to find in it insights into characteristic features of the ashram that had proved successful in the Christian environment. Although it is not known if the authors were personally active in any of the existing ashrams, as, beyond a doubt, no new ashram was established by them, they fully identify themselves with the main ideas of the Movement. In addition to the earlier-mentioned benefits, they place the emphasis on the equality of the participating Christians, regardless of social status. Therefore, in their opinion, every ashram can become a bridge overarching the gap between different social classes and also among the inhabitants of Indian towns and villages (Ibid., 219). The vision of the ashram as a new way of evangelization, which was already thematized, is surely worth paying increased attention to in their text. Now, the evangelization does not take place in the streets of cities, marketplaces or religiously exposed places where missionary preachers used to return relentlessly, albeit with relatively little success. On the contrary, in the ashram, Christ is presented through personally experienced spirituality, "not thrown from the street corners" (Ibid., 221). Fully in the spirit of the whole *Rethinking Group*, the modern missions in the ashram, de facto a mission without missions, is understood as the opposite of institutional and institutionalized dogmatism, after all, "Christ cannot be preached but can be demonstrated in life. [. . .] Asramas are discovering that to live Christ is to preach Christ" (Ibid., 220).

In the stirring conclusion of their thought-provoking book, Chenchiah and Chakkarai put forward a number of questions to which, in the opinion of both authors, Christian ashrams had not yet found clear answers. By way of cautious allusions, some unresolved or perhaps rather insolvable ideological and theological problems of this new form of indigenization of Christianity are highlighted here for the first time in the history of the Movement. First the authors point out the questionable role of the guru (Ibid., 224), his entitlement to the absolute or only partial kind of vicarious authority, which is an issue that virtually all ashramites across church denominations deal with. Further, they focus on the issue of observing celibacy as a precondition of life in an ashram (Ibid., 225–226), which is on the contrary a critical problem exclusively in Protestant churches. And, last but not least, they warn in particular against boundless "mere vague mysticism", which they also describe as "almost the equivalent of vacancy, or a mere monistic union-absolute adwaitism" (Ibid., 254). At the same time, however, they are fully aware that the experiments with spirituality seeking its inspiration in the Indian religious-philosophical environment are essential for the existence of the ashram. After all, these experiments are the real reason for its creation. The ashram is supposed to be a space where Indian Christian spirituality is revealed for the first time in the history of Christianity in India so that it could enrich Hindus with their own spiritual tradition and also Indian Christians, who on the contrary have experienced their spiritual tradition only vaguely or formally. Who is, however, targeted more and somehow primarily in this case through the adoption of the ashram style? And for whom, then, is the Christian ashram created in fact?[34] Both questions, although not directly uttered, but clearly resulting from access to the fulfilment theology, are heard from the studied book for the first time. Likewise, none of them have ever vanished from the history of the Movement since then.

An outline of the further historical development of the Protestant Ashram Movement

Both Protestant ashrams, *Christukula* as well as *CPSSA*, became a powerful inspiration for similar activities. Therefore, the first two decades after 1930 represent the first boom in ashram communities and their enthusiastic establishment.[35] The pioneers' bold attempts were imitated and further developed in them, with the general consensus that this was perhaps the so much desired, newly set direction for the development of Christianity in India. In a sense, it was as if Christian ashrams, and therefore also their whole Movement, turned into a key point of the ideological programme of Protestant churches. Interestingly, the Movement also showed an identical trajectory of the development process in the 1970s and 80s, when the role of its bearer and creator was fully taken over by the Catholic Church. However, its concept of ashrams fundamentally differed from the Protestant approach from the very beginning, as the following chapters will testify.

From among the interesting ashram projects after 1930, the *Sat Tal* ashram, located at the foot of the Himalayas, close to the now popular mountain resort of Nainital, merits increased attention. It was established by the distinguished reformer and Christian thinker Eli Stanley Jones. He was an American Methodist missionary, the author of, among others, the best-selling *The Christ of the Indian Road* (Jones 1925); a promoter of the indigenization of Christianity and an extremely active initiator of interfaith dialogue in its earliest stage. Jones quite aptly summarized the spiritual ideals and practical aspects of the life in any Christian ashram, which seemingly subsequently guided the whole Movement. In his concept, an ashram should: (1) be a place which is truly Christian and, at the same time, identically Indian; (2) where the attire, diet and dining habits are to conform to Indian tradition; (3) all inhabitants of an ashram are expected to work manually in part; (4) in an ashram, the emphasis should be placed on studying Christian and Hindu sacred texts; (5) no remuneration in the form of a salary is paid here for performed work; (6) the life in an ashram should be based on prayer, with the emphasis placed on its understanding in the Indian environment, which means quiet, often long-lasting meditation; (7) an ashram should be infused with the ideals of Indian nationalism and (8) believers of other religions are also welcome in an ashram, although no activities would be developed there aimed at converting them to Christianity (Kuriakose 2006: 347–348).[36]

In the context of the contemporaneous as well as later development of a significant majority of Protestant ashrams, it seems notable that Jones does not mention the social-reformist and charitable plane of actions and deeds of ashramites (the *seva* in the broadest sense of the word that has already been mentioned several times) in his ideological programme at all. However, Jones was also strongly influenced by Gandhi's concept of a non-violent social revolution that sought to educate Indian society and bring it to meaningful political and spiritual freedom. After all, Jones himself used to stay repeatedly in *Satyagraha*, Gandhi's first Indian ashram. Therefore, it is no surprise that Jones established a typical *seva* ashram in Lucknow in the second half of the 1930s (Ralston 1987: 79) besides *Sat Tal* and initiated a number of other ashrams through his associates and disciples. However, from its very beginning, *Sat Tal* was intended to represent a spiritual centre of a completely different type. The ashram operated merely on a seasonal basis, and its members retired to it only for the two months before the monsoon season arrived. They could discover the deeper planes of their religious life there through inner contemplation, joint and individual prayers and mutually enriching interaction. During the subsequent decades, numerous evangelizing, pastoral and interfaith conferences targeting religious professionals were also held in the ashram (Chenchiah, Chakkarai and Sudarisanam 1941: 247) but also types of spiritual summer schools for laymen designated primarily for organized groups of young Indian Christians. It is these people and their needs that the ashram serves in particular, although its influence and fame seem to be past their prime. Therefore, *Sat Tal* can be rightly described as an attempt to build a training centre of the Protestant Ashram Movement.

The preacher, missionary and voluntary social worker K. I. Mathai, commonly nicknamed Sadhu Mathai, initiated the establishment of a group in Allepey, Kerala, in 1934. It moved to the village of Manganam near the city of Kottayam in 1940 to launch the spectacular project of *Christavashram* there (Taylor 1977: 23). Mathai himself was a keen promoter of indigenized Christianity. He adopted an ascetic life in celibacy, as well as its traditional symbolic representation in the form of a saffron robe and joined the already impressive line of pioneers of the Movement (Ralston 1987: 73). Mathai had intended to build a structured community, consisting of male and female ashramites observing celibacy but also those who would pursue the ashram ideals in marriage, adhere to them and possibly also spread their ideas outside the premises of the ashram (Chenchiah, Chakkarai and Sudarisanam 1941: 241). Over the years, however, the founding father's original plans were abandoned because the emphasis placed on asceticism elicited no major response among his ashramites whom he served as a guru. From the beginning of the 1950s, the ashram transformed into a clearly profiled community of several families, living and working together. They adhered to certain aspects of the ashram lifestyle that are considered essential or even constructive by the Protestant wing of the Movement (*sandhya*, common morning and evening prayer gatherings, emphasis placed on the simplicity of life that is lived in a typically Indian cultural environment and adoption and enforcement of Gandhi's ideals of non-violence, as well as his restrained conception of asceticism as a principle of spiritual life). Definitely, *Christavashram* cannot be denied its exceptional credits in the field of social services provided to the needy, in particular to homeless children and juvenile delinquents who have been welcomed there to this day with loving and at the same time nurturing open arms. However, the question remains as to whether the ashram itself did not disappear somewhere away from those exuberant, selfless and idealistic activities long ago.

Virtually all of the Christian ashrams that newly emerged due to the Protestant initiative lost something essential of their identity, direction and even meaning alongside India achieving its independence in 1947. Let us remember that for the whole Protestant stage in the development of the Movement, ashramites identified themselves with the national liberation movement and Gandhi's ideals of empowering deprived social groups of Indian society. Ashrams could serve as an effective means for that purpose, or at least, so it seemed. But when political freedom was finally achieved and independent India set off on its journey towards a modern, democratic and secular state, the key motives for establishing further ashrams as they were understood by Gandhi, and therefore also by Protestant churches, largely disappeared. Moreover, being the strongest voice at present and during the last two or even three decades, Protestant churches had been calling for the rehabilitation of the poorest segments of society that had been ostracized and oppressed for centuries. The liberation theology stemming from this fight for the rights and freedom of the Dalits is, however, the antithesis of the ideals of the Movement in its themes, content, objectives and the means used.

It seems to be absolutely impossible and perhaps also pointless to map the exact historical development of individual ashrams emerging in the Protestant stage of the Movement. Many of them operated as ashrams for only a couple of initial years to be later transformed into more or less traditional Christian social welfare institutions devoted to charitable or educational activities in the broadest sense. Others tended to become open prayer communities over time and grew in popularity, in particular in the politically independent India after 1947, in relation to various charismatic churches and individual preachers without a clear denominational affiliation. After all, the Pentecostal Movement in general, in all of its known forms, as well as those unseen elsewhere in the world, seems to be the most vigorous expression of Christianity in contemporary India. In the context of what has been said about ashram ideals so far, some other ashrams had, quite paradoxically, placed the main emphasis on evangelization and pastoral activity from the very beginning of their existence, in particular in underdeveloped rural areas or areas inhabited by indigenous tribes. However, the title ashram that such a missionary station flaunts clearly proves to be a mere label, adopted with a not very skilfully hidden proselyte motivation. Last but not least, it is necessary to also mention the ashrams that had exhausted themselves internally after several years of promising development. Their initial founding enthusiasm had disappeared either due to differing views of ashramites, death of the founder, lack of material resources necessary for daily functioning or lack of interest of those around them and therefore also the impossibility of further development or of the vibrant life of the ashram community.

The ashrams emerging in Indian Orthodox churches underwent an interesting, largely similar and contrarily, in some cases, exactly opposite development. Some were directly founded with unconcealed evangelizing motivation, since the adoption of external signs and elements of ashram identity promised more efficient results of their missionary activities, in particular in poor, remote areas of India. Typical in this sense seem to be the two ashrams of the Mar Thoma Orthodox Church – the *Christa Panthi* ashram established in 1942 and *Christiya Bandhu Kulam* originating one decade later, which are located in Madhya Pradesh (Taylor 1979: 288–290; Ralston 1987: 80–84). Members of both of these ashrams are engaged in evangelizing work in the surrounding villages, seeking to mediate a wide range of social and educational services for their inhabitants in addition to Gospel truth. H. Ralston rightly terms them, along with a majority of Protestant ashrams, ashrams that have taken the path of action (*karma marga* or *karma yoga*) (Ibid., 82, 84). On the contrary, the vast majority of ashrams of the Syrian Orthodox Church had become closed monastic communities after their promising beginnings associated with the charismatic personality of a respective founder. The ashram ideals regarding internal and external manifestations of life in an ashram were replaced with the tradition of Western monasticism after a time. Thus, their only link to the Indian environment can be seen today in the adopted saffron robes, which monks and nuns put on in the manner of Hindu mystics and holy men, or in the consistently followed vegetarian diet.

With the benefit of hindsight, it seems as though the ashrams of Protestant and Orthodox churches could not exist on the boundary of the two cultural and religious worlds for a long period of time, that is, in the sphere they deliberately staked out within the Movement for their existence. It is as if it were beyond the strength or mere human capabilities of the ashramites themselves to endlessly adroitly balance between passive contemplative introspection, inner contemplation, life spent in prayers and, concurrently, the desire for an active presence in the world that makes selfless efforts to change and reform the world.

The Catholic Ashram Movement

In comparison with the precipitous internal development taking on the shape of the intellectual and spiritual ferment that Protestant churches were undergoing in the first half of the 20th century, the Catholic Church in India was somewhat in the doldrums at that time. The failure to respond adequately to the rapidly changing social and political conditions in a colonial country that had been slowly heading towards reaching its political freedom, or perhaps even the deliberate unwillingness to make such a response or the unacknowledged fear of it, seems to be an important characteristic of the Catholic Church at that time. The isolated voices of local educated laymen calling for substantial internal reforms had always been safely silenced until then. However, the seed that was planted by Upadhyay at the very end of the 19th century and that seemingly fell on a yet unploughed field was to bear fruit in the future.

According to the opinion of R. W. Taylor, the first Catholic ashram was established by Swami Animananda, the already mentioned main disciple, closest collaborator and later biographer of Upadhyay (Taylor 1979: 285–286). This allegedly happened at the beginning of the 1940s in Ranchi, where the ashram was supposedly located in close proximity to the local seminary. Animananda reportedly ran a boys' school there, but according to Taylor, not a single permanent pupil or disciple was recruited by him. However, without their presence, the existence of an ashram seems to be impossible in principle. Taylor bases his allegations, which cannot be found in any other information source concerning the Movement, on his personal interviews with two older Jesuits who stayed at the seminary at the time. Unfortunately, he fails to mention any other details; therefore, it seems likely that he himself considered their memories rather vague or perhaps not even very credible.

A more outright, and, in terms of information, verifiable, attempt to work out and develop the theological legacy bequeathed by Upadhyay to the Catholic Church in India is represented by the planned monumental project of the Spanish Jesuit priest and renowned historian Henry Heras. He had worked in Mumbai from the 1920s until his death in 1955, and despite his foreign origin, he personally identified with the Indian cultural environment. Although it is not supported by any explicit mention of his predecessor, the inspiration provided by Upadhyay behind Heras's intended reform of the Catholic Church in India seems to be more than evident because Heras also considered creating several types of monastic groups. Depending on their inner focus, their members would also devote themselves to three types of activities. They could dwell in the permanent contemplative seclusion of ashrams or *mathas*, or they could preach the glory of God in the environment of Indian cities and villages as wandering begging monks, that is, Franciscan "simpletons of God" akin to Hindu sadhus and *sannyasins*. Finally, they could act as scholar-evangelists using their knowledge of the local philosophical and religious thought to illuminate the essence of Christ's testimony that was also to unfold itself as the most meaningful in the Indian context (*Swami Parama Arubi Anandam* 2007: 68).[37] Heras gave his detailed project the noble title of *Saccidananda Prema Sangha*. Although remaining just a dead letter in the form of a two-volume manuscript of about a thousand pages, it represents a remarkable theoretical attempt to link Christian, or rather Catholic, and Hindu, traditions of monasticism (Ralston 1987: 110). This was a serious attempt to create a new, fully indigenized monastic way of life that would be a testimony of Christ perfectly understandable for the Indian environment and would also revive and enrich Christianity in India. The path set in the previously described manner was soon to be followed by the first Catholic pioneers of the Movement and their first Catholic ashrams.

The Saccidananda Ashram – Shantivanam

No other Christian ashram influenced the whole Movement as much as the one that originated in Tamil Nadu at the beginning of 1950. On the banks of the Cauvery River, near the town of Kulithalai, two French priests laid the foundations of the ideological centre of the Movement on March 21. No other ashram had become so influential or undergone more remarkable development – from extremely humble beginnings through a deep crisis of impending non-existence that later turned into a breathtaking rise, when many hundreds of people interested in the new form of Indian Christian spirituality flowed into the ashram for two fruitful decades, to the calming down and subsequent inertia of ashram life, when the Movement found itself in a blind alley at the end of the 20th century, out of which it has been vainly seeking a way up to now. The fortunes of *Shantivanam*, or the Forest of Peace, its history and its individual stages reflect with perfect clarity and comprehensibility the development of the idea of Christian Catholic ashrams because *Shantivanam* seems to be a byword for it.

Unlike the vast majority of other Catholic missionaries, whether from earlier or later times, the French priest Jules Monchanin[38] did not come to India to preach the word of God and thus contribute to the expansion of the local Christian community. Already at the time of his pastoral engagement in the Diocese of Lyon (1922–1939), classical Indian philosophy had made an impression on him and possibly even fascinated him. Contrary to its European sister, this world of thoughts is always consistently soteriological, at least in its underlying motives, and therefore inseparable from the world of religious ideas. The desire to live his life bearing witness to Christ in the middle of Hindu religious culture in a quiet, perhaps even unseen-at-first-sight manner, right in the heart of the sovereignly developed spiritual world of Hinduism, triggered Monchanin's decision to leave the safe intellectual environment of his native France, which was so suitable for him. However, after his arrival in South India in 1939, when he was taken under the protective wing of the ecclesiastical authority by James Mendonça, the enlightened Bishop of the Tiruchirappalli Diocese, Monchanin had to show an exceptional amount of relentless patience or rather self-renunciation. The fantasies of India he had created and absorbed in France on the basis of his studies of the Upanishads and works by great Indian philosophers led by Shankara and his concept of *Advaita Vedanta* could hardly have been more distant from the reality of the environment he was to move around in for the upcoming decade. Throughout the time he had to serve his beloved God as a common chaplain in many out-of-the-way parishes of the Diocese, among Indian Christians coming from the lowest socio-economic strata. Instead of a life consecrated to prayers, systematic contemplation and encouraging theological and philosophical discussions with religious leaders of Hinduism, he therefore had to devote himself to daily pastoral activities for the benefit of the flock entrusted to his spiritual care. Being a supreme intellectual by disposition and also the exceptionally talented theologian that he was, he did not, however, become embittered. Nor did he lose any of his initial enthusiasm and idealism arising from his deep faith, and "he continued to live on another plane and in another world, the world of ideas" (*Swami Parama Arubi Anandam* 2007: 22–23), even in the primitive conditions of Tamil villages.

The first, immature fruit of these ideals of Monchanin became *Bhakti Ashram*. It was a modest dwelling located in the immediate vicinity of the existing church in Kulithalai, where he was repeatedly engaged during his frequent transfers to various parishes of his diocese. However, Monchanin's interest was definitely not merely in the label of the ashram. Equally, he could hardly settle for a life that would take place on two parallel tracks. His idea of the ashram was much more unconditional and radical, not accepting any compromise and not admitting any possibility of concessions with regard to worldly practicality, apparent usefulness or convenient ease. He arrived in India to live there as an Indian Christian monk so that exactly such a life would become his testimony of Christ, his mission which he felt he had been called to.[39] His motives were, in their inmost essence, inherently personal, representing an existential and spiritual challenge that could not be ignored if Monchanin wanted to stay true to himself, his conscience and his faith. After all, he was convinced it was Christ himself who called him to follow him to India. He sought Christ in the religious context of Hinduism and discovered him there for himself alone, as well as for the enrichment or also fulfilment of Christianity (in India and perhaps even beyond its borders).[40] A significant mark on Monchanin's theological and spiritual profile was left by one of the most influential Catholic theologians of the 20th century, the French Jesuit and later Cardinal Henri de Lubac, who had taught at the Catholic University in Lyon for a number of decades and was one of the leading inspirational spirits of the Second Vatican Council.[41] It was Lubac who, during the fruitful discussions they had held in France and subsequently in their mutual correspondence, appealed to Monchanin to approach theology through mysticism and personal, that is totally authentic, mystical experience (Teasdale 1987: 29; Monchanin 1977: 25). And it was probably also Lubac who encouraged Monchanin to formulate his theological discoveries in the environment of India and in the light of the Indian religious experience.

To implement his ideals, Monchanin, however, needed a practical companion who would help him to turn his bold dreams into reality. The decade of patient waiting and preparations came to its end with the delivery of an inconspicuous letter from France that was submitted to Monchanin by his superior Bishop Mendonça for translation and reply. The letter responded to Mendonça's call to establish a new contemplative community in his own diocese that the bishop had already urged during his visit to Rome in 1946 and that was published as part of a longer interview by the Catholic paper *La Croix* (Jacquin 2002: 65). The letter was written from the Abbey of St. Anne in Kergonan by the Benedictine monk and priest Henri Le Saux. His desire to live out his spiritual calling in the middle of the Hindu world coincided remarkably with Monchanin's ideas.[42] Thus, a correspondence between both men, who were so different regarding their life experiences and personal profiles, was established. After one year of waiting, which was filled with lengthy formalities relating to Le Saux's conditional exclaustration, obtaining an Indian visa and long-term residence permit, Le Saux finally, in the middle of 1948, set foot on Indian soil. He was never to leave it again.

Both priests lived in the temporary *Bhakti Ashram* in Kulithalai for the following year and a half. The main activity of finding a location for the future ashram and securing the modest means necessary for its establishment was fully taken over by the more practically minded Le Saux. This preparatory phase was the initiation phase in India for him, and the Benedictine monk became very actively acquainted with the new cultural and religious environment in which he found himself. In addition to intensively studying the Tamil and Sanskrit languages and adapting his lifestyle to Indian reality, he also visited the Hindu ashram of Ramana Maharishi in the temple town of Tiruvannamalai at the foot of the sacred mountain of Arunachala several times. For the first time, he came together with Monchanin and later by himself. This direct personal experience with the live Hindu mysticism of *Advaita Vedanta* was to be of crucial importance for the following fortunes and spiritual orientation of Le Saux. It diverted his attention away from the idea of the Indian Christian monk to the notion of the Christian *advaitin*.[43] Finally, at the beginning of 1950, a suitable location was successfully found for the intended project. One of Monchanin's parishioners from Kulithalai offered both priests a neglected mango grove on the bank of the Cauvery River, less than three kilometres from the town and located in the immediate vicinity of the small village of Tannirpalli. Here, their experiment with a new form of Indian Christian monasticism was officially launched on March 21, on the feast of St. Benedict. The ashram was given the name of *Saccidananda*, or the Holy Trinity Ashram, with a recognized reference to the earlier work of Upadhyay, whom both priests admired. However, it was better known as *Shantivanam* from the very beginning. That day, both of them also dressed in saffron robes so that they could symbolically express severing their ties to the profane world and the beginning of their new life of *sannyasins* by adopting the traditional attire of Hindu ascetics. Fully in the spirit of Hindu tradition, they also chose their new Indian names – Paramarupyananda[44] in the case of Monchanin (literally, the one who feels the bliss of Supreme reality, which is without shape, i.e. unfathomable) and Abhishikteshwarananda in the case of Le Saux (literally, the one who tasted the bliss of the anointed Lord, i.e. Christ). However, Monchanin, it seems, did not use his new name much, unlike his companion. The latter, on the contrary, already as Abhishiktananda, was to become one of the most important figures of the modern history of Christianity in India. During the following decades, he turned into a religious reformer, thinker and mystic, whose major contributions to Indian theology still wait to be fully acknowledged, or rather discovered.

The Indian Benedictine Ashram

Perhaps even before the ashram was actually established, both priests had started pursuing their reflections on its constitutive document. They wanted to explain in it what their motivations had been in leading them to the ashram experiment, the methods, purposes and goals of ashram life and its expected contribution to Christianity in India. Equally, they also wished to defend its existence in the face of anticipated criticism. However, what was originally intended to be a brief document had grown to be a book of nearly one hundred pages. The book seems to be the actual manifesto (Stuart 1995:

42; Monchanin 1974: 202) of the indigenized Christianity as conceived by the Catholic Church and at the same time also a clearly worded policy statement of the Catholic Ashram Movement, at least in the first stage of its development and before the major changes that the Second Vatican Council brought to the life of the Church. The *Memorandum*, as Abhishiktananda calls the constitutive document (Stuart 1995: 42), first saw the light of day in October 1951 under the title of *An Indian Benedictine Ashram*.[45] Although both ashramites put their signatures to it in unity, except for the first chapter that Monchanin added in haste on the recommendation of a Jesuit reviewer-censor, the vast majority of the text is ascribed to Abhishiktananda (Jacquin 2002: 67; Stuart 1995: 48[46]).

The text presents the new ashram as a pioneering experiment, which had received the enlightened support of Bishop Mendonça. After all, it was the Bishop himself who wrote a blessing preface to it. In it he expressed his hope that it would be possible to merge the Indian methods of asceticism with Christian mysticism through a contemplative life. The work of both pioneers will thus bear fruit over the long term in the form of the assimilation of Christianity in the Indian environment and subsequently also the Christianization of India (Monchanin and Le Saux 1964: 4). The approach of the theology of fulfilment substantially dominates the whole pamphlet and so, entirely in its spirit, an exceptional gift of God is attributed to the Indian religio-philosophic tradition, namely "an unquenchable thirst for whatever is spiritual" (Ibid., 15). However, it first has to come to its purification in Christ so that the spiritual message firmly pressed, by the word of God and the Holy Spirit, into the depth of Indian culture could illuminate and enrich the whole world (Ibid., 24). In the opinion of the authors, it is Hindu monks in whom that spiritual message reached the brightest and deepest expression.[47] Therefore, if Christianity is to understand them, and by extension also India, it must draw inspiration from them and create a completely new concept of monastic institutions in India. Their members will be fully devoted to contemplation, as was the case in monastic communities and among hermits living alone at the beginning and in the first centuries of the historical development of Christianity. They will also be willing to come to "a total acceptance of whatever is acceptable in Indian life and manners, a total assimilation of whatever can be assimilated in Indian tradition" (Ibid., 29). Such Christian *sannyasins* will then be concurrently Christians and Indians at one and the same moment[48] (cf. Upadhyay's concept of the Hindu Catholic). Gradually, the two seemingly incompatible religious worlds will themselves become integrated in them. They will subsequently also understand how the seed already planted in the Indian soil by the word of God in the centuries before the coming of Christ and now germinating in their own spiritual experience comes to life and becomes obvious: "Spiritual paths opened by the Sages of Ancient India, cleared and cleansed, will merge at long last in the true and unique way, the Christ" (Ibid., 37).

In individual chapters of their manifesto, both ashramites seek to define the basic constitutive features of the ashram, its substantial characteristics (loneliness, poverty, prayers, work), without which it is not possible to imagine an ashram, according to their comprehension of it. Because the main author of the document was a Benedictine monk, it is hardly surprising that individual points largely correspond to the concept of the centuries-old monastic discipline laid down by St. Benedict. Moreover, Abhishiktananda himself openly admits this anchoring (e.g. Ibid., 38–39). Each of the subchapters actually somewhat followed a comprehensible methodology, gradually answering interrelated and mutually conditional questions, for example, what the prayer is, why it is important, how it should be conducted according to St. Benedict and how it can be (newly) performed in the environment of a Christian ashram. Because the text had been written in the period before the Second Vatican Council, it is certainly worth mentioning the openness of both priests to the sacred texts of Hindu religious tradition. It was really revolutionary in their time, or even rather unheard of in the environment of the Indian Catholic Church. In their opinion, monks in an ashram should be open to the Spirit of Inspiration that is present in these texts. They should use them not only for their private meditative reading (*lectio divina*) but also to venture boldly into cautious experiments with their implementation in the sacred liturgy that will bear the expected fruit after a time in the form of authentic Indian monastic liturgy (Ibid., 75). Less than two decades later, immediately after the Second Vatican Council, Abhishiktananda significantly contributed to the creation of such an order of the Indian Catholic Mass. However, it did not undergo its actual development until after his death and in a completely different ashram.

The constitutive document of the first Catholic ashram is undoubtedly a constitution. Its structure and function are quite similar to those that had already been drafted by the founders of Protestant ashrams several decades earlier. The essential difference between them lies in the absolute emphasis placed on monastic life, the newly sought-for form of which was the purpose of the ashram's being established. In this first stage of the Catholic Movement, it certainly was not a place for lay people wishing to discover their Indian Christian identity through ashram life. The ashram was not supposed to be a hospital for the poor, a refuge for the sick. Begging and wandering monks were not expected to come out of it as if from their centre, celebrating the glory of God with songs and sermons. It was not supposed to be merely a monastery, an intellectual or learning centre, and by no means at all was it supposed to be the centre of the mission and a new form of evangelization, as had been mistakenly assumed by many who thus were soon to be all the more disappointed. The monks did not grow anything in the ashram grounds to provide a living for themselves and did not engage in any charitable activities; their point was not to reform society. In fact, from its very beginning, *Shantivanam* had been "a monastic centre in the strictest sense of the word" because it sought to return to the ancient concept of monasticism, where the word "monk" primarily means a man who concerns himself solely with God, "who lives in the solitude of God [. . .] simply consecrates himself to God" (*Swami Parama Arubi Anandam* 2007: 34). The ashram was intended to fill the life of monks with the new form and content, to inject a completely new, as it sprang from Hinduism, impulse into it. Its goal was not to adapt the European type of monasticism to the Indian context, as it might appear at first sight and as finally happened in the case of other Catholic ashrams, but to incorporate the phenomenon of Hindu *sannyasa* into the life of the Indian Church, to have it take deep root in it and subsequently live it to extremes (Ibid., 37). It is here, in this radical concept of monasticism, where Monchanin and Abhishiktananda hoped to discover the spiritual plane on which Christian and Hindu mysticism would meet in shared understanding. After all, the *sannyasin*, like the Christian monk, "is the one who has been fascinated by the mystery of God [. . .] who remains simply staring at it, unable to see anything else in the universe, in his brothers, in his own heart" (Ibid., 38–39).[49]

The failing of the first Shantivanam: "Unless the Seed Fall and Rot Within the Earth, It Shall not Germinate and Bear Fruit"[50]

The beginnings, or rather the whole lengthy period of the first years of ashram life in *Shantivanam*, were, however, more than modest. The ashram utterly failed to meet one particular expectation that both founders had held. Although we do not learn much about it from their ideological manifesto, it clearly emerges from their ecclesiastical roots and even more clearly from many passages in Abhishiktananda's and Monchanin's letters to friends and sympathizers. In the full eighteen years of the existence of *Shantivanam*, until 1968, when Abhishiktananda left it for good, the ashram failed to attract any other permanent members, not even a single one, whether of Indian or foreign origin. Many adepts came and spent a number of days, weeks or even months at the ashram, but none of them joined the two Indian priests and Indian Catholic monks permanently. Most candidates were discouraged by the challenging conditions of the ascetic life of *sannyasins*. The experimentally free-floating order of the ashram did not suit others. Still others, in particular those who themselves were ordained members of the clergy, apparently refused to submit to Abhishiktananda's teaching authority. In connection with this unfulfilled expectation, we find ourselves facing the crucial paradox of the ashram and also of (almost) the entire Catholic Movement. Despite the *sannyasa* the ashramites proclaimed to have accepted, it was as if they had further seen a deeper meaning of their acts in the flourishing of the ashram community they had established and its impact on the situation of the Church in India. However, the *sannyasin* is the one who surrendered absolutely everything. He no longer attaches his entire mind to anything else but the absolute and its seeking. He is not interested in the building of any community because it necessarily has only a limited duration and prospects. From the perspective of eternity that is the *sannyasin's* point, a community is ephemeral and therefore insufficient. Hardly any modern thinker was able to capture the essence of such a radical Hindu concept of asceticism better than Abhishiktananda (Abhishiktananda 1975).[51] Nevertheless, he was not able to transcend his own Catholic shadow on the plane of real life, not the life enclosed on the pages of books, at least at the time of his engagement in *Shantivanam*. Hence, the previously mentioned paradox reveals in the full light the unresolved question about the meaning and possible limits of the adoption of key religious and philosophical concepts, in the case of *sannyasa* additionally with clear social implications, from one religious system to another.

The different personalities of both founders also significantly contributed to the failure of *Shantivanam* in its first development stage (1950–1968).[52] Despite Monchanin's initial excitement over finding a soul mate in Le Saux, agreeable with his understanding of Hinduism and intended way of monastic life, differences of opinion very soon arose between the two priests. To a considerable degree, they stemmed from their psychological profiles, different life experiences and the respective social and theological backgrounds they came from. The age difference of fifteen years also contributed to the occurrence of these disagreements (Jacquin 2002: 66). Monchanin was theologically more erudite and thoughtful but considerably passive or even impractical on the plane of everyday life, "always living in his dreams" (Stuart 1995: 89). On the other hand, Abhishiktananda was constantly driven from one location to another by something, a kind of inner spiritual restlessness or desire to discover the utmost possible reality through his activity. "Always further, always deeper, all the way over to the other side" – this is how his lifelong credo could be expressed in one sentence. This obsession first brought him to India and transformed him from a Benedictine monk into a Christian *sannyasin* and ultimately a pure *advaitin*, who relativized his Christian and clerical identity to a large extent or even deliberately utterly questioned it. In relation to Hinduism, Monchanin endeavoured to remain an observer who was involved, yet firmly grounded in his Christian set of beliefs, in particular the doctrine of the Trinity. He was looking not only for unexplored paths but also new ways of expression. For him, the religious world of India further represented "preparatio evangelica" (Schouten 2008: 176). The point of departure for Le Saux upon his arrival to India was similar to a great extent. But as early as during the first few years, already as Abhishiktananda, he was attracted by the ideological concepts of *Advaita Vedanta* not as a theologian and an observer but as a mystic, who seeks his own experience through them. Motivated by the knowledge of the sages of Upanishads, their intuitive insight into the substance of divinity and the monistic philosophy of *Advaita Vedanta* and driven by his desire for an authentic personal experience in which opposites would come together in unity,[53] he stayed alternately in Shantivanam, the meditation caves of the sacred mountain of Arunachala and among itinerant sadhus and *sannyasins*. Where Monchanin remained at the level of a theological concept, Abhishiktananda descended to searching for a specific mystical experience. While it can be accepted that both approaches are largely complementary (Jacquin 2002: 72), or even mutually enriching, for the long-term, meaningful existence of the ashram, as it was profiled in the memorandum written by the two monks, they were clearly incompatible.

Year after year, or rather with his every return to *Shantivanam* from his meditation recluses on Arunachala or at the feet of some Hindu saint, the discontent kept growing in Abhishiktananda. Incessant doubts about the meaningfulness of ashram life, not for the Church in India, but for himself, had also been growing stronger, along with the recurring frustration he felt as every unsuccessful adept left their ashram after a promising beginning. The thoughts of his own leaving *Shantivanam* start regularly appearing in Abhishiktananda's letters from 1955. It is evident in particular alongside the expectations of the arrival and subsequent longer stay of the Belgian Cistercian priest Francis Mahieu, whom Abhishiktananda had believed for some time would possibly become his deputy in the ashram (Stuart 1995: 81). However, like the others, Mahieu also left *Shantivanam* after his one-year stay there to establish *Kurisumala*, the second Catholic ashram, in neighbouring Kerala, which we will deal with in a separate chapter. The end of the long-term spiritual crisis that Abhishiktananda had been experiencing came with Monchanin's untimely death in 1957. After this, Abhishiktananda became orphaned in their common ashram. At that time, his attention as a mystical seeker was attracted to the north of India, up to the Himalayan peaks and the springs of the Ganga River, to the places which have been the home of Hindu *sannyasins* for centuries. However, the obligation to continue the work commenced beside his faithful companion and friend forced him to return to *Shantivanam* again and again. Perhaps in this very decade, from 1958 to 1968, the ashram became what it had been supposed to be from the beginning, in the first stage of its development and in spite of the vision presented in *An Indian Benedictine Ashram* – the hermitage of a single monk that was only rarely visited by a guest interested in temporarily living in its peace and in solitude with God. From there, every year, Abhishiktananda regularly set off on his several-month journey across the north. He extended the circle of his acquaintances among Christians and Hindus and also admirers and future disciples by writing numerous articles and books,[54] as well as making personal contacts. During this decade, he was also quietly transforming from an unknown priest and monk into an important teacher of the Indian Catholic Church, as was to be fully manifested in the last years of his life, and also a real Christian guru (Cornille 1991: 134).

He left *Shativanam* for good in August 1968. The burden of the life between the south and the north, where he had built himself a hermitage (*kutir*) near the Himalayan town of Uttarkashi was no longer bearable (Aguilar 2016: 68). The eighteen-year-long chapter in the life of Abhishiktananda was thus finished. He left it closed behind him with undisguised relief, though certainly not without pain and trembling with emotions (Cornille 1991: 203). Freely, as he had been dreaming about for many years, he set off towards the Himalayas that drew him with the same power as Arunachala did in the first years of his Indian life.[55] However, with this, the new and main chapter of *Shantivanam* had only just begun.

Bede Griffiths – a true guru in a true ashram

Monchanin's and Abhishiktananda's attempt ended in failure because, from the very beginning, it had not fulfilled an important condition for the existence of any ashram. Neither of the founding fathers became a guru – the only figure around whom an ashram community can grow and develop. Between themselves, no mutual teacher-student (*guru-shishya*) relationship had been naturally established, although the age difference and Monchanin's deeper experience with Hinduism, at least immediately after Le Saux's arrival in India, was instrumental in this. The absence of this relationship between the two monks is largely related to the exclusivity of the holy orders as conceived by the Catholic Church and the consequences that the holy orders bring to the further life of a priest. By his disposition alone, Monchanin seemingly was not a guru. He did not seek such a role, neither in relation to his younger fellow brother nor in relation to the guests who visited the ashram, perhaps hoping, at least subconsciously, to find a teaching authority there. On the contrary, Abhishiktananda was open to this possible role. According to Monchanin, he emphatically longed for disciples to whom he could pass on his spiritual experiences (Jacquin 2002: 69). However, because he himself was still a seeker at that time, full of inner restlessness and indecisiveness about which path to definitively take, he did not become a true guru at *Shantivanam*. On the contrary, he somewhat discouraged some of the potential aspirants from monastic life in their ashram, such as, for example, the already mentioned F. Mahieu. Being a priest himself and in addition, before he left Belgium, a spiritual mentor and confidant in novitiate, he quite understandably refused to act as Abhishiktananda's disciple. It seems remarkable that we can find only a few clerics across the whole Movement whose teaching authority had been accepted, with absolute effect and in accordance with the Hindu concept of the guru's role, by the other priests, who subsequently became their successors within the meaning of *parampara*, that is, passing the tradition from a teacher to a disciple.[56]

A personality of this type, a true guru, who transformed Abhishiktananda's hermitage into a real ashram, was the Welsh Benedictine monk and priest Bede Griffiths.[57] Already shortly before his arrival in India in 1955, he had captured the attention of the Catholic community in Britain and later also outside it by his masterfully written autobiography *The Golden String* (Griffiths 1954). It quickly became a classic of contemporary spiritual literature. Therein, in an eloquent and engaging manner, he narrates his path to faith and the Church, the twenty years he spent behind the walls of the Benedictine monastery and also his early interest in the religious and philosophical world of India, a rightful part of which he was to soon become. Like Monchanin and Le Saux, Griffiths also deliberated over the possibilities of synthesis of Christian theology with *Vedanta*. Like them, he was interested more in the direct experience of an Indian Christian monk rather than in mere intellectual cognition. Thus, when the possibility arose to join a Benedictine community which was being newly established in South Indian Bangalore, he did not hesitate. This attempt, however, ended in failure after two years. Instead, Griffiths joined the Belgian Cistercian Trappist F. Mahieu, who left *Shantivanam* in 1958, and they together established the *Kurisumala* ashram, located in the dramatic environment of the high hills of eastern Kerala. This exceptional project of an ashram monastery finally unfolded as extremely viable, in spite of the initial material hardships. However, tension associated with the pronounced, spiritually mature personalities of the two founders had been latently present in the young monastic community from its very beginning. Just as an ashram is unthinkable without a guru, it is equally clear that where there are two priests in an ashram, both aspiring to play the role of guru, the situation inevitably leads to practical and purely spiritual problems and tensions on a daily basis. Before Abhishiktananda left *Shantivanam* for good, he had asked Mahieu to take charge of the orphaned ashram and turn it into an autonomous branch of *Kurisumala*.[58] The long-term tension in *Kurisumala* thus found its natural release when Griffiths, who had transferred to *Shantivanam* together with two monks from Kurisumala in August 1968, took charge of the task. During the following years, he laid the foundations there for the golden era of *Shantivanam*, which lasted or rather progressed until his death in 1993.

Immediately after his arrival, Griffiths primarily radically reorganized the environment of *Shantivanam*. He turned the hermitage into an ashram complex, initially modest, further extended during later years to meet the growing needs and to offer monks sufficient spiritual privacy without considerably compromising the community spirit of the fellowship. Griffiths also introduced a consistent and organized rhythm into the experimenting with the elements of Hindu tradition. It continued to be based on the rules of Benedictine monastic life, while placing the emphasis on contemplative prayer. Thus, it left an open space for individualistic searching. Griffiths himself aptly gives his opinion on it in his second most famous book, *The Marriage of East and West* from 1982, when he briefly and clearly defines the essence of the ashram and a key condition for its creation and existence:

> An ashram is not primarily a community like a monastery. It is a group of disciples gathered round a master, or Guru, who come to share the prayer life, the experience of God, of the Guru. The life, therefore, centres not on the common prayer of the liturgy but on the personal prayer of each member [...] and the common prayer of the community is as it were an overflow from this.
> (Griffiths 2003: 19)

With his charisma, sensitive formative approach and in particular personal interest in anyone who visited his ashram, albeit as a temporary guest, Griffiths influenced two entire generations of Indian Christians and perhaps even more countless foreign visitors.[59] It was the latter who began finding their path to *Shantivanam* in droves from the mid-1970s to take away the religious experience that the churches in their own countries had not been able to offer them. Natural integration of some Hindu elements into the Christian liturgy (*arati*, chanting mantras, singing *bhajanas*, *nama japa*, using Hindu symbolism when decorating a chapel etc.) emerged from the *Shantivanam* inculturation laboratory. Subsequently, from the early 1980s, these inculturated elements started to be an omnipresent hallmark of most Catholic ashrams. *Shantivanam* led by Griffiths became their unofficial ideological centre.

The fundamental change of the second stage of *Shantivanam* therefore consisted of the presence of a guru and also in close relation to the guru in the openness of the ashram. Monchanin with Abhishiktananda perceived it as a pioneering attempt to establish a community of Christian *sannyasins*, which was intended to serve as a model for other monastic communities if it had been successful. On the contrary, Griffiths's ashram became a temporary spiritual home to anyone looking for a new form and content of their own religious experience. Although a group of several monks and priests of Indian origin had been formed around Griffiths during the 1970s and 80s, a kind of solid ashram core of his closest disciples and fellow collaborators, the main axis of *Shantivanam* of that period lay in the relation between the specific guru and his disciple. However, this disciple was anonymous to a large extent – while there was just one guru, the number of disciples had been respectably growing. They did not primarily consist of religious or church professionals and certainly not of *sannyasins* but on the contrary the laity coming from all corners of the world for shorter or longer periods of time. This change of emphasis in the ashram concept largely arises from the official turning of the Church towards laymen after the Second Vatican Council. Likewise, it also corresponds to the development of the Ashram Movement in the 1970s–90s, heralding it to some extent and symbolizing it in the clearest manner. Moreover, among all the previous attempts across Christian churches, this new ashram concept was closest to the Hindu approach – at least as we safely know these attempts from the development of Hinduism in the 20th century and if we leave aside all sorts of *seva* ashrams of the Gandhi type that create a completely separate development stream.

Griffiths's relation to Hinduism, and by extension also to the philosophy of *Advaita Vedanta*, was not static. It had undergone a remarkable development during the nearly forty years in which he stayed in India.[60] His point of departure also falls into the theology of fulfilment. However, since around the 1970s, probably in connection with the deeper integration of *Shantivanam* into Hindu religious tradition, the theology of fulfilment has nevertheless been turning into theological inclusion. During that period of his life, Griffiths seemed to be convinced that Christ was present in the religious thinking of other religions not only transcendently but already immanently. Therefore, these religions were not to come to their purification and completion in Christianity. In the last years of his life, Griffiths was seemingly moving closer and closer to the edge of dissolving into the mystical experience of *Advaita Vedanta*. Through an intensive personal experience of unity, every difference in religious concepts and their symbolic representation ceases to be seen. Symbols are transcended and laid aside as mere signs that have had their relevance for a certain period of time and a level of cognition but lost it when coming face to face with the utmost reality. Unlike the late Abhishiktananda, at the time after *Shantivanam* and in particular in the last year of his life, Griffiths, however, never definitively crosses this boundary.[61] He does not let himself be devoured by the absolutized demand for non-duality that relativizes not only his accepted sacrament of priesthood, Christ's exclusive divinity, but also the mystery of the Trinity because its concept of unity in plurality is untenable in the context of *Advaita Vedanta*. Through the theocentric theology of pluralism (Schouten 2008: 180), Griffiths attempts to teeter on the brink where the tension between Christianity and Hinduism remains permanent in principle yet, in his opinion, precisely because of this, creatively fruitful – after all, it is the result of the marriage of East and West.

Shantivanam in its second development stage became not only a sought-after centre of a new potential form of Christianity in India but also the target of sharply worded criticism. This came from both traditional and conservative circles of the Catholic Church, notably from priests, bishops and also many laymen (e.g. Kulanday 1988), as well as chauvinistically hateful nationalistic Hinduism. The latter was becoming intensely aggressive towards Christianity and even more so towards Islam, in particular during the 1980s in connection with the development of the political atmosphere and the growth of communalistic sentiments in society.[62] The most important themes of this criticism will be mentioned in the next part of this book, dealing with the Christian ashram as a phenomenon, so let us leave them aside for now. From the perspective of the historical development of the Movement, however, this criticism is related to the problematic status of the ashram and its spiritual leader in the Church structures. Throughout the 1970s, *Shantivanam* was considerably unanchored from the point of view of the Church institutionalization. It continued to officially come under the authority of the Bishop from Tiruchirappalli, who, however, did not view Griffiths's experiments with great enthusiasm. Concerns about the future fate of the ashram therefore led Griffiths to intensively search for a Benedictine community that would take *Shantivanam* under its protective wing. In 1982, the ashram thus teamed up with the Italian Camaldoli congregation of St. Romuald. It gave him not only the institutional support and background, but also a considerable degree of internal freedom (Pattathu 1997: 220), which is characteristic for the Camaldoli offshoot of the Benedictine order. In the immediate neighbourhood of *Shantivanam*, even a women's community of nuns subsequently grew up, and in addition, during the 1980s as well as 1990s, numerous shoots sprouted from the ashram in the form of further independent ashrams established by Griffiths's disciples both in India and abroad (United Kingdom, United States, France etc.) (Ralston 1987: 136–137).

Shantivanam after Griffiths's death – the memorial of the Movement?

Bede Griffiths died in *Shantivanam* in 1993, surrounded by a community of devoted monks and disciples. By that time, nine permanent members along with several novices and postulants had already been living in the ashram (ashram booklet *Saccidananda Ashram*, undated).[63] However, the ashram did not cease to exist with Griffiths's departure, as might be assumed with respect to his exceptional role of guru. After all, many Hindu ashrams likewise do not disappear from the world after their founder's death. His place is taken either by the most significant disciple, who is often determined by the guru himself in advance, or the leadership of an ashram takes on a collective form with a purely formally constituted superior. It was this latter option that arose in the case of *Shantivanam*, while the final decision on what would happen to the ashram from that moment onwards was thus postponed to the indeterminately distant future. The interest of local and foreign visitors had considerably faded from the second half of the 1990s. The path to the ashram at that time was found in particular by those who were influenced by Griffiths, either through their previous personal contact with him or just by reading his inspiring books, and so the ashram de facto turned into Griffiths's living memorial. After all, the whole Movement had apparently passed its prime during the 1990s and at the turn of the millennium. The personalities dominating the Catholic movement in the 1970s and 80s had passed away one by one and new theological and socio-economic issues had been raised in the mainstream of Indian Christianity. The Movement had become internally exhausted and had lost the key themes that stood at its beginning as well as during its remarkable rise lasting a full three decades.

A small but still active ashram community with members gathered from all over India, however, continues relating itself to *Shantivanam* as its ideological centre. This claim is proved by numerous specialized conferences that are held in the ashram or the original studies dealing with Hinduism influenced by Christian spirituality that are occasionally published here. In this context, the minor as well as extensive texts of the Indian Camaldoli monk John Martin Sahajananda[64] are worthy of our increased attention. He is one of the main disciples of Griffiths and acts at the ashram as its unofficial spiritual leader today, without aspiring to the role of guru in the full sense and without his fellow ashram brothers expecting him to play such a role. In fact, Sahajananda builds upon Abhishiktananda and his attempts to understand Christianity from the point of view of *Advaita Vedanta* without any additional conditions more than upon his teacher Griffiths (Collins 2006: 137). Perhaps also for these reasons, this once-promising student of the theological seminar in Bangalore did not accept holy orders and took refuge under Griffiths's teaching wing in 1984. He can spread his radical theological opinions, which are a pure example of the theology of dissolution of the Christian identity, more freely from the position of a mere monk than a Catholic priest.[65]

Although the future of *Shantivanam* seems unclear today, it still forms an arch on the bank of the Kaveri River after seven decades of its existence, like a bridge connecting both worlds, Hinduism and Christianity. Ashramites themselves are not worried about future development, at least outwardly; after all, in their words "birth, growth, and decay are inevitable stages of the cosmic process. Ashrams too are within this all-embracing cosmic process. Any death or decay is only the beginning of a new existence" (Ayyanikkatt 2002: 3).[66]

The Kurisumala Ashram monastery

Kurisumala, located near the village of Vagamon in the foothills of the Western Ghats in Eastern Kerala, is chronologically the second Catholic ashram. It came into existence on the initiative and with the support of the local bishop of the Syro-Malankara Church, Zacharias Mar Athanasios, and was founded by the Belgian Cistercian Trappist Francis Mahieu in 1958.[67] Mahieu arrived in India in 1955 to join the two pioneers in *Shantivanam*. The considerably liberal, de facto individualistic approach of Monchanin and Abhishiktananda to monasticism as practised in the everyday life of the ashram, however, sharply diverged from his ideas and plans that brought him to India. In cooperation with Griffiths, he thus tried in Kerala to transfer the monastic tradition of Oriental Orthodox Christianity, which West Syrian liturgy authentically refers to and which had been formed by mystical texts of the desert fathers, into the Indian context. The deep symbolism of rituals, colourful poetic images of prayers and religious songs, alongside the emphasis placed on the simplicity of an introspectively oriented life lived in the closest possible contact with untouched nature – it was as if all this had been predestined for an enriching confrontation with the religious experience of India. From its beginning, their ashram had been more of an oriental monastery (Ralston 1987: 95). After all, it originated in the institutional framework of the Syro-Malankara Church, which was not (re)united with the Roman Catholic Church until 1930 and which followed the Eastern rite in liturgy. According to Mahieu, it is this very rite that corresponds more closely with the monastic tradition of India; can influence it more easily and, in a completely natural way, become an instrument of the assimilation of the ascetic and contemplative heritage of India (Acharya 1984: 208).

Both founders could hardly have chosen a more impressive place for their ashram than this. *Kurisumala* is situated at the foot of the ancient pilgrimage Mountain of the Cross, from which *Kurisumala* also got its name and up the hillside of which individual Stations of the Cross ascend to the top. A cross rises there – far away from civilization, in the breathtaking environment of lush, wooded mountains, in the ubiquitous, captivating atmosphere of silence, which utterly calls for concerted contemplation, deep prayer and "an experience of the presence of God" (Ralston 1987: 95). The beginnings of the ashram were extremely difficult. Just a handful of monks built it practically without any assistance, using their bare hands, under the adverse conditions of the strong monsoons that mercilessly lash the Western Ghats mountain range year after year (ashram booklet *Kurisumala Ashram* 2009: 4).[68] However, very soon, new adepts began to find their way to the ashram, seeking an appropriate response to their spiritual calling. The community of monks and novices was quickly expanding; some aspirants even had to be turned away because of the limited capacity of the ashram (Schouten 2008: 178). Nevertheless, the number of its permanent members has been around twenty for several decades. Also in this respect, in its long-term viability, *Kurisumala* seems to be a notable exception among virtually all Catholic ashrams. This is undoubtedly the result of two factors acting simultaneously – the far-sighted decision to establish the ashram community as a monastery and the extraordinary character of the founding father. Being attentively led by Mahieu and, side by side with him, also by Griffith until 1968, the monastic community of *Kurisumala* had been fully adapting itself to its surrounding living conditions. It started with the strictly vegetarian diet and austere decoration of the chapel and the residential quarters with minimal furnishings and ended with the Indian manner of celebrating Mass and the saffron-coloured monastic robes. Frequent *satsangs* (evening community gatherings) with the singing of mantras and *kirtans*, regular contemplation of sacred Hindu texts as part of the daily monastic discipline (*lectio divina*)[69] and serious studies of various Indian philosophical movements that all of the local postulants of monkhood had undergone for many years speak volumes about a life that is fully dedicated to dialogue between the two religions.

The personality of the founder of *Kurisumala* seemed to comprise a rare combination of purely practical, intellectual and contemplative qualities. While *Shantivanam* had always remained existentially dependent on the support of its sympathizers, whether from abroad or from India, Mahieu, fully in compliance with his original order membership, had sought to build a self-sustaining monastic community from the very outset. The dairy farm, started in the immediate neighbourhood of *Kurisumala* and operated as just an experiment during the first years, is already well established today. It secures adequate financial means for the ashram and, in addition, offers employment opportunities to the poor inhabitants of the surrounding villages (Acharya 1974: 117). Francis Acharya (Teacher),[70] as Mahieu was deservedly called by his monks, was at the same time actively involved in courageous reforms of Indian liturgy. The heterodox Christian circles had already been flirting with them from the beginning of the 1960s, and their bold attempts subsequently evolved into the Indian mass, the so-called *Bharatiya Pooja*. This integrates in itself, in a remarkable way, elements of Hindu and Christian liturgical symbolism, liturgy relating to God. It is an everyday part of the Eucharist sacrifice nowadays and remains a vitalizing source of the ashram community, from which the community draws its spiritual strength and through which it also acquires its full meaning. Also in this regard, which considers the Eucharistic celebration to be the basis of ashram life, *Kurisumala* remains a traditional monastic community and as such sets itself significantly apart from many other ashrams.

During several short study trips to the Middle East, Mahieu also systematically searched for the original texts of the Syrian Christian tradition. The four-volume publication of *Prayer with the Harp of the Spirit*, a monumental work of selected Syrian prayers of the Antiochian rite intended for the everyday needs of monastic communities and individuals, marks the climax of more than twenty years of his efforts as a translator. At first glance, it may seem that the life in *Kurisumala* is clearly dominated by the connection of practical activities (*seva*) with intensive devotion (*bhakti*), which is, in line with the dominant Christological orientation of Oriental Christianity, focused mainly on the divine person of Christ the Saviour (Schouten 2008: 179). However, Mahieu always reminded his monks as well as the occasional visitors to the ashram of the vital importance of contemplative meditation (*dhyana*) for any spiritual growth. His own understanding of the Indian ascetic tradition and the basic religious and philosophical texts of Hinduism is eloquently demonstrated by the large number of small contributions published in Indian theological journals. The most remarkable in this sense is his pamphlet *Meditation: Hindu-Christian Meeting Point*, which is subtle yet very significant due to its inspirational character (Acharya 2006).[71]

In 1998, Mahieu's long-time dream was fulfilled when *Kurisumala* was returned into the arms of his original religious order community. It obtained the status of the autonomous Abbey of the Order of Cistercians of the Strict Observance (so-called trappists), and Mahieu himself was officially ordained a year later as its first Abbot (ashram booklet *Kurisumala Ashram* 2009: 5). When Mahieu died in 2002, he left behind not only a firmly established, internally coherent monastic community growing at a healthy and sustainable rate but also several other ashrams in Kerala and the neighbouring Tamil Nadu. They were newly established at Mahieu's instigation or with his blessing by Kurisumala monks and priests, aspiring to further develop the work of their teacher.[72] None of these ashram offshoots, however, managed to put down strong roots, and all of them are likely to become a one-generation project of their respective founding fathers and a tiny circle of their followers. Nevertheless, the crisis of the Ashram Movement that occurred at the turn of the millennium and in particular over the past decade has apparently not concerned *Kurisumala* itself so far. After Mahieu's death, the position of Abbot was taken over by one of his oldest disciples, the charismatic monk and priest Yesudas Thelliyil. *Kurisumala* monks have related to him as a rightful and authoritative *acharya* with the same humility and respect as they showed their first teacher. It seems therefore that the *parampara* of this ashram remains uninterrupted so far. Of course, the question is whether this is happening because it is the ashram monastery.

The Christian Ashram Movement in the context of the Second Vatican Council

The revolutionary changes brought into the life of the Church by the Second Vatican Council marked a turning point in the history of the Movement – regarding the approach of official Church representatives to ashrams and in terms of the self-understanding of ashramites themselves. What had been happening on the periphery of the Church's interest for many years, what had been tolerated or rather suffered thanks to some liberal-minded bishops, suddenly came under the spotlight and became one of the possible means of a sovereign Indian response to the noble ideals that the Council formulated. The transformation of what had been a somewhat spontaneous search for the relationship of Christianity to Hinduism and what was to become a deliberately set up and safely demarcated form of such a relationship, however, contributed to the failures or even the end of the Movement in the long term.

Although the representatives of Indian bishops participated in the pre-conciliar and even the conciliar sessions themselves in large numbers, their involvement was significantly passive, revealing their great willingness to accept but not assertively offer or give (Leeuwen 1990: 5).[73] The first general session of the Catholic Bishops' Conference of India, the CBCI, after the termination of the Council was held in the autumn of 1966 and is usually classified as truly historic. It was decided at the session to establish a national centre that was to become an instrument for the implementation of the ideas contained in the conciliar decrees. The way for the renewal of the Church in India was thus opened. This decision had laid the foundations for the National Biblical, Catechetical and Liturgical Centre[74] that commenced its operations in Bangalore, South India, in February of the following year.

Elected to its lead as its director and concurrently as the secretary of the CBCI Commission for Liturgy was D. S. Amalorpavadass, a Tamil priest, who was studying and working in Europe at the time the Council was held. His ideas and experiences concerning the new forms of the global and national Church therefore extended beyond the horizon of the Indian perspective. Amalor's contribution to the Catholic Church in India can hardly be appreciated enough. In particular, it was he, during the entire period of the 1970s, who set out the direction for future development – with his countless texts, lectures, organizational work and so on. After all, his scope is unusually broad, covering liturgy, spirituality, theology, missiology, ecumenism, catechesis, pastoral care, the relationship between culture and religion, interfaith dialogue and more. After the four "fathers of the West", it was predominantly through him that the Movement ceased to be the domain of foreigners and became an authentic self-expression of Indian Christians.

One of the primary tasks of the new centre should be to create an indigenized or inculturated, hence local in the true meaning of the word, liturgy. It should contribute to the restoration of the liturgy relating to God, as it is determined by the conciliar document titled *Sacrosanctum Concilium*. The three successive, mutually conditioned phases of the interculturation process were set out by Amalor (Amalorpavadass 1976: 214; Leeuwen 1990: 70).[75] Subsequently, they were also approved as an imaginary schedule for the plan of liturgical renewal at the second session of the CBCI Commission for Liturgy at the beginning of 1969. At this meeting, the Committee formulated the so-called Twelve Points of Liturgical Adaptation and subsequently presented them to the entire episcopate of the CBCI for approval. Since a two-thirds majority voted in favour of their adoption, the President of the CBCI referred the matter to the Congregation for Divine Worship and the Discipline of the Sacraments in the Vatican. It is certainly worth mentioning that the chairman of the CBCI Commission for Liturgy, the Archbishop Lourdusamy, an older brother of Amalor, personally conveyed the request of the Indian episcopate to the Congregation. He also gave a detailed explanation of the individual points of the adaptation and consequently celebrated mass in the Vatican in which the points were included. All this happened with the active participation of the members of the Congregation and to their full satisfaction (Amalorpavadass 1978: 75–76; Leeuwen 1990: 70–71). The Twelve points of adaptation, which were experimented with in *Shantivanam*, *Kurisumala* and other early ashram communities for nearly two decades, were thus definitively approved and were to become part of the liturgical life of the Catholic Church in India.[76]

It was, however, obvious to some of the participating bishops as well as involved priests and lay people that the adopting of the Twelve points that would help to create an Indian atmosphere during a Church service (Amaladoss 2005: 8) was only the beginning of the inculturation of the liturgy and renewal of Church life. However, the plans conceived by Amalor and his NBCLC and the ideas of the CBCI, daring as they were at that development stage, were more far reaching. The Second Vatican Council really set the long static mechanism of the Indian Church in motion. Of course, those who had already been bringing the ideas of inculturation to life over a longer period of time, or perhaps more accurately whose own lives had been a credible testimony about the meaning and possibilities of inculturation, could not stay on the sidelines. If we turn our attention to Abhishiktananda, the first mention of new impulses in the Indian Church can be found in his letters from the end of 1966 (Stuart 1995: 189). Many years of his experience of a Christian *sannyasin* and his growing reputation in liberal Christian circles cast him as an indispensable adviser to the CBCI Commission for the Liturgy. Therefore, although still hidden away in his ashram or in the seclusion of his Himalayan hermitage for most of the time, he unwittingly found himself at the very centre of Church developments during 1967–1969.[77] This was the period when extensive study and organizational preparations were underway for the All-India Seminar on the Church in India Today, which had been convened by the CBCI, and Abhishiktananda as well as Mahieu were significantly involved in them. Prior to the Seminar, which can without exaggeration be evaluated as the most significant historical event in the modern history of the Indian Catholic Church, Abhishiktananda had still managed to publish an important contribution regarding the life of the Church and the need for its transformation (Abhishiktananda 1969, 1970).[78] This, he thought, however, must take place not only at the level of the sacred liturgy but also in the form of complete theological renewal, which would completely change the relationship of Christians with the Indian religious environment.

The ideas presented in the previously mentioned critical essay had become an inspiration for many participants in the Seminar, as they largely anticipated the future developments and accurately named the main purpose and objectives of the Seminar. Abhishiktananda sees the decrees of the Second Vatican Council[79] as an open appeal to national Churches to reflect their own situation. In his opinion, this should lead primarily to the establishment of study centres that will examine the local religious context so that their knowledge could become an expert basis for the "local adaptation of pastoral work, worship, religious life and Church legislation" (Abhishiktananda 1969: 27). Without good knowledge of the context, there can be no dialogue with members of other religions that the Council had repeatedly called for and the fruit of which should not only be the spreading of the Gospel, that is, evangelizing, but also enriching one's own religious knowledge (Ibid., 32). The task of the renewed Church is not one of being a new missionary tactic (Ibid., 24). The Church "is not destined simply to fill a religious vacuum" (Ibid., 32) in a given country but, through the understanding of what is foreign, to understand where its brand-new mission lies in modern times. It is not too surprising that Abhishiktananda ascribes a key role in this mission and also a wide spectrum of opportunities for operation to Christian ashrams. Paradoxically, at the same time, he left his own dreamed-of ashram project in *Shantivanam* because it had become a burden for him. However, Abhishiktananda's personality comprised many such paradoxes (Aguilar 2016: 47).

Thus, he dusts off the ashram concept in the previously mentioned contribution; however, his current rendition differs significantly from the older *Benedictine ashram* in many important details. Still, this should be a place primarily devoted to a contemplative way of life; however, his personal experience forced him to rethink the role of a guru, whom he now sees as the cornerstone of the ashram (Ibid., 46–47). Where there is no guru, there is no ashram; however, the question of who the guru is still remains. Abhishiktananda himself admits that there are very few individuals who meet the demands placed on the founder of the ashram, who would be simultaneously a genuine teacher and the one who guides his students along the path to God in a meaningful way (Ibid., 53).[80] With prophetic validity for the entire Movement, he also points out that in many cases, there are more ashram founders who would like to play the role of the guru than their potential disciples (Ibid.). However, at this point in his thoughts, Abhishiktananda makes a seemingly minor concession. It will launch a completely new stage of Catholic ashrams in its consequences, that is to say the Seminar's conclusions on ashrams that he himself undoubtedly contributed to significantly, as well as in the further historical development of the Movement:

> Let the Church encourage, if not actual foundations, at least the call to live an ashram-life in the case of priests, religious or lay people [sic!] who feel a genuine call to it. [...] Ashrams will be quite diverse among themselves. We can never repeat enough that the needs of India are many and very diverse, even apparently contradictory, according to conditions and particular situations. Some ashrams should by all means be conducted after the pattern of the Gandhian ones, with more concern for social work, for example, among labourers or villagers. Some will devote their activities to education, reviving the old tradition of gurukulas [...] Some ashrams will be almost exclusively devoted to contemplative life and spiritual training, according to the most traditional pattern of ashrams.
> (Ibid., 54)

Associated with the last ashram type is also Abhishktananda's remarkable yet never fully implemented idea of a "pilot seminar", which would represent a temporary ashram training school, an "ashram seminar" for priests, monks or preferably theologians. There, they would receive systematic ashram training and education focused on studying sacred Hindu texts. The language of the Church service would be exclusively Sanskrit, while the language of instruction and communication would be one of the vernacular languages. Adepts of the seminar would be led along the well-worn paths of Hindu spirituality and mysticism so that it would be there where the truly indigenized – because arising from the depths of the Indian environment – local theology would come from.[81] Not a single mention is made in Abhishiktananda's reflections of the ashram seminar producing Christian gurus, as Abhishiktananda's intended project is mistakenly and misleadingly presented by C. Cornille (1991: 142) on the basis of another, never-published Abhishiktananda text.[82] Despite this, it is clear from the comparison of the previous quote about possible ashram types and Abhishiktananda's theological thoughts what internal controversy of opinion and at the same time spiritually existential contradiction reigned in the mind of a Catholic *sannyasin*. On the one hand, the quest for a deep reform of the Church, with which there was still a vital personal relationship. On the other hand, the conscious crossing of the institutionalized religion, including all of its sacraments, which are regarded as a mere sign from the perspective of an *advaitin*. On the one hand, life in the world and in the Church that wants to serve the world and bring it the news of the salvation of Christ. On the other hand, the desire to withdraw from the world to a meditation retreat and gradually blend in with the unity, which is represented by *Saccidananda*. It is this incompatible contradiction that seems to be the neuralgic point of the theology that originated in Catholic ashrams.

All-India Seminar on the "Church in India Today"

The All-India Seminar of the Catholic Church took place in Bangalore in May 1969 after more than two years of preparation. It was ascribable to the reform impulses of the Second Vatican Council and the assertive Indian response to them. Even before the Seminar began, its primary objective had been set by the Preparatory Commission that identified in its official pronouncement the existing failure of the Church in India to integrate into the Indian environment as its biggest problem (*All India Seminar* 1970: 8).[83] A similar view, but this time as a hopeful invitation to change, was also presented by the Archbishop, S. Pignedoli, Papal legate and the Secretary of the Congregation for the Evangelization of Peoples (Ibid., 440–449). In particular the emphasis that he placed regarding the quest for renewal of the Church in India, on inner spiritual life, contemplative prayer and monastic communities firmly grounded in the tradition of Indian spirituality, aroused the enthusiastic amazement of many participants on the very first day of the Seminar and perhaps exceeded every expectation of the supporters of inculturation.[84] A brief mention at the end of his speech about the urgent need for small ashram communities[85] then became an important inspiration or direct invitation addressing the working groups dealing with spirituality and liturgy. In their conclusions and subsequently also in the final declaration of the Seminar, the ashram issue then inevitably had to find its inalienable place.

There were 600 representatives of a wide variety of ecclesiastical lifestyles participating in the Seminar. To enhance the efficiency of their work, they were divided into sixteen groups that dealt with various aspects in which the Church in India should achieve renewal or at least arrive at an adequate response to the newly formulated challenges of the modern world.[86] The conclusions of the Seminar, which were divided into the Declaration and Resolutions in terms of the texts, summarized the interim findings and recommendations of individual working groups, turning to the responsible ecclesiastical authorities, priests and monks, as well as the lay community, thus creating a true manifesto of the Indian Church. The main tasks set in the Declaration are as follows: 1) to deepen spirituality, 2) to spontaneously express this spirituality in liturgy, 3) to inculturate liturgy, 4) to create Indian theology reflecting Indian religious tradition and adequately responding to the heritage of the sacred literature of India, 5) to mobilize laymen, 6) to support monastic professions and the establishing of ashrams in cities and villages and 7) to support ecumenical efforts in their widest possible range (Ibid., 241–243). In the more extensive text of the Resolutions, the increased emphasis placed on contemplation as a genuine expression of relating to God reoccurs at the forefront (Ibid., 249–250). Invitations to experiment in liturgy (Ibid., 252) and integrate authentic elements from Indian rituology into Christian liturgy (Ibid., 254) are further reiterated, alongside the requirement for overt support of the Church in establishing ashrams, where spiritual traditions of Christianity and India would be wedded.[87] Thus, ashrams as envisioned by the Seminar participants were to become places of dialogue (Ibid., 259), small units where the life of Indian Christians would acquire a new external form as well as inner content, thus contributing to the formation of an entirely new identity of Christians. It seems remarkable that the Catholic Church had arrived, after almost 50 years, at conclusions similar to those of the Protestant churches regarding the possible function of the ashram, the only difference being that its universal character better allowed the unification of the up-to-then-independent activities of individuals and sub-trends within the Movement.

All-India Consultation on Ashrams

A positive attitude towards the phenomenon of ashrams, in particular to their importance for the life of the Church, was also confirmed at meetings and conferences held by the CBCI and other conferences taking place in the first half of the 1970s.[88] The Catholic ashrams had experienced a real boom during this period. However, it cannot be determined precisely how many of them had emerged in the course of just a few years, because traditional monasteries, pastoral centres, subject-area institutes of Catholic universities or their departments dedicated to interreligious dialogue and spirituality and even some theological seminaries started adding the term *ashram* to their official names. The ashram became part of the Church's renewal programme, and almost every diocese had to have at least one to meet the organizational line newly set by the Seminar. The bishops therefore directly commissioned suitable priests to establish ashrams on predetermined sites (Ralston 1987: 121–122), although two of the fundamental principles of the formation and existence of ashrams, that is, spontaneity and the leadership role of a guru, were thus totally refuted.

The uncoordinated mass character of the Movement at this stage of development resulted in, apart from the obvious increase in the number of ashrams, emptying the content of the ashram concept. Various ashram communities were at the same time bearers of ongoing attempts to inculturate liturgy, which had become a considerably controversial issue from about the middle of the 1970s. Therefore, the need of the Church's oversight over the whole Movement or the correct interpretation of the meaning and function of the ashram for the Church and ashramites themselves emerged.[89] The question of what an ashram is, which arose at the very beginning of the Movement, whether in the rendition of the Protestants Jesudason and Forrester-Patton or the Catholics Monchanin and Abhishiktananda, stood at the forefront once again. But this time the reason for its updating was not only to name the requisite characteristic features of the ashram, to set the conditions for its establishment and purpose, but at the same time to determine what religious institutions were not ashrams. In 1976, the CBCI Commission for Liturgy obtained authorization to coordinate and support the Ashram Movement (Leeuwen 1990: 182). Because the issues concerning ashrams kept reoccurring in 1976 and 1977 (Ibid.: 183), in particular thanks to incentives from ashramites themselves and also from the Secretary of the Commission, Amalorpavadass, it was decided to organize an internal, closed debate on the role of ashrams in the Catholic Church under the auspices of the CBCI in the premises of the NBCLC in Bangalore.

The debate itself, titled the All-India Consultation on Ashrams, was held on June 7–11, 1978. It had been preceded by a three-day meeting of about twenty ashramites from different regions of India,[90] who also managed to create an authentic ashram atmosphere on the premises of the NBCLC. After all, Amalorpavadass, the mover of events and the main initiator of the debate, had been intentionally building the NBCLC campus from its very origin as an ashram of its kind or the nerve centre of the Movement.[91] Amalor also formulated the key points of the meeting of ashramites and the subsequent debate when the ashramites were joined by more than sixty other representatives of the Church. These came from the ranks of bishops, priests, monks, nuns and lay people and represented virtually all regions of India (Irudayaraj 1978: 279). Naturally, the main general purpose of the meeting was to comprehend ashram tradition and find a unique place for it in the context of the Indian Church. However, emphasis was also placed on the evaluation of the development of ashrams from the time when the Seminar was held, the issues related to the attractiveness of ashrams for foreign visitors and the search for the institutional anchoring of ashrams in the Church organization so that ashrams could remain completely free in their activities and, at the same time, a legitimate and meaningful part of the Church.[92] Three panel discussions were devoted to the practical and spiritual experiences of ashramites from Hindu and Christian ashrams. Nevertheless, the floor was also given to those who were not members of ashrams but had personal experience with them because they had briefly stayed in them. The conclusions of the meeting were succinctly summarized in the official *Statement of the All India Consultation on Ashrams* (NBCLC 1978). It became the new constitution of the Movement and was rightly called the Magna Carta of the Ashram Movement by Paul Pattathu, providing an authoritative description (Pattathu 1997: 193). Thanks to the co-operative creativity present during the meetings, the contemplative atmosphere and unprecedented openness of the participating bishops and the priests who had not been engaged in the Movement until then, many participants considered the whole debate an epochal event in the life of not only ashrams but also the whole Indian Church. According to some of them, it even offered the possibility of influencing events in the universal Church in the future (Vandana 1978: 358–359). Although such expectations soon proved overly optimistic, the meeting of ashramites in Bangalore undoubtedly marked another important milestone in the history of the Movement.[93]

Ashram Aikya, an Association of Ashrams

Even during the previously mentioned three days preceding the official part of the debate, a decision had been taken spontaneously to create an ashram organization that would unite the ashrams and their members. An understandable motivation seems to be the truly first historic meeting at the all-India level. Ashramites from various regions found themselves side by side with those whom they had known only from their fleeting visits or, even more often, from accounts of them. For three inspirational days, they were able to mutually share their spiritual and practical experience, findings from experiments with Indian spirituality and liturgy from everyday ashram life and the lofty ideals or common human desires that guided them to their respective ashrams. The association of Catholic ashrams was given an interim, or rather merely working, title of *Bharatiya Kristashram Sangha* (Leeuwen 1990: 185)[94] but was established as *Ashram Aikya (AA)* or the Association of Ashrams as soon as the end of the debate and publication of the official statement.[95]

AA was established with the aim "to foster unity among Ashrams, to give mutual support and stimulus and to represent their needs to those concerned" (Amalorpavadass 1985: 6). Membership in *AA* had been voluntary from the beginning, open not only to ashramites but also to all those interested in the Movement or the ashram way of life. During the following decades, the number of its participants and sympathizers ranged from a few dozen to a hundred or so at the beginning of the new millennium (Painadath 2003b: 124). *AA* works completely independently of the organizational structures of the Catholic Church. Its administration is ensured by the elected team composed of the president of the Association, his deputy and the executive secretary – the leaders of the Catholic Movement have taken turns in these functions since 1978. The most important and visible activities of *AA* undoubtedly include organizing regular bi-annual meetings of all members, so-called *AA satsangs*. Their programme is usually brought under the umbrella of one or more selected topics, to a greater or lesser extent concerning the Movement; for example, the ashram as a place of contemplation (second *satsang*), the relationship to non-Catholic ashrams (fourth *satsang*), fundamentalism and dialogue (fifth *satsang*), the issues and problems of the *guru-shishya* relationship (sixth *satsang*), Christian ashrams and *Hindutva* (eighth *satsang*), the relevance of *sannyasa* in modern times (ninth *satsang*), great spiritual figures of Indian history (eleventh *satsang*), evaluation and the future of the Movement (thirteenth *satsang*) and Brahmabandhav Upadhyay (fifteenth *satsang*). According to the original intention, *satsangs* should have taken place in a different ashram each time so that participants would have the possibility "to live the life of that Ashram"[96] and so extend their own ashram experience or even enrich their daily practice thanks to inspiring motivations. However, these meaningful rotations in individual ashrams were never carried out, as *satsangs* were held recurrently in only a few places. This was also for purely practical reasons, because only a few ashrams had sufficient capacity in their premises that would allow them to accept twenty to eighty guests. The agenda of *satsangs* is governed by the rules of the ashram way of life. Therefore, it includes as its integral part prayer meetings and a celebration of the Eucharistic sacrifice in the inculturated liturgy (always in accordance with the customs of the respective ashram). The length of time between individual sessions, during which the speaker presents his topic and a discussion follows, is also dedicated to individual contemplation, spiritual reading or its joint reflection. From 1995, regional *satsangs* began to be occasionally organized within *AA*, when ashramites of a respective Indian state or broader regions met. Their content noticeably corresponds to the concept of national *satsangs*, only the numbers of participants are of course lower. In 2003, on the occasion of the twenty-fifth anniversary of the founding of *AA*, the final version of the so-called *Handbook of Ashram Aikya* was created and subsequently approved at the thirteenth *satsang*. The *Handbook* maps the previous history of *AA* in a well arranged way and also aims to be a sort of a constitution of this ashram association (*Handbook of Ashram Aikya* 2003). It offers one more authoritative interpretation of the content of the concept of the ashram, but this time arising solely from the experiences and opinions of ashramites themselves.

The second most important activity of *AA* is the publishing and distribution of the *Ashram Aikya Newsletter*, which is intended for internal use by the members of *AA* and thus represents a crucial source of information.[97] The journal is published twice a year, with occasional delays. Its editor in chief is usually the respective secretary in *AA*, but all interested ashramites may also contribute to its content. There thus appear short reports about the activities of their ashrams; papers relating to Indian spirituality, the new form of which they have been de facto forming in their ashrams and plans for upcoming *satsangs* or, on the contrary, additional reflection on the *satsangs* that have already been held. In its earlier editions, especially those published before 1995, the main space in the journal was held by brief vignettes of newly constituted ashrams where the motives for their origin, original aspects, daring visions and plans for the future were described. The informational relevance of these contributions, however, is extremely debatable; after all, their enthusiastic authors were usually the founders themselves. In this respect, somewhat more remarkable are the messages from the pens of other ashramites who visited the respective ashrams within their ashram pilgrimages. This is an interesting trend in the development of the Movement, in particular from the second half of the 1980s. To strengthen their own identity and deeper integration, ashramites not only meet through *satsangs* but also thanks to mutual visits (e.g. the long ashram pilgrimage of the then-secretary of *AA*, Mariananda, who visited all the ashrams associated in *AA* at the turn of the millennium; see his travel report in No. 38 and 39).[98] Significant space in the journal is taken up by the personal creeds of ashramites. They frankly retell their lives and fates and outline the various circumstances that led them to the ashram. In fact, these contributions are often spiritually intimate confessions as to why it is in the ashram where they discover the fulfilment of their spiritual journey. Well-deserved attention is also devoted to portraits of key figures of the Movement throughout its history. As many as four editions of the *Newsletter* (no. 47–50) dealt with Upadhyay and his life and legacy left to the Catholic Church; some others are dedicated to Abhishiktananda, Griffiths and Amalor after his untimely death in 1990. A separate category of topics consists of contributions of a more specialized nature, original as well as previously published. They deal with some of the important aspects of inculturation in the broadest sense of the word, for example, the relation of Christians to the Hindu sacred texts (No. 32), the relationship between Christianity and Zen Buddhism (No. 39), Christ as a cosmic principle (No. 53), interfaith dialogue and definition of the *sannyasin*. There can be also found interesting reflections on religious documents relevant to the Movement or, on the contrary, *AA*'s official response to new developments in the Church related to ashram issues (e.g. a letter of *AA* to the Asian Synod of Bishops in No. 33, which advocated the ashram idea). Individual issues of the journal, in chronological order, are thus a direct testimony to the development of the Movement after 1978. They are a polyphonic testimony of hope, which had been put into the concept of the ashram, to the disappointment when the much anticipated public interest of the Christian public did not appear, and finally to the stagnation and feelings of doom when the Movement apparently reached a critical point of its existence in the early years after the turn of the millennium. The theme of the failure of the Movement, finding its causes and the painstaking attempts to redefine the concept of the ashram so that it could offer new possibilities for implementing the ashram ideals, dominate in particular the last ten editions of the magazine. The most important themes of this courageous self-criticism will be duly taken into account in the next part of this book devoted to the phenomenon of the Christian ashram.

An outline of the development of the Catholic Ashram Movement after 1978

As in the case of ashrams arising from the Protestant initiative, with regard to the Catholic ashrams existing in the high and late periods of the Movement, it is virtually impossible to mention them all, let alone capture their development. Michael O'Toole, the author of one of the first investigative works, *Christian Ashrams in India* (1983), offers a geographically structured list and description of ashrams. It was meant to serve as an instructive manual for those interested in the spirituality of ashrams, in particular from among their young foreign visitors. His "practical guide to ashrams" does not distinguish between church denominations, but among the fifty ashrams presented in the guide, more than half belong to the Catholic Church. The numbers given in other information sources differ substantially. For example, the prejudiced critic of the Movement Sita Ram Goel presents a list of 108 ashrams, once again without distinguishing whether they are Catholic or Protestant (Goel 1994: 209–213). Helen Ralston, who conducted her sociological research of the ashram scene in the middle of the 1980s, visited fourteen Catholic ashrams (Ralston 1987: 123). Sebastian Painadath, one of the leading figures of the Movement from the 1990s and the president of *AA* during 2005–2009, presents autobiographical portraits and personal confessions of nearly thirty ashramites from various ashrams (Painadath 2003a: 2–112).[99] Finally, the official list of the Catholic ashrams that are members of *AA*, based on figures from 2004, when they were last published on the pages of the *AA Newsletter* (no. 45: 17), comes to forty-three items.[100] The directory of the Indian Catholic Church from 2005, a sort of Yellow Pages of all Christian institutions in India, including their addresses and other contact information, lists 127 Catholic and 22 Protestant ashrams, although the methodology of selecting and adding an eligible institution to the list seems to be more than questionable. It is actually completely impossible to find one's way around such a maze of real and wannabe ashrams.

In the outline of the further historical development of Catholic ashrams, we will therefore briefly introduce those that are or have been in many ways exceptional, whether due to the purpose of their establishment, the personality of the founder or notable developmental fates, and also those that the ashram community itself considers crucial for the later stage of the Movement. The present selection is subjective, based on the direct personal experience of the author, the knowledge he obtained during his research and the opinions provided by his informants from among the ashramites. But it also captures to a large extent the trends that the Movement went through after 1978.

Aikya Alayam

Shortly before the Seminar took place, in Madras, Tamil Nadu, an attempt had been made amid the hustle and bustle of the city to implement, in a sense, Abhishiktananda's idea of the ashram seminar. After all, Abhishiktananda himself participated in the inauguration of the *Aikya Alayam* ashram immediately after he left *Shantivanam* for good in 1968 (Stuart 1995: 204). The ashram was founded by the Jesuit priest Ignatius Hirudayam, a major supporter of inculturation in its early stage and a promoter of interfaith dialogue. An urban environment was deliberately chosen for the site because the function of this ashram, unlike many previous ones, was supposed to consist primarily in "the intellectual apostolate" (Dhanaraj 1990: 43[101]), which was to be carried out through the ashram way of life. During its first four years, the ashram operated in makeshift premises. From 1972, when it was relocated, it started to be systematically built up, also in terms of its architecture, as "an Inter-faith Research Dialogue centre" (Ibid., 33), which aims to engage in direct interaction with the academic environment and representatives of non-Christian religions. Regular seminars on the new form of Indian Christian spirituality, short-term study programmes dealing with sacred texts of various religions, theological aspects of the dialogue and so on also continued to be held in the ashram after its founder died in 1983. After nearly thirty years, interfaith meetings were once again organized there on a yearly basis, during which representatives of Christianity and Hinduism stayed, prayed, debated and shared their religious experiences together for several days (Ibid.: 35).

Due to the founder's order membership, the ashram also started to serve as a college for theology students from among Jesuit seminarians from the end of the 1970s. However, the efforts to interconnect their theological and priestly formation with ashram life and integrate them into it more deeply failed. After all, the mainstream of the theology pursued in the theological seminars of India was dominated by completely different topics even at that time. It drew increased attention to and subsequently also placed absolute emphasis on social aspects of the apostleship, in particular in the form of the Dalit theology of liberation. The sparse ashram community managed to continue resisting the constant tension between the two considerably different approaches to the Indian cultural and religious environment for a number of following years, perhaps in particular due to the all-India and international fame of the founder. Before the ashram wound up its activities for good towards the end of the 1990s and its premises became a part of the Jesuit seminar, a number of foreign researchers, making use of its very well-equipped library, or temporary ashramites, studying at some of the Madras universities, regularly stayed there.

Jyoti Niketan

One of the oldest still-functioning ashrams was established in the North Indian state of Uttar Pradesh near the city of Bareilly as early as in 1954. The Anglican pastor Murray Rogers, one of the most active and best-known representatives of the Protestant Movement, had lived there with his family until 1971, when he left India to establish an ashram of a similar type in Jerusalem. From the beginning of its existence, the ashram was guided by Gandhi's utopian ideals and designed as a small self-sufficient community. It kept surviving in modest material conditions but in accordance with the spiritual testimony of the Gospel that was not proclaimed but lived there, moreover, in a way that aspired to be fully understandable for the poor rural environment in which the ashram was set. Although the ashramites contributed to some degree in improving the living conditions of the villagers, and so it was possible to include their ashram under the *seva* category, its purpose was not "to do something so much as to be something" (Vandana 2004: 108). According to Vandana, this should apply in the most general sense to every Christian ashram. Also, *Jyoti Niketan* is inextricably linked to Abhishiktananda. Being a close friend of Rogers, he had stayed in the ashram many times from the early 1960s and had changed it through his influence into one of the few truly ecumenical ashrams. Thanks to Abhishiktananda, among others, two significant meetings of representatives of Hinduism and Christianity took place in the premises of the ashram as part of the attempt at interfaith dialogue (Ralston 1987: 40, n. 7). Fully in line with the concept of Protestants, Rogers never acted as the guru of the ashram. The leadership was thus de facto collectively anonymous, which is also suggested even by the official status of the ashram as a foundation. After the departure of Rogers from India, the Foundation went over to the Church of North India into the hands of the Catholic Church, and the role of Administrator was entrusted to the Franciscan Capuchin priest R. Deenabandhu. With respect to the legacy of the founder, the ashram did not change its original profile under his leadership. It remained a small open community whose members divided their time between selfless service to the needy and unpretentious testimony of their Christian faith, clothed in Indian attire. However, due to the ageing members of the ashram, it inevitably went defunct some time ago.

Anjali Ashram

The most active, the best-planned, and from its beginning also the best-organized ashram project not only after 1978 but perhaps also throughout the whole history of the Movement was started in 1979. Amalorpavadass, the first director of the NBCLC, who has already been mentioned multiple times, added to his numerous activities the function of professor of Christianity at the University of Mysore. Amalor's holistic and all-encompassing concept of human spirituality and religious experience, however, could not be limited to the intellectually theorizing academic perspective. He strived to interconnect this new role with "a genuine Christian community life, lived in an Indian tradition, context and atmosphere, following an Indian life-style which an Ashram is" (ashram booklet *Anjali Ashram*, undated: 7). A small community was thus established in rented premises in the immediate vicinity of the University. It offered, under the leadership of the guru whom Amalor had become in the full sense of the word in that period, a space for meditation, prayer and dialogue to students, Christians from the city and also the general public. In 1983, *Anjali Ashram*, under the pressure of the growing interest of Amalor's students and people interested in the courses in Indian spirituality organized by him, began to move into newly built premises on the outskirts of Mysore. They were and still continue to be symbolically located at the foot of Chamunda, the Hindu sacred mountain. From here, Amalor launched and fully developed the activities of his ashram as a centre devoted to liturgical experiments and experience-based training or systematic training in Indian Christian spirituality. *Anjali* is usually considered the university of this spirituality, and justly so (Pattathu 1997: 245).

Similarly to when he was building the campus of the NBCLC, Amalor paid great attention to the layout of the ashram. Its architecture, appearance and the arrangement of individual buildings in the overall plan, as well as their names, are packed tight or even oversaturated with the religious symbolism of inculturated Christianity. Everything here has its precisely marked out and thought-out place, from an open gate that never closes through the entrance tower (*vishva gopura*), the meditation and assembly pillared hall (*satsang mandapa*), small meditation caves (*guha*) and sacred fig trees, to the Saccidananda shrine, which represents a demonstration of high sacral Christian art in contemporary India. Its gloriole was seemingly formed by the twenty or so simple bungalows (*kutir*) arranged in a circle and intended to accommodate participants in the offered courses.[102] *Anjali* is probably the largest Christian ashram and is able to provide shelter for up to 120 visitors.

In this ashram, there is not even a trace of spontaneity (Ralston 1987: 101), chaotic intuition in experimenting with Indian liturgy and spirituality or flexibility or freedom in following somehow vaguely set up rules of everyday life as it used to be and still is the case in most other Christian and Hindu ashrams. Amalor brought into the ashram phenomenon a settled and strictly followed system and meaningful ashram rules. It all starts from an original and, in the history of inculturation, probably the boldest and best-worked-out concept of the Indian mass (*An Order of the Mass for India*, undated)[103] up to the courses of Indian spirituality, which are comprehensively arranged, planned in the minutest detail and many days long and which the ashram has been offering to interested trainees month after month for four decades. No other ashram in India is so "organized and organizing" (Cornille 1991: 145). While elsewhere the ashram primarily represents a place of freedom and tranquillity for the implementation of one's own spiritual practice (*sadhana*), and so the activity is left fully in the hands of ashramites, here, they are provided with the best practices and resources which they adapt to. The two most popular study and experiential spiritual programmes, called *Atma Purna Anubhava* and *Brahma Sakshatkara Anubhava*,[104] have already been completed by thousands of adepts under the leadership of Amalor and his successor at the head of the ashram.[105] Most of them are from the ranks of religious professionals, priests, seminarians, monks, nuns and novices, but each of the implemented programmes has also always been attended by several lay people. After all, many of them have applied for admission to the courses repeatedly for several years, and they understand them as a regular part of their own spiritual renewal.

Amalor knowingly targeted the general Christian public, striving to renew and mobilize it for the Church, as well as in the Church, just as the whole Catholic Movement did in the latter phase of its development after 1978. The effects of Amalor's activities are multiple. He significantly influenced in particular the urban intellectual and middle-class strata of Christians from the States of Karnataka and Tamil Nadu, and many of his pupils, who view him as a true guru, still continue his work. Although the NBCLC sidelined the inculturation direction of their main aim during the 1980s, it is Amalor's disciples who are the key intermediaries and carriers of the lay apostolate, the centre of which the NBCLC continues to be, whether it is the All-India Catholic Union or the very active Christian Renewal Movement of India (*Anjali Ashram's God-Experience, Dialogue – Service* 2005: 23).

The guru of *Anjali* tragically died in a car accident in 1990, and his community and a wide circle of devoted disciples were suddenly orphaned.[106] After three years of uncertainty and dithering, the head of the ashram, as the major *acharya*, became a Tamil priest and one of Amalor's disciples, A. Louis (Swami Gyanajyoti). Along with the nun Mariella, he nowadays forms the core of the small community that still successfully builds on the work of its teacher. The visions and goals of the *Anjali ashram*, which Amalor set upon its establishment, remain valid and seem also to inspire other ashram communities that were formed along the lines of *Anjali* to a certain extent:[107] 1) creating a multi-faith community connecting men and women coming from all social and economic strata; 2) supporting further enhancement of Indian spirituality; 3) striving for dialogue across religious communities;

4) cooperating with the academic sphere; 5) supporting social activism leading to the elimination of social oppression and injustices rooted for centuries in Indian society; 6) educating future leaders, in particular from among lay persons and 7) creating the ashram as a place open to all who are seeking radical change in their spiritual life and lifestyle (ashram booklet *Anjali Ashram*, undated: 7–13). As is evident, in Amalor's concept and also at this stage of the development of the Movement, the idea of the ashram was significantly expanded so that its scope could take up virtually all of the challenges that Christianity is currently facing.

Matridham Ashram

Varanasi, in religious terms the most prominent place within the whole of India, has attracted the attention of Christian missionaries for centuries. Starting a victorious campaign for the Christianization of India right here, in the heart of Hinduism, seemed to be a prospect too enticing to resist. In 1953, the Catholic Indian Missionary Society, IMS, was established in Varanasi. A year later, its Superior General J. Fernandez established the *Matridham* evangelistic centre in the suburbs of the holy pilgrimage city, which was to adapt its character and external form to the cultural features of the surrounding environment. The inspiration for this first attempt became the Protestant ashrams built at that time in accordance with Gandhi's model throughout India (ashram booklet *Prarthana Manjari*, undated: 2).[108] Although *Matridham* had already been abandoned in 1960, one of the priests who also spent a year in the novitiate of the IMS was Ishwar Prasad. Later he was to become a significant promoter of inculturation and the Ashram Movement in North India (*Ashram Aikya Newsletter*, no. 49: 7).

Immediately after the end of the Seminar, the then progressive Bishop of Varanasi, P. D'Souza, one of the bright stars of the Seminar, strove for the renewal of *Matridham*. However, this time, ashrams became part of the official programme course of the Church renewal, as the Christian ashram. This did not happen until 1976 under the leadership of a member of the IMS, Swami Dayananda, who had obtained his previous ashram experience in the tiny *Krist Panthi* ashram. The aforementioned Prasad operated this ashram in Varanasi from 1971 for several years on the inspiration of Bishop D'Souza.[109] It was Prasad who took *Matridham* over in 1983 and turned it into the most important ashram of North India during the ten years of his time as the main *acharya*.

The objectives of *Matridham*, as defined in the ashram booklet, appear to be all embracing. They cover interreligious dialogue, Indian Christian spirituality, inculturation, spiritual renewal of the laity and religious professionals and also social assistance for the needy (ashram booklet *Matridham Ashram*, undated: 5–10). Under the leadership of Prasad, the ashram acquired quite a new external appearance thanks to the overhauling of the complex and several newly constructed buildings, which displayed classic features of inculturated Christian architecture. Just as with *Anjali* at the same time in South India, *Matridham* also started to act as a training ashram centre for Indian Christian spirituality. The essential difference between the two ashrams, however, lies in their subsequent fates, which were to a large extent influenced by the different situations of Christians in South and North India. The Christian community in the South is a safely established part of the religiously pluralistic society due to historical circumstances, and many local Christians are today a rightful part of the numerous middle class despite their lower social origin. On the contrary, the North Indian Christians, if we venture to generalize, belong to the lower economic and social groups in the vast majority of cases. In addition, they also struggle on a wider scale with regular manifestations of religious intolerance from the side of the majority Hinduism. It bears a grudge against religious minorities of non-Indian origin under the banner of *Hindutva*, aiming to achieve its nationalist-political goals at their expense. The spiritual needs of the Christians from Tamil Nadu and Karnataka, who have found their way to *Anjali* in the hope of meeting them, are simply inherently radically different from the needs of the poor Christians of Uttar Pradesh. Thus, although *Matridham* under the leadership of Prasad attracted multitudes of priests, monks and nuns who had completed courses of spiritual renewal there to subsequently enrich the life in their congregations or parishes with the obtained impulses and deeper religious experiences, the ashram started quickly changing after Prasad left it in 1993.[110]

The change was enforced in a non-violent manner by local Christians themselves. Under their pressure, the ashram became a popular charismatic centre, a place of ecstatically expressed personal devoutness, where collectively experienced religious ecstasy and also miraculous curing occurred during prayer assemblies (public *satsangs*).[111] *Matridham* continues to be an ashram, with a sparse ashram community living there in a typical ashram style,[112] having been led by the main *acharya* and also a member of the IMS, Anil Dev, since 1995. His interactions with the world outside now take place primarily for the needs of "Khrist Bhaktas".[113] Moreover, Hindus from the wide surrounding area often appear in their ranks crowding the ashram premises Sunday by Sunday. Paradoxically, in the context of the ideas and ideals of the Movement, it is this form of Christian spirituality that appeals to them. They understand it, unlike the complex and ungraspable mystic-philosophical planes of *Advaita Vedanta*, the abstractions of Upanishads or the demanding requirements of contemplative meditation. This surprising finding, of where and what the ashram turned into, was reached by participants of the fifteenth *satsang* of the AA, which was held in *Matridham* in 2007. The entire ashram community seemingly suddenly discovered to their amazement that, while their own ashrams had been becoming desolated and had not been attracting the interest of Christian laity and certainly not of

Hindus who would be willing to enter into an interfaith dialogue with them, this local ashram could only just manage the onrush of both groups with some degree of difficulty. The remarkable evaluation report about the *satsang* taking place that appeared on the pages of the *AA Newsletter* (no. 50: 13–16) incorporates the unspoken, yet obvious questions. Does the *Khrist Bhaktas* movement represent one of the possible development streams of the interaction between Christianity and Hinduism (San Chirico 2014: 27)? Is it a new challenge for the existing Christian ashrams? Is it this very direction in which the whole Movement should be oriented and thus pull it out of the deep crisis in which it finds itself today?

Jivandhara Ashram

No outline of the development of the ashram scene after 1978 would be complete without mentioning the ashram that, in its focus, returned to the concept of the late Abhishiktananda and, to some extent, Griffiths, too, and above all without making a more extensive comment about its founder. In the chapter dealing with the Ecumenical *CPSSA* ashram in Pune, it was stated that Vandana, a nun from the Catholic Society of the Sacred Heart (RSCJ), participated in its renewal in 1972. However, in 1974, she and her faithful companion Ishapriya, a nun of English origin from the same monastic order community, left *CPSSA* and spent the next five years staying in many Hindu ashrams for varying periods of time.[114] During her ashram journey, Vandana was significantly influenced in particular by the Shivananda Ashram in Rishikesh, North India. A deep personal friendship and mutually shown spiritual respect teamed her up with Shivananda's successor in the position of the guru of the ashram, Swami Chidananda. The northern part of Rishikesh, the area called Lakshman Jhula, is the very place where Vandana settled down at the end of the 1980s. There, on a small piece of donated land, a few huts were built, for which the name of *Jivandhara kutir* became usual. The community that had come together around Vandana and originally had just a few members started attracting many new ones interested in her spiritual leadership. Because the *kutir* in Rishikesh did not provide enough space, the emerging ashram moved to the higher altitudes of the Himalayas, to a place known as Jaiharikhal, in 1984. Here, in the breath-taking surroundings, offering spectacular views of the snow-capped Himalayan Mountains, *Jivandhara Ashram* subsequently grew under the leadership of Vandana as its *mataji*.[115]

The core of the ashram, its permanent community, remained small. Nevertheless, visitors from among Indian priests, nuns, Indian laity, Hindus and also many foreigners regularly found their way to it. They received something similar here as in the South Indian *Shantivanam* under Griffiths's leadership, only in a female version, perhaps with even greater maternal sensitivity and understanding but definitely with the absolute emphasis placed on meditation as the basis of life in the ashram. Meditation completely sidelined any liturgical inculturation experiments. On the contrary, according to Vandana's concept, it is the very sustained and concentrated search for God and personal experience of unity with God that constitute the essence of the ashram and are, therefore, above all the Christian sacraments, including that of the Eucharist.[116] Thanks to such a radical attitude towards the ashram phenomenon, Vandana was willing to exceed her own Christian identity, just as Abhishiktananda was after his departure from *Shantivanam*, and her religious affiliation if the Church in the form of her order community would have prevented her from continuing to live the life of an ashramite she had chosen. The distinction between the Hindu and Christian ashram is also losing relevance to that effect, because the freedom that a *sannyasin* enters by relinquishing everything goes beyond the narrowly defined categories of denominational or religious affiliation. In comparison with Griffiths, Vandana had not sought to find a solid and safe place in the Church structures for her ashram, nor was she worried about the future fate of the ashram. An ashram as she understood it was not a place but a relationship – a relationship of absolute trust and allegiance between the guru and a disciple, the relationship of freedom and love that mirrors the relationship between God and man.

The *Jivandhara Ashram* was in operation on a seasonal basis because the community would return to *kutir* in Rishikesh during winter months. Both Vandana and Ishapriya very often spent that period among their disciples in India and abroad, where they dispensed their concept of ashram ideals by giving lectures and spiritual lessons and performing other awareness-raising activities. In 1994, they definitively abandoned the Himalayan ashram to permanently settle in Rishikesh. The ashram came under the administration of the Carmelite order that continues operating it as a place for long-term individual meditation stays. In the words of Vandana, the time of inner quietening was now to come for her, which would provide her with a space "to practise herself what she has preached for years to others" (*Ashram Aikya Newsletter*, no. 33: 8). Her active role of guru ended, although she lived in Rishikesh for many years and willingly received all serious candidates seeking a base for their spiritual practice.

The limits of inculturation, the limits of Church support for the Movement

The beginning of the end of the Church's support for any efforts to adapt the life of Indian Christians to the local environment occurred in conjunction with the inculturation of liturgy, since the latter was most apparent on the outside. It happened, paradoxically, at the same moment when it was officially authorized. Already the publication of the Twelve points of the outer liturgical adaptation, which were to become part of the celebration of the Eucharistic sacrifice in India by decision of the Vatican Congregation for Divine Worship and the Discipline of the Sacraments, provoked controversy, both in the ranks of the general public and between bishops and priests.[117] For many of them, such a novelty was too radical; neither the Church nor the faithful were properly prepared for it. In their opinion, the danger of Hinduization of the Church was particularly alarming. Others questioned the mandate of the CBCI Commission for Liturgy; the validity of the voting carried out at the level of the CBCI, which approved the adaptation; the results of the work and the meaning of the establishment of the NBCLC. Some, as in a number of other places around the world, were very critical about the doctrinal conclusions and recommendations of the Second Vatican Council. This resulted in a divergence of opinions in the Congregation of Indian bishops, and so adaptations were supported in some dioceses and banned in others (Saldanha 1997: 61–62). The rather vague formulation of the Congregation in the confirmation letter, which played into the hands of different interpretations, was probably also to blame.[118] Although the CBCI Commission for Liturgy did after some time manage to dispel doubts regarding the legality of adaptations, the shadow of fear loomed over them from then on. As a result, the Indian bishops became more cautious about all of the next steps in the process of inculturation. However, from the perspective of the laity active in the life of the Church and being critical about the adaptation, the question has never been resolved: is inculturation desirable for a religious minority at all, or, on the contrary, does its implementation weaken the already fragile identity of Indian Christians as a separate and exclusive social and religious community?

The promoters of inculturation encountered a clear and insurmountable obstacle in the mid-70s, when they tried to move from the outer adaptation to inner liturgical changes that would take inspiration from the tradition of Indian religious texts. Bishops were invited by the Vatican's Congregation to create an Indian anaphora, which is the heart and soul of every Eucharistic Sacrifice. Such an anaphora had already started acquiring its form from 1968. In several meetings of the CBCI Commission for Liturgy in the early 1970s, the drafted text had been adapted many times so that the entire College of Bishops could vote about its final version in 1972. Although sixty of the eighty bishops present took a stand in favour of its adoption, a dispute concerning the exact amount of the required majority subsequently broke out.[119] Hence, the submitted text was not officially approved by the CBCI and therefore not sent to the Vatican Congregation for further analysis and possible approval of its implementation.[120] However, in experimental communities, for example, in some ashrams, it began to be commonly used. The bishops who supported the anaphora appreciated its deep understanding of Indian religious tradition, comprehending this tradition as a meaningful part of the history of salvation, and therefore its sensitively implemented integral connection with the Gospel message. On the contrary, the critics reproached it for using direct quotations from Hindu religious texts (Saldanha 1997: 64) and religious-philosophical terms that keep carrying along with them their quite specific theological meaning. They acquire it in the context of Hinduism, and that is in principle incompatible with the doctrinal anchoring of the Christian faith.[121]

However, another problem soon arose in addition to the unresolved issue of the Indian anaphora when the CBCI Commission for Liturgy tried, through its NBCLC laboratory, to unleash a theological debate on the possible use of the sacred texts of non-Christian religions during the Liturgy of the Word. In 1974, Amalorpavadass organized a research seminar on non-biblical scriptures in the NBCLC. It was attended by leading Indian theologians, some bishops and also two representatives of the papal throne (among others, the Secretary of the Vatican Secretariat for Non-Christians). In its conclusions, the seminar recommended such utilization when, in the opinion of the seminar participants, passages from the Vedas, Upanishads, *Bhagavadgita* and so on could be incorporated into Mass. They were allowed to appear in its order in the form of readings, communal prayers, songs or quotes in the homily and even as an integral part of the anaphora (Leeuwen 1990: 141–146). From the perspective of the Church liturgical tradition but also from the perspective of theological implications, it was a truly revolutionary opinion. Amalor, therefore, published all documents relating to its content (*Research Seminar on Non-Biblical Scriptures* 1974) immediately after the seminar, perhaps with a sincere desire to play an open game with the highest ecclesiastical authorities. However, the adverse reaction of the Vatican was not long in coming. This appeared in the form of the famous letter of Cardinal J. Knox, prefect of the Congregation for Divine Worship and the Discipline of the Sacraments. He called on the CBCI in 1975 to unequivocally and by means of an official declaration ban the use of non-biblical texts in liturgy, as well as the Indian Eucharistic prayer (anaphora), during Eucharistic Sacrifices celebrated both publicly and in private (Saldanha 1997: 71) The Congregation of Indian bishops took fright at the uncompromising tone of the letter. As a result, any further support from the Church for any following attempts at liturgy renewal, inculturation and experiments (Leeuwen 1990: 79), the bearers or rather pure embodiment of which were Christian ashrams, was de facto ended by this in India.

From the perspective of the total number of newly emerging ashrams, the 1980s was the most fruitful time for the Movement. However, its history was already inexorably heading towards its end at that time. This fact became absolutely obvious during the international theological conference which was held in Delhi in 1981. The Ecumenical Association of Third World Theologians, EATWOT, was established in Tanzania in 1976 and brought together 50 participants from 27 countries. Its aim was to find ways to relevantly form theology in the context of their countries and the challenges of the modern age. The official conclusions of the fifth EATWOT Conference in Delhi spoke critically about the theology of fulfilment. Its approach to religious diversity was a starting point for the Movement at its very beginning. However, in the opinion of the EATWOT representatives, the theology of fulfilment did not take into account the poverty of countries in the Asian region. While focusing its attention on Christ present in various religions, it failed to recognize the Christ of the poor (*Statement of the Fifth Conference of the EATWOT* 1982: 92). But it is he who is the relevant theological theme of Christianity in third world countries. To sideline him means to overlook the essential needs of their population, both Christians and members of other religions. The Ashram Movement as understood by the EATWOT and those to whom modern theology originating in the environment of Asia have to respond were thus at odds with each other because ashramites were expressing only "a passive solidarity with Asia's poor and oppressed without actually participating in their struggle" (Ibid.). In the decisions of the Conference, a clearly articulated reproach was also directed towards the conception of inculturation that was false from its beginning. Its advocates identified with a layer of Indian culture that is the cause and source of the continuing social and economic oppression of the poor. The emerging Dalit theology of liberation received a significant impulse and authoritative defence in it. It became evident that the much-awaited Indian theology would probably not arise in the environment of ashrams or even, in the opinion of some critics of the Movement, must not arise.[122]

The Catholic Christian Ashram Movement had already been blamed from the end of the 1960s, when it gained traction, for ignoring the real interests of the vast masses of Indian Christians. The Movement was offering them an unsolicited and, with respect to their hardships, completely ineffective cure in the form of contemplative escape and the pursuit of their own salvation, regardless of the distressing everyday social problems that Christians in India must face (Cornille 1991: 182). In the course of the 1980s, these objections accumulated and turned into severe attacks. The defenders of ashrams gradually became not very efficiently defensive under their pressure. However, finally, from the beginning of the 1990s, they started asking themselves increasingly urgent questions as to whether the selected course was the right one. The topics of the relevance of ashram ideals in the face of a multitude of Christian Dalits, genuine lay people, to whom the Movement, in accordance with its own perceptions, wanted to turn its attention and draw into the life of ashrams, appear repeatedly on the pages of the *AA Newsletter* and in the discussions during the *satsangs* conducted in the past 30 years. Was a mistake made in the very early days of the Movement when the main, or rather the only, source of its ideological inspiration became the elite layer of Hinduism, which was, in addition, laboratory-extracted from the literary tradition? On that account, did ashrams not break faith with the message of the Gospel that brings freedom, salvation and new life to all those downtrodden, suffering and on the margins of society?[123] The empty ashrams that were closed after the departure of their founders, transformed into priest seminaries or affiliated to one of the Church orders or parishes seem to be convincing evidence of the unmet expectations:

> The glamour about Christian ashrams is gone. As the founders and pioneers of the Christian ashram movement are fading away, there seems to be a sense of emptiness enveloping the Christian ashrams; there is a sense of disappointment among theologians, social activists and Church personnel, as the ashram movement did not pick up the momentum they had expected. Even those of us who are in the ashrams do not seem to have a clear idea where we are going.
> (Ashram Aikya Newsletter, no. 55: 3)[124]

Trends in the Christian Ashram Movement

As perhaps sufficiently clearly emerged from the presented history of the Movement, it cannot be considered static or not subject to developments. These take place in close association with the changes of context – social, political, cultural and theological. The resulting form of the idea of the Christian Ashram and the attempt to implement it therefore differed quite considerably in the various stages of the Movement. However, this evolution, no matter how dramatic its consequences, has seemingly been overlooked by those who have studied the Movement so far. Unknowingly, they ignore it because they are themselves part of the Ashram Movement, whether as its direct, and thus interested, participants; its apologists or its sympathizers. Perhaps they focus their attention solely on one specific aspect related to the phenomenon of ashrams and therefore inevitably cannot see the whole picture which eludes their selected snapshot. Or they already formulated their insights and conclusions several decades ago, when the Movement was on the uptrend and still represented an active and vivid manifestation of Indian Christianity. The temporal, spatial and ideological detachment, through and thanks to which this book has been written, does, however, enable us to understand the history of the Movement as a closed chapter of the history of Christianity in India. Therefore, we are able to name different tendencies of approach in its individual stages.

The baseline theme of the first, Protestant period was the *crisis of evangelization*. It enforced a search for new ways in which Christianity could present itself in an attractive and confident manner on the dynamically developing religious scene of the early 20th-century India. The main task of the newly outlined direction of evangelization was seen in the *creation of such a Christian identity*, which would be masterfully and confidently *built on Indian foundation*. It would match the Indian environment and be a rightful part of it, not just the result and manifestation of the political domination of the colonial power. Therefore, all sorts of *attempts to indigenize* Christianity, one of which became the Ashram Movement, took hold. The next stage was dominated by the approach of the *theology of fulfilment* which unfolded as incredibly influential in India. In shaping the identity of Christians, the attention at that moment shifted from external assimilation in the local environment to a deeper understanding of it and later on also meaningful integration into the context of Christian teaching. In a global dimension, the history of religious thinking started to be understood as a common history of salvation. Non-Christian religions, the intuitive religious cognition of which develops to finally reach its meaningful completion or fulfilment through Christianity and nothing else, also contribute their share. However, they have not been aware of it so far and thus have not been able to reflect on it. Mainly thanks to the impulses from representatives of the early Catholic ashrams, the theology of fulfilment in its next phase started elaborating upon considerations connected, contrarily, with *the fulfilment of Christianity itself* under the influence of other religious traditions. Such thoughts were growing, finally and actually rather inevitably, into the *theology of religious pluralism*. From the perspective of the Movement, this theological approach to religious diversity represents a phase when bridges were genuinely built between Christianity and Hinduism. Under this approach, the ashram seems to be not only a place of dialogue but dialogue itself, a pure personification of dialogue. The ashram is an authentic expression of faith that God does not reveal himself exclusively in any of the existing religions. Therefore, it is not possible to talk about the fullness and partialness of revelation in this or that religious cognition. God is incomprehensibly always present in all of them at the same time, and the Christian comprehension of God is only one of many possible versions. The *theology of the dissolution of Christian identity* has its source in such construed religious pluralism. It consciously refers to the mystical planes of religious experience where any differences between religions become meaningless since the sole aim of the life in an ashram is to achieve the awareness and experience of oneness with God. Threats or, on the contrary, opportunities regarding the theology of dissolution actually stretch across almost the entire Movement. Its sympathizers and critics are well aware of them. They can be even understood as never-expressed concerns about how far actually to go in the inculturation of Christianity. The most obvious is the struggle with dissolution of his own identity and at the same time fascination with such a possibility in the late Abhishiktananda. What is more, in his case, as was already mentioned, it was not mere intellectual theologizing but a real conflict in his life. While Griffiths approaches the dissolution of Christian identity with caution as a risk and is willing to consider communion with God only if individuality is not totally lost in the process, Vandana and Sahajananda, on the contrary, consider the approach of the theology of dissolution a method they consciously embraced. For both of them, it is not an unpleasant and unexpected consequence of the radical concept of the ashram phenomenon. In their view, the *sannyasa* and meditation leading to the unconditional union with God (Vandana) or the painstaking search for the Kingdom of God (Sahajananda) mean more than any religious identity. However, at this stage in its development, the Movement encountered a bottleneck, because it apparently ceased to be the *Christian* Ashram Movement.

Notes

1 In actual fact, the affiliation of CMI's members with the order is a more convoluted issue. Originally, the community was called the Congregation of the Servants of Mary Immaculate of Mount Carmel; in 1860, it was affiliated with the Discalced Carmelite order (in Latin: Ordo Carmelitarum discalceatorum, OCD) as their Third Order (Third Order of Discalced Carmelites, TOCD). Therefore, CMI is more a designation of this community as a church institution than the official name of a religious order. CMI is for men, but since 1866, it has also had a female branch, the Congregation of the Mother of Carmel (CMC).
2 K. Chavara drew up the history of his order in a four-volume work written in Malayalam (Chavara 1981–1982).
3 The Sanskrit term *prayaschitta* means a ritual through which a member of a higher Hindu caste strives for cleansing from the defilement that he may have suffered, for example, through frequent contacts with foreigners, a long-term stay outside the territory of India, crossing a sea or an ocean, conversion to another religion and so on. The result of all of these serious offences against Hindu religio-social codes is always loss of the caste status and thus de facto exclusion from Hindu society. Upadhyay underwent the cleansing ritual a few months before his death, in the context of his "defiling" journey to Europe, which he performed in the years 1902–1903. However, he had already informed those around him about his intention related to *prayaschitta* for several previous years.
4 These three pioneering works, published in the same year, cannot be missing in the bibliography of any publication dealing with virtually any aspect of Christianity in modern India (Baago 1969; Boyd 1969; Thomas 1969).
5 In this sense, for example, his article "Conversion of India – An Appeal", published in the October issue of *Sophia* magazine y. 1894, spoke volumes (Lipner and Gispert-Sauch 2002: 175–178). Here, he draws attention to the fundamental errors of previous methods of evangelization and outlines, for the first time, the plan of missionaries-*sannyasins* that will lead him to an attempt to establish an ashram community five years later. However, Upadhyay will undergo a fundamental transformation with respect to the indigenous philosophical tradition during these five years. While in 1894, he utterly rejects the monistic belief of *Advaita Vedanta* in the essential substantial unity of God and man, after 1898, he already uses the terminology and philosophical principles of *Vedanta* as a pure method for expressing the relation to God. During these five years, the open appeals for conversion also gradually disappear from his magazine contributions, being replaced with the idea of evangelization in the form of lived testimony, which means without direct conversion demands.
6 However, Upadhyay was not the first to use a similar concept; for its genesis, see Tennent (2005: 10, n. 18).
7 "The Hindu mind is extremely subtle and penetrative, but is opposed to the Graeco-Scholastic method of thinking. We must fall back upon the Vedantic method in formulating the Catholic religion to our countrymen. In fact the

Vedanta must be made to do the same service to Catholic faith in India as was done by the Greek philosophy in Europe". From Upadhyay's "The Clothes of Catholic Faith" article in the August issue of the *Sophia* magazine y. 1898 (Lipner and Gispert-Sauch 2002: 207).

8   For Upadhyay, *Vedanta* means the *Advaita Vedanta*, as it was developed by Shankara and his followers.

9   For the best reflections on Upadhyay's revolutionary theological concept of *Saccidananda*, see Tennent (2005: 208–299) (Chap. 5: "Brahmabandhav and Shankara's Advaitism: Building Christian Theology on the Foundation of Philosophical Hinduism") or the rather more sceptical and restrained Lipner (2001: 178–204) (Chap. 8: "Light from the East? Constructing a Hindu, Platform of Belief and Practice").

10 Tennent, for example, draws attention to the existence of the fragment of Upadhyay's translation of *Panchadashi*, a classic teaching manual of *Neo-Vedanta*, dating back to the 14th century, written by Vidyaranya (Tennent 2005: 231, n. 63).

11 For an erudite analysis of the whole hymn, preferably see Gispert-Sauch (1972: 60–79).

12 "Protestantism has created a deep-rooted impression among the people that Christianity is synonymous with denationalization. People have a strong aversion to Christian preachers because they are considered to be destroyers of everything national" ("Conversion of India – An Appeal" in Lipner and Gispert-Sauch 2002: 177).

13 The general report on the results of this search, which can already be interpreted as one more defence of the project, is provided by Upadhyay himself in his "Our New Scheme" article, which appeared in the July issue of *Sophia* in the same year (Lipner and Gispert-Sauch 2002: 204–205).

14 Upadhyay perhaps chose the Sanskrit word "matha" for his monastery because it probably better matched his idea of the tradition of Indian monasticism and its semantic correspondence with the early Christian monasticism of the Western type. The era of ashram development was not in sight in the late 19th century, either. Their true popularity and the associated mass expansion of the mythologized concept of the ancient ashram, which was to become an alternative to modern times full of technological achievements, came about no earlier than before Gandhi's return to India. However, this will be properly addressed in the following chapters. Upadhyay's missionary centre nevertheless corresponds quite accurately to the concept of an ashram, although he decided to call it *matha*.

15 "The Sanskrit words ka and sthala mean 'time' and 'land' respectively. If we join the two words and form an adjective we get the compound *kashthalika*, which means "pertaining to all times and lands". Hence *kashthalika* or Catholic faith is a faith which extends to all ages and climes" ("The Clothes of Catholic Faith" in Lipner and Gispert-Sauch 2002: 205).

16 Lipner mentions some personal traits of Upadhyay that could play their role – impatience, temper, restlessness, instability and pronounced individualism, which was bolstered by a life of celibacy (Lipner 2001: 222–223).

17 P. Pattathu, an isolated, albeit somewhat critical historian of the Movement, who moreover personally participated in it, even talks about a "crisis of evangelization" (Pattathu 1997: 178).

18 In this connection, some authors speak about the so-called Indian Christianity Movement, the beginnings of which are usually dated to the last decades of the 19th century and which culminated in the first decades of the 20th century in an (unsuccessful) attempt to create a single and unified Indian National Church (e.g. Ralston 1987: 27).

19 "Rethinking Christianity in India" represents a loose grouping of South Indian, in particular Tamil Protestant, missionaries and pastors of domestic origin and also the laity. This grouping released a publication of the same name in 1938, trying to build the relationship between Christianity, or more precisely Christ separate from Christianity, and Hinduism on a completely new plane (see, e.g. Boyd 1994: 159–160). One of the members of this intellectual circle and the authors of the influential publication was also S. Jesudason, the co-founder of the first Protestant *Christukula* ashram in Tirupattur, Tamil Nadu, which is discussed in greater detail subsequently.

20 The phenomenon of an ancient ashram or rather its literary rendition that we have available through the previously mentioned text resources is more broadly thematized in Chapter 4, which deals with the question of what an ashram actually is.

21 Dr. E. Forrester-Patton is, besides S. Jesudason, who was referred to in note 19, the second co-founder of *Christukula*, the oldest Protestant ashram in Tirupattur, Tamil Nadu.

22 Taylor erroneously states the year 1901.

23 The ashram was established several months after Gandhi's return to India in 1915, in a village near Ahmadabad, and only two years later, it was moved to Sabarmati (Gandhi 1997: 329).

24 For the first time, we come across the key term of *khadi* here, opposing the *kavi* ashrams. The typology of Christian ashrams on the basis of this terminology pair was determined by Taylor (1977: 19–37).

25 Compare with the division into two categories (*bhakti karma* and *gyana karma*) as conceived by Pattathu (1997: 122).

26 The significant difference of inspirational sources is also proved by direct personal experiences and life stories of the leading spirits of the Movement – while J. Winslow, the founder of the important Protestant ashram *Christa Seva Sangha* located in Pune, visited Gandhi's ashram *Satyagraha*, the Benedictine Swami Abhishiktananda, the key figure in the Catholic concept of Christian ashrams, repeatedly stayed in meditation caves of the sacred Tamil mountain of Arunachala, in the local ashram of Ramana Maharshi or at the feet of his Hindu guru, Vedanta mystic Gyananda.

27 The National Missionary Society was established in 1905 by Indian Christians belonging to various churches of non-Catholic denominations. The agenda of the Society, which was significantly affected or even primarily motivated by the Indian nationalist movement, consisted of building a purely domestic, that is, a fully indigenized and united Indian church, which, in all respects, would be completely independent of the original church centres located abroad; see Boyd (1994: 87–88) and Philip (1946: 265).

28 Taylor (1979: 284) states the title "God's Darbar", while Ralston (1987: 29) states "Darbar of the Lord Jesus Christ".

29 This is a key source for the early history of that first ashram, which is a kind of balancing activity report after the first sixteen years of its existence.

30 Jesudason himself talks only about the assistance and advice of several people from the NMS and subsequently about his own decision to cooperate with the Society (Jesudason 1937: 44). The words of P. O. Philip, who was the Secretary General of the NMS at that time and encouraged both founders of *Christukula* in their decision, are similar (Philip 1946: 266). However, R. Taylor, who is usually well informed, already describes them as missionaries of the NMS (Taylor 1977: 22).

31 The sensitive issue of requisite or voluntary celibacy in ashrams aroused a number of disputes among Protestants in later years, even leading to schisms of ashram communities, as will be outlined subsequently.

32 This change in the concept of the ashram is clearly evident, for example, from the retrospect report of *CPSSA* published in 1937, authored by the successor of Winslow, the Anglican priest Bill Lash (1937: 53–54, 57). See also the document from 1934, founding the ashram with a new name, which the previously mentioned word "prema" was added to, but in particular with a distinctly new aim and internal organization, *From the Rule of Christa Prema Seva Sangha, 1934* [online]. [Quotation 11/03/2019]. Retrieved from: www.yumpu.com/en/document/view/7282006/from-the-rule-of-christa-prema-seva-sangha-1934

33 In his voluminous and intellectually rich theological work, Aiyadurai Jesudasen Appasamy, a significant Indian theologian, sought to relate Christian tidings to the Hindu tradition of *bhakti*, in particular as it was philosophically worked out by Ramanuja, the leading representative of *Vishishta Advaita*, in the 11th–12th century.

34 Cf. "The Hindu sees only the commonplace Christianity in us. He does not find that there is anything in Christianity corresponding to the deeper levels of Hindu spiritual experience. [. . .] Hindu religious experience mapped out in Yoga, takes man from height to height. Similar heights in Christianity, the Christian himself has not explored. There are certain valued experiences of the Hindu in the pilgrimage of the soul to God. Of parallel experience in Christianity he is not aware. Of the Holy Spirit, of living with Christ and in Christ, we have not told him. Asramas, if they would not belie their promises, have their main work in this direction" (Chenchiah, Chakkarai and Sudarisanam 1941: 257).

35 For one of the first attempted chronologically organized lists of the fifteen early Protestant ashrams originating between 1921 and 1942, see Thomas (1977: 209). In his information-packed paper, the author surveys the causes of the Movement, its ideas and ideals, presenting very brief portraits of the major ashrams and putting their contribution, as well as the contribution of the whole Movement to the shaping of the new form of Christianity in India, through critical, albeit too-brief reflection. In the supplement to his paper, he presents a list with as many as thirty-two ashrams that had been established by 1958 (Ibid.: 219).

36 It is a selection from the fourteen points defined by Jones in establishing *Sat Tal* in 1930.

37 It is a revised reprint of the memorial pamphlet issued in the same place in 1959, in memory of the late J. Monchanin. Although the original text was published without mentioning the author, it comes from the pen of Henri Le Saux–Swami Abhishiktananda, a co-founder of the *Shantivanam* ashram.

38 For the personality, fortunes and work of Monchanin, see Monchanin (1977); also the memorial pamphlet titled *Swami Parama Arubi Anandam: A Memorial* 2007 or the comprehensive collective work *Jules Monchanin (1895–1957) as Seen from East and West* 2001.

39 "I think the essential point of my mission to India will be to create a contemplative life" (Monchanin 1977: 22). See also Schouten (2008: 173–174).

40 For the first time, we are dealing here with a kind of second development phase of the theology of fulfilment, which, however, as it seems, has not yet gone through any deeper theological reflection. The traditional concept of the theology of fulfilment opens its arms to all non-Christian religions (sometimes also called *natural* religions as opposed to *revealed* Christianity). Their teaching is understood as a natural preparation for the acceptance of Christ and his liberating message. Only in this theology will these archaic, intuitive and therefore, according to the teachings of the Catholic Church, necessarily imperfect religions achieve their completion and fulfilment. They will reveal their deep meaning, which has been non-obviously present in them since the very

beginning, through Christ. The second development phase of the theology of fulfilment, which many theological reflections emerging in Catholic ashrams are based on, however, seemingly largely built up expectations of an exactly opposite result from the process of the interaction between Christianity and other religions (mainly Hinduism), whether happening consciously or otherwise. On the contrary, Christianity is to be enriched and fulfilled. It can achieve perfection through understanding the theological and philosophical meaning of other religious worlds – this is through recognizing Christ's presence in them, however, not for the benefit of their devotees but for Christians themselves.

41 Lubac dedicated a memorial pamphlet to the memory of his friend; see Lubac (1967).
42 For the first letters between Monchanin and Le Saux, in which the first considerations appear about their future joint plans for creating a contemplative community in India and where the personality of Le Saux is also very clearly revealed in the context of his then nearly twenty years' experience of being a Benedictine monk, see Stuart (1995: 14–20). Together with the spiritual diary (Abhishiktananda 1998), it is the most important resource about the life and work of Le Saux–Abhishiktananda.
43 The first two visits are authentically rendered in the letters written by Le Saux (Stuart 1995: 29–32). See also the whole first chapter in the later printed reflection in Abhishiktananda (1979b).
44 Var. Parama-arūbi-ānanda.
45 The first edition of 1951, numbering 500 copies, was followed by a translation into French in 1956, reviewed and considerably extended (Monchanin and Le Saux 1956). In 1964, the first edition was reviewed by Abhishiktananda and published under an abbreviated title (Monchanin and Le Saux 1964). Due to the unavailability of the first edition, we refer in our work to this second English edition. According to Abhishiktananda's own words found in its introduction, it remains completely faithful to the original from 1951.
46 Here, additionally in footnote no. 13, is a list of the author contribution of Monchanin according to the information provided by Abhishiktananda in 1970.
47 "Monasticism has been for ever the most genuine fruit of her [i.e. India's] heart" (Monchanin and Le Saux 1964: 24). Such an observation, however, not only greatly romanticizes the figure of an ideal Hindu monk but depicts the Indian religious reality rather univocally, through the prism of Orientalism, which is so much criticized today. Above all, it raises the question of whether the words "monasticism" or "monkhood" that are clearly semantically defined in the Christian context are adequate expressions for the Hindu concept of *sannyasin*. It seems that Catholic thinkers, like their Protestant counterparts, seek and find in the complexly organized Hindu tradition primarily what they want to find there. Only the fruits of such a quest can be quite different.
48 Throughout their pamphlet, the authors treat the terms of "Indian" and "Hindu" rather loosely. They practically do not distinguish between the two categories.
49 However, it must be noted with respect to this quote that it is the opinion of Abhishiktananda who had already had eight years' experience with India and its majority religion, Hinduism. During that time, he underwent a major spiritual transformation, whether in *Shantivanam*, in the meditation caves of Arunachala Mountain or at the feet of his Tamil Vedanta guru, Gyanananda.
50 It was with this reference to the words of the Gospel that Abhishiktananda concluded his commemorative writing dedicated in memory of the deceased Monchanin (*Swami Parama Arubi Anandam* 2007: 61). Although by using them, he had in mind the seemingly unsuccessful Indian mission of his fellow

brother and ashram companion, they can be most aptly related to the whole first stage of the existence of *Shantivanam*.
51 The first chapter of this late Abhishiktananda work, not published until after his death, deals with the concept of Hindu *sannyasa* and is highly rated by Indian Christian theologians and liberal-minded Hindus alike.
52 According to Taylor, the main cause of the failure dwelt in the fact that both monks and their ashram remained too bound by the rules governing the life of the Benedictine order, which cannot be combined with the concept of an Indian ashram (Taylor 1979: 286). However, relevant sources, such as the letters written by both priests, do not give the merest cause for such assessment. Therefore, Taylor's opinion can be rather considered to be based on the Protestant concept of the ashram.
53 The dramatic nature of Abhishiktananda's inner spiritual struggle that he had lived through for many years is very intelligibly depicted in his posthumously published spiritual journals (Abhishiktananda 1998).
54 Abhishiktananda was a very prolific writer. Some of his books were first written in his native French and only then translated by Abhishiktananda himself into English, or their translation was significantly edited by him, while in the case of others, the process was exactly the opposite. Apart from those already mentioned, his most important titles undoubtedly include (we state the original English versions and translations that are more readily available, in chronological order): *Prayer* (1967), *Hindu-Christian Meeting Point – Within the Cave of the Heart* (1969), *The Church in India: An Essay in Christian Self-criticism* (1969), *Towards the Renewal of the Indian Church* (1970) and, last but not least, the masterpiece of *Saccidananda: A Christian Approach to Advaitic Experience* (1974). However, none of Abhishiktananda's books offer a comprehensive theological system. After all, the author himself did not consider himself a theologian but a spiritual mentor. Thus, all his books are more autobiographies in which Abhishiktananda depicts his experiences with spirituality that take place in the little-surveyed terrain between Christianity and Hinduism. A number of contemporary and later authoritative theologians, in particular R. Panikkar and J. Dupuis, however, took his views very seriously.
55 A number of researchers and popularizers have already dealt with the personality, life and work of Abhishiktananda. Nevertheless, the most significant work still remains an extensive monograph written by the Catholic priest E. Vattakuzhy (1981), one of the leading representatives of the Movement and the founder of the Kerala ashram *Shantisadan*.
56 Leaving aside Abhishiktananda, who, as has already been mentioned, did not become a guru until the last years of his life and moreover outside of the ashram environment, there are actually only three priests who have emerged as such charismatic personalities throughout the whole history of the Movement: F. Mahieu, B. Griffiths and D.S. Amalorpavadass. They will all be properly discussed subsequently.
57 There are a large number of works dealing with the life and work of B. Griffiths, among which the following are undoubtedly the most important (in alphabetical order): Anandam (1998), Rajan (1989) and Teasdale (1987). For a popular Griffiths biography see Du Boulay (1998).
58 For the process of this development, see Stuart (1995: 192–193, 197, 203–204). However, the original condition laid down by Abhishiktananda, that Mahieu himself take charge of *Shantivanam*, was not fulfilled. Their mutual relations after Mahieu left *Shantivanam* in 1958 improved significantly to culminate in a very narrow cooperation towards the end of the 1960s in shaping the new Indian Catholic liturgy and also preparing and implementing an India-wide seminar for

renewal of the Church in India, which is discussed in a separate chapter here. The relationship between Abhishiktananda and Griffiths, however, was noticeably cooler. This emerges from minor allusions in the memoirs of the still-surviving witnesses-ashramites, who were important sources of information for the author of this book. It is also evident while reading between the lines in the texts written by both men, when they comment on or contrarily are silent about one another. There is clear evidence then that Abhishiktananda had "escaped" from *Shantivanam* before the arrival of a group of three monks led by Griffiths, who came to take over the ashram but found it already abandoned. As has been seen, strong personal antipathy or mutual rivalry can exist even between holy men, *sannyasins* and Christian monks. It can be also heightened by the fact that they are both respected spiritual leaders with their own circle of supporters and admirers.

59 The popularity or rather worldwide reputation of Griffiths as a respected spiritual leader of modern Christianity also grew thanks to his extensive activities as a writer. Leaving aside a large amount of shorter contributions in theological journals, his most important book titles include *Christian Ashram* (1966), *Return to the Centre* (1976), *The Cosmic Revelation: The Hindu Way to God* (1983), *A New Vision of Reality: Western Science, Eastern Mysticism and Christian Faith* (1989). However, Griffiths's works do not represent any coherent theological views, either. They more attempt to popularize Indian Christian spirituality.

60 This development is revealingly and quite critically analyzed by L. Anandam (1998) (in particular 258–267).

61 For a notable comparison of the theological approaches adopted by both men and their development, see Collins (2006: 132–137).

62 Probably the most significant precursor of the *Hindutva* ideology in relation to Christianity was the Hindu activist Sita Ram Goel. He even devoted a whole book to criticism of the Ashram Movement, mainly as perceived in its Catholic conception, because it was more clearly organized and, in his opinion, also more dangerous (Goel 1994).

63 This ashram booklet is largely an updated version of the booklet from 1975. Similar promotional information materials, mostly only of several pages and without any expensive layout or editing, are published by virtually all ashrams. They usually provide a brief history of the respective ashram, introduce its founder and the site itself and set out the main points of the ashram programme.

64 The two most important works of Sahajananda are represented by the following titles: *You Are the Light: A Rediscovery of Eastern Jesus* (2003) and *A Brief Comparative Study of Sankara and Master Eckhart* (2005).

65 Sahajananda's remarkable essay *Mission without Conversion* seems to be sufficiently illustrative in this sense; see Sahajananda (2008).

66 The author of this introduction, a Dominican priest, is the previously mentioned formal superior of *Shantivanam* following Griffiths's death.

67 For the so far only published biography, see Mahieu-De Praetere (2008).

68 For information about the beginnings and the first ten years of *Kurisumala*, see Griffiths (1966a) and Mahieu (1958–1959).

69 See the exactly set out daily schedule in the ashram booklet. A similar time schedule, with slight variations arising from the specifics of the given ashram, is set out by almost every existing ashram, but hardly anywhere is it followed with such precision and consistency as in *Kurisumala*. The description, characteristics and critical analysis of the content of the life in Christian ashrams are, however, dealt with in separate chapters of the next part of this book.

70 This is a title semantically alternative to the more common appellation of guru. Nevertheless, the question of whether Mahieu chose it deliberately to weaken

the serious theological tension, affecting every Christian, present in the absolute claim of the title of guru, remains unresolved. After his naturalization in India in 1968, the Acharya honorific became de facto Mahieu's new surname.
71 First published in the form of three articles in the magazine *Southern Chronicle*, August–September–October 1982, it has already seen several editions.
72 For their listing see Acharya (1984: 209–210).
73 This unique, priceless work is an essential source of information concerning the establishment, functions and development of the NBCLC in the first 15 years of its existence.
74 "B" was added to the original NCLC in 1971, when the biblical apostolate was placed in the care of the centre.
75 In a general sense and also from the pre-conciliar context, see Amalorpavadass (2009: 269). Amalorpavadass (1978: 74) already states only two phases when he relates the goals of the third phase, that is, implementation of the readings from sacred texts of other religions to the liturgy of the Word also to the second phase.
76 The Twelve points of adaptation cover the external aspects of the liturgy. Individual points refer, for example, to the posture of a priest during Mass, who is, in line with Indian tradition, allowed to sit; the greeting of peace exchanged by clasping one's hands together (*anjali hasta*) and slightly bowing; using *arati* as an expression of respect for the celebrant of the Mass and towards the congregation; the replacement of certain objects of worship by those that are used for religious purposes in the Hindu environment; the use of flowers, incense and oil lamps as gifts presented on the altar during the service, which means not only as decoration and so on. For the complete list, with brief commentary explaining their symbolism and meaning in the order of the Mass, see Amalorpavadass (1978: 81–86). For the approval letter of the Congregation, see *Ibid.*: 87–88.
77 For information about the first contacts with Amalor, his considerations relating to the inculturated liturgy and also the future form of the Indian anaphora, see Stuart (1995: 192). See also an article outlining the possibilities of liturgical experiments in the context of Hindu religious symbolism (Abhishiktananda 1968).
78 The themes of both books, and often entire passages, overlap to a large extent. They both summarize the author's ideas, germinating for many years, on the future of the Church in India. As is evident, despite the lifestyle of a Christian *sannyasin* he adopted, Abhishiktananda had been unflaggingly interested in the fate of the Church.
79 In particular *Lumen Gentium*, *Gaudium et spes*, *Ad Gentes* and *Nostra Eatate*.
80 Abhishiktananda literally speaks about the "vocation of being a guru".
81 For the first extensive description of the intended project, see Abhishiktananda (1969: 48–52). However, Abhishiktananda repeatedly returned to the idea of the seminar in the following years, but it seems that his demands on the teaching staff in it and on the possible candidates from the ranks of seminarians were impossible to fulfil. After Abhishiktananda's death, the idea was restored and temporarily implemented in a modified form under the guidance of the Catholic priest Iswar Prasad in his briefly existing *Khrist Panthi* ashram and also in the significant and still functioning *Matridham* ashram, located on the outskirts of Varanasi (Prasad 1993: 47).
82 Abhishiktananda wrote his unpublished article titled "An Ashram Seminary" on the initiative of Bishop P. D'Souza, who expressed his interest in 1971 in implementing such a workshop in his diocese of Varanasi; see Stuart (1995: 248–254, 335).

83 A voluminous document (627 pages) describes the sequence of events leading to the organization of the Seminar, its actual progress and subsequent evaluation. This significant source includes interim conclusions of individual working groups, adopted recommendations and also official declarations of the Seminar.

84 "With the aim of encouraging a robust interior life, I do not fear to say monastic life would have a function of primary importance in the India of today and tomorrow. [. . .] A monastic institute should be an oasis of renewal of culture and interior life" *All India Seminar* (1970: 448).

85 "Small ashrams, with few members, from three to six, men and women, should be spread in the cities and in the country areas" Ibid.

86 The most important working groups of the Seminar, besides the two already mentioned at the end of the previous paragraph, were among those engaged in evangelism, dialogue, Indian culture and education or civil-political life.

87 "We recommend immediate steps be taken to promote an authentic contemplative and monastic life in keeping with the best traditions of the Church and the spiritual heritage of India, and all encouragement be given to those who show signs of a special vocation for the life of prayer and silence, or prayer and service, in an ashram setting, even if they are already leading a priestly or religious life" *All India Seminar* (1970: 253).

88 The two most important were The International Theological Conference on Mission Theology and Dialogue, held in 1971 in Nagpur, and The All-India Consultation on Evangelization, which took place in 1973 in Patna. Both conferences repeat in their conclusions and recommendations the arguments of the Seminar and also call for establishing further ashrams (Pattathu 1997: 191–192, 198–200).

89 At the fifth all-India meeting of the CBCI Commission for Liturgy held in 1976, ashrams were identified as places suitable for experiments with inculturated liturgy (Leeuwen 1990: 81).

90 The so-called "Get-together and live-together of ashramites".

91 Under the leadership of Amalor, the NBCLC was to become a kind of showpiece or the embodiment of the inculturation of Christianity in India. The ingeniously thought-out architecture loaded with symbolism remarkably connects motifs of many Indian religions. Although the campus consists of the main chapel, which is quite understandably called Saccidananda, and many other secular administrative buildings, the boundary between the mundane and the sacred is completely wiped away here. Everything is interconnected into a meaningful whole, fully in accordance with Amalor's holistic approach to life. Perhaps no other place in India can boast so many examples of modern Christian, fully inculturated art. Best see *NBCLC Campus. Milieu of God-Experience. An Artistic Synthesis of Spirituality* 2005.

92 For the eight points, as they were defined by Amalor at the meeting of ashramites as well as to introduce the debate, see Irudayaraj (1978: 278), Vandana (1978: 361) and Amalorpavadass (1985: 5; this is Amalor's important contribution to the third satsang of *Ashram Aikya*, held in 1983; the text was first published in *Word and Worship* in 1984).

93 G. van Leeuwen, who himself represents an internal source from the NBCLC, states that some ashramites had held considerable reservations from the very beginning about the decision of the CBCI to establish the Liturgy Commission as the patron of ashrams (Leeuwen 1990: 186). Similar traces of doubt, however, do not appear in any of the available contributions evaluating the importance of meetings and debates. All of the later works dealing with the history of the Movement or some of its aspects also keep quiet about them.

The enthusiasm over the conclusions of the debate probably silenced any potential doubts.
94 Leeuwen once again mentions this title as the only source.
95 Non-Catholic ashrams also have a similar association. It was created under *The Inter Ashram Fellowship* title towards the end of the 1940s, uniting the ashrams of protestant Churches, the Indian Mar Thoma Church, the Syrian Orthodox Church and ecumenical ashrams. Members of this fellowship meet annually in an attempt to coordinate their activities, especially in the field of medical education of ashramites so that their *seva* would be meaningful. In 1982, the Fellowship published its statutes in the *Inter Ashram Review* magazine, which has been regularly published since then with occasional fluctuations and serves in particular as an information source for the internal purposes of the Fellowship. From the perspective of the history of the Movement, the activities of the Catholic association of *Ashram Aikya* appear to be weightier because their changing trajectory faithfully reflects the evolution of Christian ashrams – both in terms of the expectations of their members and the subsequent disappointment when the hopes pinned on the ashram idea did not come to fruition.
96 The letter of invitation written by the then-president of *AA*, Vandana, to all members before the second *satsang* was held in *Shantivanam* in 1980, dated October 20, 1980 (the first *satsang* is considered the meeting of ashramites in the NBCLC mentioned previously); a copy of the letter is in the archives of the author.
97 The information and conclusions about the *Ashram Aikya Newsletters* in the following paragraph reflect no. 1–55 of the journal and thus cover the period from 1978 until 2010.
98 Fully in the spirit of the ideological and conceptual interpretation of the arbitrariness, which often occurs within the framework of the ideology of the Movement, these ashramites wandering from ashram to ashram are called *parivrajakas* (*Ashram Aikya Newsletter*, no. 32: 4).
99 The last portrait included in this publication presents the ashram, located in the United States, that was established under the influence of B. Griffiths (Painadath 2003a: 113–118). The Christian ashrams existing outside India are a remarkable phenomenon of the past 30 years, which, however, goes beyond the thematic scope of this book.
100 However, some important ashrams, which decided on their own initiative to stand outside the activities of *AA*, for example, *Kurisumala*, are missing from the list.
101 This is a specific type of ashram booklet, which is more extensive compared to others and was not compiled until after the death of the ashram founder, mostly from his previous texts. The material presents not only the ashram itself and its architecture and visions but also the person of the founder.
102 For the plan of the ashram, see the ashram booklet *Anjali Ashram*, undated: 11, the authoritative interpretation of its symbolism from the pen of Amalor, Ibid., 13–28.
103 The Eucharist is celebrated according to this Missal in the ashram every day.
104 Both programmes also have book forms; see Amalorananda (2000) and Amalorananda (2009).
105 For a brief description of the contents of both programmes and also the exact numbers of their graduates in each of the years in 1983–2004, which allow forming a clear idea of the impact of this ashram, see *Anjali Ashram's God-Experience, Dialogue – Service* (2005: 9–14).
106 A more detailed report on this tragic accident, which dealt an incurable blow to the entire Catholic Church in India, is given in the letter by the ashram representative Pat Astudillo which was sent to the *AA* ashram community

and Amalor's friends; a copy of the letter is in the archives of the author. The last farewell to the deceased took place in the *Saccidananda* ashram shrine, in the crypt of which Amalor is buried. The Requiem Mass was celebrated by Amalor's brother, Cardinal Lourdusamy and five other archbishops, and about seventy priests also concelebrated with him – this also speaks sufficiently about the importance of Amalor for the life of the Catholic Church in India.

107 For example, *Vidyavanam ashram* established in 1996 near Bangalore; see Vineeth (2003: 208).

108 A number of the ashram booklets also contain, in addition to a brief history of the ashram, the texts of inculturated prayers and Christian *bhajans*, as evidenced by the title of the cited.

109 The best account of the complicated ashram path chosen by Ishwar Prasad, which turned the enthusiastic evangelist-missionary pursuing a single goal, namely religious conversions, into a defender of inculturation and ashram ideals, which are dominated by bearing witness to Christ rather than preaching him, is given by Prasad himself (Prasad 1993: 45–48).

110 Ishwar Prasad established another ashram, *Bharat Mata*, in 1996. It is located in the state of Hariyana, near the city of Kurukshetra. This ashram was also established as part of the IMS's inculturation activities and aims to be a centre for interfaith dialogue, liturgical experiments and theological answers newly formulated in the face of Hindu religious tradition.

111 The charismatic orientation is also clearly outlined in the ashram booklet; see ashram booklet *Matridham Ashram*, undated: 7–8.

112 The rules of life in the ashram and everyday timetable are not fundamentally different from other ashrams (Ibid., 11–12).

113 A comprehensive analysis of the *Khrist Bhaktas* phenomenon was introduced by the Indian Catholic priest C. J. Kuttiyanikkal in his doctoral thesis (2014); see also San Chirico (2014: 21–44).

114 The early fruit of this long ashram journey was her book, first published in 1978, *Gurus, Ashrams and Christians*, that belongs among the classic works stemming from the environment of the Movement.

115 In the ashram tradition, it is a title equivalent to guru, but it is intended for his female counterpart.

116 The remarkable and extremely informative letter Vandana wrote to Griffiths dated July 16, 1990, in which Vandana argues with many of Griffiths's opinions concerning the ashram principles of the entire Movement; a copy of the letter is in the archives of the author.

117 The Vatican had given its approval to the Twelve points of adaptation only one month before the Seminar was held. Naturally, it was the Seminar during which Masses which included changes were repeatedly celebrated then to the complete satisfaction or even elation of the majority of the Seminar participants. Controversy broke out immediately afterwards, when information about the adapted liturgy appeared in the pages of the Church and secular press, and so the interested Catholic public was acquainted with it. For details, see Leeuwen (1990: 72–73); for the further development of the controversy, see also Amalorpavadass (1978: 77–79).

118 "The above-mentioned adaptations can be put into effect by the Episcopal Conference and local hierarchies in places where they see fit and at the degree and measure that they think fitting for the faithful". Official Document of the Holy See Approving the Twelve points of adaptation. In Amalorpavadass (1978: 88). In the opinion of some conservative or hesitant bishops, it was this very sentence that put the implementation of the adaptation fully under their competence, and they therefore based their rejecting opinion on it.

119 For the fates of the Indian anaphora, see Leeuwen (1990: 74, 76, 79–80).
120 Probably the only published text of the anaphora (An Indian Eucharistic Prayer) can be found in Aguilar (2016: 174–181).
121 For the summary of the consistent criticism of the anaphora and the entire Indian Mass, which was published in 1974 and continues to be celebrated in this form, without the controversial anaphora, in many places in India, in particular in ashrams, see Collins (2006: 228–234).
122 See the letter of the respected Indian Jesuit, theologian and critic of the Movement G. Soares-Prabhu, which he sent to Vandana before the seventh *Satsang of the AA* was held in 1991. To the credit of Vandana and the whole ashram community, it must certainly be mentioned that the objections raised regarding the Movement in the letter became one of the key topics of the *satsang* and the text of the letter subsequently appeared in its book reflection (Vandana 1993: 153–156).
123 Cf. Amaladoss (2005: 10, 12).
124 With these words, the current *acharya* of *Anjali Ashram*, A. Louis, invited the whole ashram community to an extraordinary meeting of the *AA*, where the crisis of the ashram identity and the essence and meaning of the Movement was intended to be the main, or rather the only, topic.

References

Abhishiktananda. 1968. "A Study of Hindu Symbolism." *Word and Worship* 1 (8): 298–300, 305–307; 2 (2): 77–79.

Abhishiktananda. 1969. *The Church in India: An Essay in Christian Self-Criticism.* Madras: CLS.

Abhishiktananda. 1970. *Towards the Renewal of the Indian Church.* Bangalore: Dharmaram College.

Abhishiktananda. 1974. *Saccidananda: A Christian Approach to Advaitic Experience.* New Delhi: ISPCK.

Abhishiktananda. 1975. *The Further Shore.* New Delhi: ISPCK.

Abhishiktananda. 1976. *Hindu-Christian Meeting Point: Within the Cave of the Heart.* New Delhi: ISPCK.

Abhishiktananda. 1979a. *Prayer.* New Delhi: ISPCK.

Abhishiktananda. 1979b. *The Secret of Arunachala.* New Delhi: ISPCK.

Abhishiktananda. 1998. *Ascent to the Depth of the Heart.* New Delhi: ISPCK.

Acharya, Francis. 1974. *Kurisumala: A Symposium on Ashram Life.* Vagamon: Kurisumala Ashram.

Acharya, Francis. 1984. "Silver Jubilee at Kurisumala Ashram." *Vidyajyoti Journal of Theological Reflection* 48 (4): 208–212.

Acharya, Francis. 2006. *Meditation: Hindu-Christian Meeting Point.* Kurisumala: Kurisumala Ashram.

Aguilar, Mario I. 2016. *Christian Ashrams, Hindu Caves and Sacred Rivers: Christian-Hindu Monastic Dialogue in India 1950–1993.* Philadelphia: Jessica Kingsley Publishers.

All India Seminar: Church in India Today, Bangalore, 1969. (undated, probably 1970). New Delhi: CBCI Centre.

Amaladoss, Michael. 2005. *Beyond Inculturation: Can the Many Be One?* New Delhi: Vidyajyoti Education & Welfare Society/ISPCK.

Amaladoss, Michael. 2008. *Beyond Dialogue: Pilgrims to the Absolute*. Bangalore: Asian Trading Corporation.
Amalorananda. 2000. *Atma Purna Anubhava*. Mysore: Anjali Ashram.
Amalorananda. 2009. *Brahma Sakshatkara Anubhava*. Mysore: Anjali Ashram.
Amalorpavadass, D. S. (undated, probably 1976). "Indigenous Liturgy: Indian Christian Worship." In *Praying Seminar*. Edited by D. S. Amalorpavadass. Bangalore: NBCLC, pp. 207–216.
Amalorpavadass, D. S. 1978. *Gospel and Culture, Evangelization and Inculturation*. Bangalore: NBCLC.
Amalorpavadass, D. S. 1985. *Ashram Aikya: Whence and Whither*. Bangalore: NBCLC.
Amalorpavadass, D. S. 2009. *The Destiny of the Church in the India of Today*. Mysore: Anjali Ashram.
Anandam, Lourdu. 1998. *The Western Lover of the East: A Theological Enquiry into Bede Griffiths' Contribution to Christology*. Kodaikanal: La Salette Publications.
Animananda, B. (undated, probably 1946). *The Blade: Life and Work of Brahmabandhab Upadhyay*. Calcutta: Roy & Son.
Anjali Ashram's God-Experience, Dialogue: Service. (undated, probably 2005). Mysore: Anjali Ashram.
Arun, C. Joe. 2007. "Revisiting de Nobili's Mission to Tamil Nadu." In *Interculturation of Religion: Critical Perspectives on Robert de Nobili's Mission in India*. Edited by Joe C. Arun. Bangalore: Asian Trading Corporation, pp. 1–18.
Ashram booklet. (undated). *Anjali Ashram*. Mysore: Anjali Ashram.
Ashram booklet. 2009. *Kurisumala Ashram*.
Ashram booklet. (undated). *Matridham Ashram: At the Service of God's People*. Varanasi: Matridham Ashram.
Ashram booklet. (undated). *Prarthana Manjari. Bharat Mata Ashram*. Kurukshetra: Bharat Mata Ashram.
Ashram booklet. (undated). *Saccidananda Ashram*.
Ayyanikkatt, Dominic. 2002. "Introduction: Striking Roots and Spreading Out." In *Saccidanandaya Namah: A Commemorative Volume*. Thanirpalli: Saccidananda Ashram Shantivanam, pp. 1–5.
Baago, Kaj. 1969. *Pioneers of Indigenous Christianity*. Bangalore: Christian Institute for the Study of Religion and Society.
Barnes, Michael. 2004. *Theology and the Dialogue of Religions*. Cambridge: Cambridge University Press.
Bergen, Van. 1978. "Contemporary Christian Experiments in Ashram Life." *Journal of Dharma* 3 (2): 174–194.
Boyd, Robin. 1994 (reprint, the 1st edition 1969). *An Introduction to Indian Christian Theology*. New Delhi: ISPCK.
Chavara, Kuriakose Elias. 1981–1982. *Chavara*. Mannanam: St. Joseph Press.
Chenchiah, Pandipeddi, V. Chakkarai and A. N. Sudarisanam. 1941. *Asramas Past & Present*. Madras: Indian Christian Book Club.
Collins, Paul. 2006. *Context, Culture and Worship: The Quest for "Indian/ness"*. New Delhi: ISPCK.
Cornille, Catherine. 1991. *The Guru in Indian Catholicism: Ambiguity or Opportunity of Inculturation?* Leuven: Peeters Press Louvain.
Cronin, Vincent. 1959. *A Pearl to India: The Life of Roberto de Nobili*. New York: Dutton.

Dhanaraj, R., editor. (undated, probably 1990). *Aikiya Alayam Towards* . . . Bangalore: Aikiya Alayam.
Du Boulay, Susan. 1998. *Beyond the Darkness: A Biography of Bede Griffiths.* London: Rider.
Forrester-Patton, Ernest. 1952. *The Christian Ashram Movement in India.* Tiruppatur: Christu-Kula Ashram.
Gandhi, Mohandas Karamchand. 1997. *An Autobiography or the Story of My Experiments with Truth.* Ahmedabad: Navajivan Trust.
Gispert-Sauch, George. 1972. "The Sanskrit Hymns of Brahmabandhav Upadhyay." *Religion and Society* 19 (4): 60–79.
Goel, Sita Ram. 1994. *Catholic Ashrams: Sannyasins or Swindlers?* New Delhi: Voice of India.
Gravend-Tirole, Xavier. 2014. "From Christian Ashrams to Dalit Theology: Or beyond: An Examination of the Indigenisation/Inculturation Trend within the Indian Catholic Church." In *Constructing Indian Christianities: Culture, Conversion and Caste.* Edited by Chad M. Bauman and Richard Fox Young. New Delhi: Routledge, pp. 110–137.
Griffiths, Bede. 1954. *The Golden String: An Autobiography.* London: The Harvill Press.
Griffiths, Bede. 1966a. *Christ in India: Essays towards a Hindu-Christian Dialogue.* New York: Charles Scribner's Sons.
Griffiths, Bede. 1966b. *Christian Ashram.* London: Templegate Publishers.
Griffiths, Bede. 1976. *Return to the Centre.* London: Collins.
Griffiths, Bede. 1983. *The Cosmic Revelation: The Hindu Way to God.* Illinois: Templegate Publishers.
Griffiths, Bede. 1989. *A New Vision of Reality: Western Science, Eastern Mysticism and Christian Faith.* London: Collins.
Griffiths, Bede. 2003. *The Marriage of East and West.* Tucson: Medio Media Publishing.
Handbook of Ashram Aikya. 2003. (place of publication not specified): Ashram Aikya.
Hedlund, Roger E. 2000. *Quest for Identity: India's Churches of Indigenous Origin: The "Little Tradition" in Indian Christianity.* New Delhi: ISPCK.
Irudayaraj, X. 1978. "A Report of the Consultation." *Word and Worship* 11: 277–282.
Jacob, Plamthodathil S. 1979. *The Experiential Response of N. V. Tilak.* Madras: CLS.
Jacquin, Francoise. 2002. "Jules Monchanin and Henri Le Saux: Their Mutual Complementarity." In *Saccidanandaya Namah: A Commemorative Volume.* Tannirpalli, Kulithalai: Saccidananda Ashram, Shantivanam, pp. 64–74.
Jesudason, Savararirayan. 1937. *Ashrams, Ancient and Modern: Their Aims and Ideals.* Vellore: Sri Ramachandra Press.
Jones, Eli Stanley. 1925. *The Christ of the Indian Road.* New York: Abingdon Press.
Jules Monchanin (1895–1957) as Seen from East and West. 2001. New Delhi-Tannirpalli, Kulithalai: ISPCK-Saccidananda Ashram, Shantivanam.
Kulanday, Victor J. F. 1988. *The Paganization of the Church in India.* Madras: Galilee.
Kuriakose, M. K., editor. 2006. *History of Christianity in India: Source Materials.* New Delhi: ISPCK.
Kuttiyanikkal, Ciril J. 2014. *Khrist Bhakta Movement: A Model for an Indian Church? Inculturation in the Area of Community Building.* Zürich: Lit Verlag.

Lash, Bill. 1937. "Christa Prema Seva Sangha Ashram, Poona." In Jesudason, Savararirayan. *Ashrams, Ancient and Modern: Their Aims and Ideals.* Vellore: Sri Ramachandra Press, pp. 52–58.
Leeuwen, J. A. G. Gervin van. 1990. *Fully Indian: Authentically Christian.* Bangalore: NBCLC.
Lipner, Julius J. 2001. *Brahmabandhab Upadhyay: The Life and Thought of a Revolutionary.* New Delhi: Oxford University Press.
Lipner, Julius J. and George Gispert-Sauch. 1991 (vol. 1), 2002 (vol. 2). *The Writings of Brahmabandhab Upadhyay.* Bangalore: United Theological College.
Lubac, Henri de. 1967. *Images de l'abbé Monchanin.* Paris: Aubier.
Mahieu, Francis. 1958–1959. "Kurisumala Ashram: An Experiment in Monastic Life." *The Clergy Monthly Supplement* 4: 202–204.
Mahieu-De Praetere, Marthe. 2008. *Kurisumala. Francis Mahieu Acharya: Pioneer of Christian Monasticism in India.* Kurisumala: Kurisumala Ashram.
Monchanin, Jules. 1974. *Mystique de l'Inde, mystère chrétien.* Edited by S. Siauve. Paris: Fayard.
Monchanin, Jules. 1977. *The Quest of the Absolute.* Edited by J. G. Weber. London: Cistercian Publications.
Monchanin, Jules and Henri Le Saux. 1964. *A Benedictine Ashram.* Douglas: I. O. M. Times Press.
Monchanin, Jules and Henri Le Saux. 1956. *Ermites du Saccidânanda.* Tournai: Casterman.
NBCLC Campus: Milieu of God-Experience: An Artistic Synthesis of Spirituality. 2005. Bangalore: NBCLC.
An Order of the Mass for India. (undated). Mysore: Anjali Ashram.
O'Toole, Michael. 1983. *Christian Ashrams in India.* Pune-Indore: Ishvani Kendra-Satprakashan Sanchar Kendra.
Painadath, Sebastian, editor. 2003a. *Solitude and Solidarity: Ashrams of Catholic Initiative.* New Delhi: Ashrama Aikya/ISPCK.
Painadath, Sebastian. 2003b. "The Spiritual and Theological Perspectives of Ashrams." In *Solitude and Solidarity: Ashrams of Catholic Initiative.* Edited by Sebastian Painadath. New Delhi: Ashrama Aikya/ISPCK, pp. 120–148.
Pattathu, Paul. 1997. *Ashram Spirituality.* Indore: Satprakashan.
Philip, P. O. 1946. "The Place of Ashrams in the Life of the Church in India." *The International Review of Mission* 35: 263–270.
Prasad, Iswar. 1993. "Inter-Religious Dialogue and Ashrams." In *Christian Ashrams: A Movement with a Future?* Edited by Vandana. New Delhi: ISPCK, pp. 42–49.
Pulsfort, Ernst. 1989. *Christliche Ashrams in Indien, Zwischen dem religiösen Erbe Indiens und der christlichen Tradition des Abendlands.* Altenberge: Telos-Verlag.
Rajamanickam, S. 1972. *The First Oriental Scholar.* Tirunelveli: De Nobili Research Institute.
Rajan, Jesu. 1989. *Bede Griffiths and Sannyasa.* Bangalore: Asian Trading Corporation.
Ralston, Helen. 1987. *Christian Ashram: A New Religious Movement in Contemporary India.* Lewiston/Queenston: The Edwin Mellen Press.
Research Seminar on Non-Biblical Scriptures. 1974. Edited by D. S. Amalorpavadass. Bangalore: NBCLC.

Sahajananda, John Martin. 2003. *You Are the Light: A Rediscovery of Eastern Jesus.* Winchester: O Books.
Sahajananda, John Martin. 2005. *A Brief Comparative Study of Sankara and Master Eckhart.* Thanirpalli: Saccidananda Ashram.
Sahajananda, John Martin. 2008. *O Lord, Make Us Instrument of Your Peace: Mission without Conversion: An Open Letter to the Christians.* Thanirpalli: Saccidananda Ashram Shantivanam.
Saldanha, Julian. 1997. *Inculturation.* Mumbai: St Pauls.
San Chirico, Kerry P. C. 2014. "Between Christian and Hindu: Khrist Bhaktas, Catholics and the Negotiation of Devotion in the Banaras Region." In *Constructing Indian Christianities: Culture, Conversion and Caste.* Edited by Chad M. Bauman and Richard Fox Young. New Delhi: Routledge, pp. 23–44.
Sauliere, A. 1995. *His Star in the East.* Edited by S. Rajamanickam. Madras: Anand.
Schouten, Jan Peter. 2008. *Jesus as Guru: The Image of Christ among Hindus and Christians in India.* Amsterdam: Rodopi.
Scott, David C., editor. 1979. *Keshub Chunder Sen.* Madras: The Christian Literature Society.
Statement of the All-India Consultation on Ashrams. 1978. Bangalore: National Biblical Catechetical & Liturgical Centre.
"Statement of the Fifth Conference of the EATWOT." 1982. *Vidyajyoti Journal of Theological Reflection* 46 (2): 81–96.
Stuart, James. 1995. *Swami Abhishiktananda. His Life Told through His Letters.* New Delhi: ISPCK.
Swami Parama Arubi Anandam: A Memorial. 2007. Tannirpalli, Kulithalai: Saccidananda Ashram, Shantivanam.
Taylor, Richard W. 1977. "From Khadi to Kavi: Toward a Typology of Christian Ashrams." *Religion and Society* 24 (4): 19–37.
Taylor, Richard W. 1979. "Christian Ashrams as a Style of Mission in India." *International Review of Mission* 68: 281–293.
Taylor, Richard W. 1986. "Modern Indian Ashrams." *Religion and Society* 33 (3): 3–23.
Taylor, Richard W. 1990. "Ashrams and the Kingdom of God." *Vidyajyoti Journal of Theological Reflection* 54 (1): 19–27.
Teasdale, Wayne Robert. 1987. *Toward a Christian Vedanta: The Encounter of Hinduism and Christianity According to Bede Griffiths.* Bangalore: Asian Trading Corporation.
Tennent, Timothy C. 2005. *Building Christianity on Indian Foundations: The Legacy of Brahmabandhav Upadhyay.* New Delhi: ISPCK.
Thomas, M. M. 1969. *The Acknowledged Christ of the Indian Renaissance.* London: SCM Press.
Thomas, Philipos. 1977. "Christian Ashrams and Evangelisation of India." *Indian Church History Review* 2 (3): 204–221.
Vandana. 1978. "Ashramites' Satsangh." *Indian Theological Studies* 15 (4): 358–366.
Vandana, editor. 1993. *Christians Ashrams: A Movement with a Future?* New Delhi: ISPCK.
Vandana. 2004. *Gurus, Ashrams and Christians.* New Delhi: ISPCK.
Vattakuzhy, Emmanuel. 1981. *Indian Christian Sannyasa and Swami Abhishiktananda.* Bangalore: Theological Publications in India.

Vineeth, V. F. 2003. "Inculturation and the Ashram Ideal in India." In *Christian Commitment to National Building* (Papers of the Indian Theological Association 2002). Edited by Anthonyraj Thumma. Bangalore: Dharmaram, pp. 195–212.

Winslow, Jack. 1923. *Narayan Vaman Tilak: The Christian Poet of Maharashtra.* Calcutta: Association Press.

Županov, Ines G. 2001. *Disputed Mission: Jesuit Experiments and Brahmanical Knowledge in Seventeenth-Century India.* New Delhi: Oxford University Press.

Županov, Ines G. 2005. *Missionary Tropics: The Catholic Frontier in India (16th–17th Centuries).* Michigan: The University of Michigan Press.

4

THE PHENOMENON OF THE CHRISTIAN ASHRAM

When describing and analysing Christian ashrams, one will inevitably run into a problem lying in the extraordinary diversity of their concepts. As has already been said and suggested several times, every ashram is unique, having distinctive, unmistakable characteristics resulting primarily from the personality and ideas of its founder. There is absolutely no unanimity among the researchers and ideologists of the Movement about the basic characteristic features of the Christian ashram. They differ significantly in the emphasis they place on specific aspects or even the very essence of the ashram way of life. The functions they assign to ashrams are also varied, whether they are impacts felt by individuals, communities, the Church or the whole of society. Similar diversity can also be found in the daily operations and schedules of individual ashrams, which as a result represent different ashram types.

The objective of this part of the book is therefore to characterize the Christian ashram phenomenon by means of generalization. First of all, it strives to indicate the anticipated constitutive features of this indigenous Indian religious institution. Concurrently, it seeks to highlight the agreements as well as the shifts in meaning of the Christian interpretation when compared to the ancient Indian ashram model and Hindu tradition, which the Movement representatives creatively relate to. The presented conclusions primarily adopt a Christian perspective because it is relevant to the theme of the Movement. Nevertheless, they point to the more crucial problems associated with the conflict between the Indian and Christian concept of religiousness, both regarding their general understanding of the nature of the ashram and the comprehension of its constituent elements. Unlike the so-far rarely mapped history of the Movement, the ashram phenomenon is a key topic of virtually all scholar and popular works dealing with Christian ashrams as well as countless minor texts produced in ashrams themselves. This rich, although considerably confusing and moreover often ideologically inconsistent, literature is, along with the information gathered through field research, the main information source for this part of the book.

What the ashram is about

The Sanskrit word *āśrama* can be interpreted in several possible ways. The verb base (√*śram-*, *śrāmyati*) that it is derived from conceals a fairly wide variety of meanings – "to make efforts", "to exert oneself", "to strive", "to try to overcome", "to conquer" and "to humble" but also "to get tired" or "to get exhausted" in the pre-classical period of Sanskrit. The noun (*shrama*) created from this verbal base therefore names some effort. It means endeavour or strain associated in particular with the performance of various religious practices, including asceticism or mortification, but also exerting oneself and exercising, which quite logically can lead to fatigue and exhaustion. The prefix *ā-*, which modifies the meaning of the noun, poses an interpretation problem. In theory, it is possible to evaluate it as an association of the long *ā-*, with the meaning of fullness, completeness and unity, and the short *a-*, which Sanskrit uses to create antonyms negating a word's meaning. *Āśrama* could then be the absolute absence of fatigue and exhaustion, the lack of any effort or exertion, which could perhaps mean the perfect peace of mind and body and also a place where such a condition occurs. Although this interpretation may seem inconsistent with the fact that the ashram, on the contrary, is a place intended for continuing efforts to achieve the desired objective, it cannot be entirely ignored. In particular, when we take into consideration some descriptions of ancient ashrams as they are found in the Sanskrit literary tradition, where they are described as an oasis of serenity and inner calm in which it is as if time and all human toil have stopped. The second and generally accepted interpretative possibility is the simple combination of the long *ā-*, with the previously mentioned modifying meaning, with the noun *śrama*. In this concept, *āśrama* therefore indicates some vehement effort, enduring quest, renunciation, self-denial, self-control, asceticism (*tapas*) and, according to the Sanskrit texts throughout historical development, also a place where such activities are fostered in the long term. In some texts, however, *āśrama* also appears as a plain shelter or refuge where victimized or abandoned people can find safety and protection without necessarily having to undergo any practice of asceticism. The same term also took root, apparently in the first centuries before Christ, in the ideal and considerably idealized division of human life into four unequally long stages. Within them, certain activities and the locations where they are performed are attributed to every person, always closely connected to his particular caste or rather to his position in the *varna* system.[1] The semantic ambiguity of the Sanskrit term that we have briefly outlined here may seem confusing and even contradictory. Nevertheless, each of the described aspects contributes equally to creating the ancient ashram phenomenon and to its Christian conception in the 20th century.

In ancient Sanskrit literature, different ashrams can be found across literary genres, styles and the subject areas covered by the relevant works. According to P. Pattathu, who tried to track down the references to ashrams in the Upanishads, the two great Epics, the Dharmashastras and the Puranas (in all of these, undoubtedly, just selectively), it is even possible to talk about some kind of "ashram literature" (Pattathu 1997: 21). According to his assumptions, it was in the ashram settings where this type of literature came to existence. The ascetic sages and saints who were their authors painted, somewhat unwittingly, a colourful picture of the ideal ashram. They also set several key conditions for its existence. In this concept, the ashram represents the forest hermitage (*tapovanam*), which implies that it is always located away from the hustle and bustle of civilization and its everyday mundane concerns. The aspirants to genuine, liberating knowledge (*brahmavidya*) retire to it so that they may practice some of the chosen spiritual means (*sadhana*) at the feet and under the emphatic leadership of their teacher (*guru*), who has already acquired such knowledge.[2] Although Pattathu devotes substantial space in his exceptionally contributive work to the description and resourceful analysis of the essential personality features of the teacher and the disciple (Pattathu 1997: 28–29, 76–82) and to the defining of fundamental ashram activities (Ibid.: 33–35, 41–47), the concept submitted by him covers only a small part of the ancient ashram phenomenon. There are numerous references to ashrams that bear little relation to the proposed idea that are still left unnoticed by the author and disregarded in his text analysis and subsequent conceptual synthesis.

Due to its spontaneous character developing in a non-organized manner, the Hindu religious and cultural tradition has never created any clearly defined religious institute in the Christian sense of the word that Pattathu and other ideologues of the Ashram Movement would like to see, although they do not openly admit they may have such an expectation. The Sanskrit literature actually very often uses the term "ashram" to refer to the hermitage of a single holy man who stays there alone, without any contact with the outside world for many years, practising his asceticism. The relationship between the teacher and the disciple, which is key to the concept of the Movement, in particular of its Catholic stream, but equally the loving relationship of the whole community in the Protestant ashrams cannot, however, be considered in such a case. On the other hand, many ashrams were apparently functioning as community centres established in association with a major temple or a place of pilgrimage. Their ashramites participated in local everyday religious acts and events, without any of them holding the position of guru; it is rather the specific deity that their collective religious practice referred to that can be considered to be the guru.[3] There is also textual evidence supporting the existence of ashrams focused on a certain type of artistic activities or a scientific area. The guru may hold a prominent position there, however, not as a spiritual leader but primarily as a teacher leading his disciples towards perfect mastering of a given type of art or knowledge. The residents of such ashrams can hardly be classified as ascetics, whether in the life stage of *vanaprastha* or *sannyasin*. This is so because whole families or widespread clans live there together, and the characteristic of their everyday life unequivocally falls into the *grhastha* stage. Apart from the obligatory spiritual practice, the residents in some of the ashrams which we learn about from the Epics and the Puranas also devote themselves to considerably secular exercises, for example, archery and martial arts in general.[4] The majority of ashrams are described in a way giving the impression that they have no ties or have even intentionally severed their ties with the world, a specific historical period and the broader region in which they are set. At the same time, it is conceivable that certain ashrams, despite their Brahman origin (Olivelle 1993: 22), would in fact become centres of revolutionary socio-political movements (Ishanand 1999: 132–136) and thus seedbeds for outstanding reformers or at least ideas that marked the historical development of India. Last but not least, shelters for the sick, abandoned and dying, set up particularly at important places of pilgrimage, should be noted. Under the name of ashram, they de facto represented the ancient concept of the modern hospice.

Moreover, the ashram phenomenon as well as everything else in ancient India experienced the intricate developments proceeding from the cultural and religious reality of Indian civilization. Today, we are unable to conclusively determine what the relationship was between the ashram and historically probably earlier *gurukula*. The second term, in a considerably general sense, denotes the teacher's family, under the wing of which disciples took sanctuary in the life stage of a student (*brahmacharin*) for various lengths of time.[5] Under the teacher's leadership, they not only spiritually evolved there but in particular educated themselves in many scientific areas necessary for their further professional career and overall life after the end of this phase. It seems that some of the ancient ashrams apparently fulfilled both functions, while others did not. Some were open to all people regardless of their age and status, with their gurus raising simultaneously or in parallel several *brahmacharins*, including their own sons. Others, especially those located in or near cities, served exclusively as a family boarding school, strictly reserved for a specific caste community, in particular from Brahmana *varna*. The concept of *gurukula* as a practised method of education closely linked to the Brahman culture perhaps conformed more to religious orthodoxy in certain stages of the development of Hinduism. On the other hand, ashrams hidden in the depths of forest silence, far away from civilization and open to individualistic speculative seeking, could be perceived as a hotbed of heterodox ideas. The advent of Buddhism and Jainism with firmly established monastic communities, fettered by the rules of monastic orders, also affected the ashram phenomenon to some extent. On that account, ashrams have been emerging since the turn of the Common Era, with features that more resemble monasteries (*matha*).

Therefore, a clear depiction of the ideal ancient ashram, which would serve as a model for similar institutions in modern times, obviously cannot be found. A large number of the distinctive features that are quite stereotypically ascribed to ashrams in the Sanskrit texts are additionally highly poetic, formulated with obvious poetic hyperbole. At random, let us mention, for example, the so much-proclaimed environment-friendly approach of the ancient ashramites (Ibid.). It is seen in stereotypically recurring descriptions of ashrams as places where, thanks to the holiness of the guru residing there, wild beasts become tame, trees and shrubs overflow with fruit and one can see plants which normally blossom in different seasons flowering in a single moment. It is therefore misleading to deduce from the similar conditions anything indubitable about the practical everyday operation of the ashram; its residents; their motives, values and activities or the religious and societal role of ashrams in ancient India. However, at the same time, this fact opens up a wide area regarding the original concept of the ashram. Indeed, it frees the hands of all persons interested in the ashram way of life during their attempts always to grasp the phenomenon of the ashram from scratch in their own contemporary context and in the context of current needs (Amaladoss 2008: 161). As was sufficiently shown by the history of the Movement, the vaguely defined ashram idea is exceptionally prolific, both on the side of modern Hinduism and Christianity.

What the Christian ashram is about

It is understandable that nearly all ashramites and indeed the authors who deal with the Movement feel an urgent need to express an opinion on the principles of ashram life and its core and purpose. The efforts to clearly formulate the motives, conditions and distant goals of the newly perceived Christian life in the ashram are the founding basis of the Movement. Nevertheless, they also keep emerging repeatedly in individual stages of its historical development. Older definitions are then reviewed, and the previously mentioned aspects differ only slightly, often overlapping each other; however, a new aspect is added to them here and there, or the emphasis placed on one of them increases. The prerequisite of any ashram activity seems to be spontaneity and the inner freedom of the person who performs it. Therefore, the sought-after essence of the ashram means something different for each of the participants. It is always related to the context of their own socio-cultural backgrounds, theological grounding, life experiences and spiritual preferences, as shown in the following overview of various definitions and insights as they were originally formulated by important representatives of the Movement.[6]

Already in her early contributions on issues related to ashrams and the Movement, Vandana highlights a string of key features, which would not disappear from her concept in the following decades despite her personal development and transformations in relation to the Church. According to Vandana, the ashram is primarily "a power-house of the spirit, with a prophetic and spiritual ministry for the re-creation of man" (Vandana 1978: 15). The life-giving centre of the ashram should not be the Eucharistic prayer, which only Christians can be involved in and contribute to, but contemplative prayer (Vandana 2004: xxiv). Ashram does not necessarily mean a specific place, and certainly not an institution, but a community of people seeking God. It is open to all regardless of their gender, age, social and economic status, religion or position in the Church (Vandana 1978: 17–18). Such an absolute degree of openness brings about an array of consequences, whether it is the adoption of a simple lifestyle (Vandana 2004: 54) that blurs distinctions among people; a high level of flexibility in prayer and liturgy, the principle of which is freedom, not any fixed order rules (Ibid., 55) and, in the long run, also the temporariness of the ashram (Ibid., 58). However, the latter is hardly understandable and acceptable from the perspective of the traditional religious understanding of newly established Christian institutions. Logically, this raises the question of why so much effort should be exerted on something which should be, by definition, impermanent. However, Vandana bases her statement on two arguments; their importance for the understanding of ashrams would continue to grow for her in subsequent years. She believes that the ashram appears and vanishes with a charismatic guru personality, around whom a community is spontaneously formed (Vandana 1978: 16–17; Vandana 2004: 58). And in the same breath, she also warns against the ashram being established by the Church authority, because this would negate two basic guiding principles of the Movement, which are spontaneity and charisma (Vandana 1978: 15). It is thanks to these that ashrams can differ significantly from the Church's congregations. However, institutionalizing such a free endeavour, even if in good faith and in an attempt to ensure some degree of autonomy and stability for it through its inclusion in the ecclesiastical structure, would in effect mean crushing the entire ashram (Ibid.).

Amalorpavadass also unreservedly agrees with the impermanent nature of the Christian ashram, existentially dependent on the guru's personality (Amalorpavadass 1980: 10). In his conception, refined to perfection in tens of minor or more extensive contributions, the ashram represents primarily "a state of intense and sustained spiritual quest for the Absolute" (ashram booklet *Anjali Ashram*, undated: 3). It is not a place but a way of life, a concerted effort bringing man to a certain motion-movement. Thanks to a combination of the activities of individual ashrams that are partial, yet focused on a common goal, it is possible to think and talk in terms of the Ashram Movement in the outcome. The ashram is also a place for dialogue, or more precisely dialogue itself, which is "a new form of Christian presence and the Church's mission" (Amalorpavadass 1985: 2), building new relationships with other religions through and in the ashram. As the most active promoter of the ideals of inculturation in India, Amalor declares the ashram to be its purest form. He goes even further in this sense when seeking "to transcend the distinction of Christian mysticism and Hindu mysticism, Christian ashrams and Hindu ashrams, Christian spirituality and Indian spirituality" (Ibid., 3) in the environment of ashrams. Ashrams seem to be the most suitable place for such a task because their ambience of serenity and liberating self-denial (Amalorpavadass 1990: 30) offers an ideal space for seeking and finding God and experiencing God's imperishable presence (ashram booklet *Anjali Ashram*, undated: 4). However, Amalor's idealistic expectations, seeing in the ashram the prototype of a new society (Amalorpavadass 1985: 2) and the spiritual centre of nationwide resurgence, could not be fulfilled. The absolutization of the functions that the ashram should play in his conception and also according to the ideas of many other representatives of the Movement proved to be too heavy a load. After all, even the influence of Hindu ashrams on the historical developments in India across the centuries can hardly be demonstrated. In modern times, spiritual and social reform in part arose from Gandhi's ashrams, profiled, however, in a completely different way. But not even these became a model for the perfect functioning of contemporary Indian society.

Another of the leaders of the Movement, and also an extremely prolific author, B. Griffiths holds ideas in line with most of the previously mentioned characteristics of the ashram. For him, the ashram is primarily a place of prayer, "but a place of prayer conceived according to Indian tradition, as a place where people come to 'realise' God" (Griffiths, undated: 218). Such a purpose requires an ambience of serenity, silence and seclusion, so that a space "for being alone with God", a space for "active inactivity" would be created (Ibid., 219). At the same time, it must be a place where a community creates its living core because "to realise God is to realise the presence of God in your neighbour" (Ibid., 221). The ashram community should not only be open to all but also should not be bound by a firmly constituted internal structure. For Griffiths, the freedom in the life of the ashram is expressed through the option available to its members to leave any time or stay in the ashram for only a short period of time or repeatedly in accordance with their own spiritual needs and in various periods of their life. In accordance with Vandana, Griffiths gives precedence to contemplative meditation over liturgies and the socially beneficial action of ashrams. It is the emphasis placed on vivid spirituality that India expects from Christianity according to his vision (Ibid., 219, 221). Alongside Amalor, he calls for extensive, freely undertaken experiments with various types of such spirituality (Ibid., 220) that will draw their inspiration from the richness of Hindu religious tradition and daily practice.

It would appear understandable that at the moment of experiencing a crisis, strenuous attempts are made to reinvent or redefine the meaning of the activity that has resulted in the crisis. So it is possible to understand the little book written by M. Jeyaraj, a long-time ashramite in the Madras *Aikya Alayam*. He tries to concisely and clearly define the Christian ashram, including its essential characteristics, therein, and so it is actually another in a series of ashram manifestos. Paradoxically, however, it was created at a time when ashramites from the Catholic community began to concern themselves over an identity crisis and the related question of why the Movement had not fulfilled the expectations of the late 1960s and '70s. Despite the freedom and spontaneity that were so much proclaimed earlier, this publication aims "to provide some guidance which will be accessible and useful to our Ashramavasis; setting out clearly the goal of the ashrams and the means with which to pursue it" (Jeyaraj 2001: foreword). Interestingly, the effort to institutionalize and control ashram activities did not emerge from the environment of superior ecclesiastical authorities but from ashramites themselves. Jeyaraj aptly defines the Christian ashram as "a place, where seekers relentlessly, strenuously, seriously and sincerely employ themselves, devote themselves and dedicate themselves to the pursuit of God experience with the grace of God and under the guidance of a guru with suitable sadhanas" (Ibid., 3). He furthermore summarizes the essence of the ashram, its characteristic features and the methods which may help to achieve the objectives pursued in several points, dedicating the major part of his pamphlet to their description and resourceful analysis. In his conception, the ashram comes into existence through the following: 1) contemplation; 2) asceticism in the form of accepted *sannyasa*; 3) the life of the community whose members bear witness to Christ and at the same time are open to a newly sought relation to believers of other religions; 4) through a voluntarily chosen life of poverty, chastity and obedience; 5) a necessary attribute of every ashram is the ambience of silence that creates a space for meditation; 6) the lifestyle of ashramites is utterly simple, whether in terms of food, clothing or equipping their homes; 7) the ashram must always be open to all so that everybody who enters it is shown hospitality; 8) the ashram should have a clearly set but not slavishly observed daily schedule and 9) the guru is the most important aspect of any ashram (Ibid., 4–31).

S. Painadath, an eminent Jesuit theologian, the founder-guru of the *Sameeksha* ashram in Kerala and from the mid-1990s one of the most active representatives of the Catholic Movement, built on Jeyaraj to a large extent. His vision of the ashram as "a congenial place for respecting the diversity of religions and promoting the unity in spirituality" (Painadath 2007: viii) clearly illustrates how far the ashram idea had already travelled on its journey from the initial approach of the theology of fulfilment. Painadath, just like Vandana, even believes that in the strict sense of the word, no ashram should be Christian or Hindu in terms of its denominational identification. But a spiritual site which claims to be identified as the ashram needs to be open to members of all religions without distinction, even if in its early days it was established on the initiative of any of them (Ibid., 97). Of the characteristics that Painadath adds to those previously mentioned, his belief that ashrams must awaken a desire for mystical enjoyment and experiences in the Church (not only in India) is worth mentioning. Across its historical development, Christianity has always excelled in creating complex and effectively functioning structures of religious organizations and communities, in the conceptually conceived formulations of theological thoughts and in the development of mass education and social work of any kind and type. Christian mysticism had seemingly been sidelined, marginalized or even become an object of persecution all the time (Ibid., 102). It is the ashrams that can rediscover the lost "mystical dimension of the Church and point to the eschatological horizon of the Church" (Ibid., 113). However, the spirituality cultivated in the ashram needs to be holistic at the same time (Ibid., 109), needs to take into account the whole human being, with all the goals of his or her life and the means he or she has available to achieve them. Spiritual life in the ashram should therefore be holistic and fully integrated so that there can be mutual balance and interconnectedness in the theological paradigm of *gyana-bhakti-karma* proposed by Painadath (1994: 41) – the knowledge acquired through contemplation and love for God and man, which becomes apparent in selfless service to others, should embrace each other. Because, according to Painadath, the ashram is primarily a movement – "a movement of the divine Spirit in the human spirit" (Painadath 2007: 114).

The guru in the Christian ashram

In the relatively rich literature arising from the environment of Christian ashrams or dealing with ashrams and the Movement, perhaps no other topic arouses so many varying opinions as the figure and role of the guru. Similar to the case of the ancient ashram, the concept of the guru in Hindu tradition is also quite extensive, and Christianity drew its inspiration from it. The guru can be any religious teacher passing on his knowledge. His more or less accidental disciples, however, do not necessarily have to have any fixed personal ties established to him. The family priest who performs life cycle transition rituals (*samskara*) and also the teacher-educator whose house is a shelter for a teenage boy for several years in the life stage of *brahmacharin* are often referred to as gurus. The guru is also the one from whom a disciple receives initiation (*diksha*) if the guru finds him already sufficiently spiritually developed. However, the same title is frequently attributed to any authoritative personality deserving respect, including one's own father or other family members. From the many possible options, Christianity in India, and not only that recognized in the environment of ashrams, has chosen the one that follows from certain passages of the Upanishads. In these, the guru acts as a personal spiritual leader and mentor who has already experienced God's existence himself and is able to pass on this knowledge of his to others. According to Amalor's fitting words, the guru has the experience (*anubhava*) of both the *guha* and *rupa* type – the guru is the one who discovered God "in the cave of his heart (*guha*) and who is capable of giving expression to it (*rupa*), by sharing it with others and leading them to it" (ashram booklet *Anjali Ashram*, undated: 3). The absolutization of the guru figure in this conception, which most probably happened from the late Upanishad period in certain religious and social layers of Indian society, gradually led to the identification of a human guru with God himself. Without a doubt, this resulted from the extracted Gnostic idea of the Upanishads, that he who knows God reaches God and becomes God. The guru thus became a mysterious person, possessing sacred knowledge and power beyond the natural realm, the supreme teacher and a mediator between man and the absolute. Such deification of a mortal human being is, however, hardly acceptable for Christianity.

The first Christian ashrams set up as a Protestant initiative refused to deal with the issue of a guru in such a highly charged sense (Taylor 1977: 27). The essence of the ashram in their understanding was represented in particular by a community of equals who related to Christ jointly and individually. Although, for practical reasons, the head of an ashram was usually its founder, he did not arrogate to himself religious or spiritual authority, nor was such a role expected from him. In the long run, the role of the founding leader was expected to be replaced by the ashram community itself, which would then make all decisions together (Chenchiah, Chakkarai and Sudarisanam 1941: 224). The constitutive relationship of *guru-shishya*, that is, the teacher and the disciple, which is the basic condition of the establishment and existence of most Catholic and modern Hindu ashrams, was thus replaced by the Christ-*shishya* relation with the Protestants.

Attempts to identify the guru with the figure of Christ were made much earlier by distinguished personalities of Christianity in India, whether it was de Nobili, who is usually ranked first in this connection (he used the Tamil word *kuru*) (Cornille 1991: 95–96),[7] B. Upadhyay or N. V. Tilak (Ibid.: 99; Pattathu 1997: 303, n 72). Thus approached, Christ is given different names in theological and evangelizing texts (*paramaguru* – the highest teacher, *jagadguru* – the teacher of the world, *jivanmuktaguru* – the teacher who has reached redemption in this birth etc.). Most often he is referred to as the *Sadguru* (the true or real teacher) (*Statement of the All-India Consultation on Ashram* 1978: item no. 7; Abhishiktananda 1997: 201, 202, n. 5), so that sufficient attention would be drawn to the fundamental difference between his sovereign authority and human gurus, whether those from Hindu or Christian ashrams (Cornille 1991: 158). In the opinion of S. Painadath, it is in the mystical experience of Christ as *Sadguru* where the most important contribution of ashram spirituality lies. In ashrams, this experience of Christ is awoken in us, not as an object worthy of respect but as a subject forever present in ourselves "as the inner master, the Sadguru, who inspires us from within the cave of the heart" (Painadath 2007: 101). This inner Christ (*antaryamin*) is a measure of all theology, inspiration for art, a source for liturgy and motivation for any social service. The function of an ashram, then, is to draw concentrated attention to this highest value that every person carries in himself or herself.

On the contrary, in the environment of Catholic ashrams, the question of the guru played a key role, and the development of the answers provided to it has been remarkable in the case of some ashramites. Vandana started her ashram journey in the *Christa Prema Seva Sangha* ecumenical ashram in Pune. Following the initial attempt of J. Winslow, the ashram was restored as an egalitarian fellowship, not a community of devoted disciples gathered at the feet of an exceptional teacher. After several years of her personal experience with the practice in Hindu ashrams, she however came to believe that "ashrams cannot be "opened" the way we had done [in Pune] by our own will, nor by the will of religious superiors or Bishops. An ashram has to be born. And we learnt that it is only born when a God-experienced person is asked by one or more persons if he/she might come and live with her/him" (Vandana 1993: 7, 2004: 35). In this opinion of hers concerning the *guru-shishya* relationship as a cornerstone of the ashram, Vandana remained consistent for the rest of her life; in fact, it probably even gradually increased in importance for her. However, for the existence of an ashram, both subjects in the relationship are essential. Just as it is not possible to consider an ashram without a guru, until a guru has at least one disciple, the place where he lives cannot be an ashram.[8]

A similar shift in opinion can also be noticed in Abhishiktananda. In the constituent manifesto of the Benedictine ashram in *Shantivanam*, the figure of a human guru is not yet thematized. As has already been said, it is most likely that neither Monchanin nor Abhishiktananda felt qualified to play a similar role at that time. However, Abhishiktananda's attitude changed with his growing experience with the environment of Hindu ashrams and their spiritual leaders. Thus, so-called *karanaguru*,[9] in the figure of a charismatic, mortal guru, becomes a tool that helps his disciple to discover the immortal guru, *Sadguru* in himself (Abhishiktananda 1990: 85). In the last two years of his life, Abhishiktananda came to the understanding of the mystical character of the relation between a teacher and a disciple, as it is perceived in Hindu tradition and that is fundamentally different from seemingly similar relations in Christianity, for example, between a priest and a believer. Thanks to the young French student of theology, Marc Chaduc, who became his only disciple in the full sense of the word, Abhishiktananda could experience the monistic character of both subjects in this relationship, just as it is understood in *Advaita Vedanta*.[10] The guru in this concept is nothing more than a human form through which the ultimate, indeed the only, reality (*brahma*) reveals itself so that it will open a disciple's eyes and he can understand the consubstantiality of himself, the guru and God (Stuart 1995: 256).

A similar mystical experience of consubstantial mutuality is, however, exceptional, and not only in Christian ashrams. Many of their founders or spiritual leaders are reluctant to use the title guru because they consider it to be associated too strongly with Hindu religious reality and thus non-transferable to the Christian context. A number of Church representatives ardently refuse to accept the concept of the guru. This is partly due to a lack of suitable people who could play such a role and in no small way also due to the fear of entrusting such vast power that the guru is endowed with in Hindu tradition to a single person. According to the cautious words of Griffiths, who himself undoubtedly acted in the capacity of guru in *Shantivanam* and is still seen as such by his disciples, in the case of Christian ashrams, it is more appropriate to think about a group of several *sannyasins*. These have "some experience of prayer and contemplation, and can form the nucleus of the community" (Griffiths, undated: 220), because while the guru-disciple relationship is primary in Hindu ashrams, for Christians, it is a mutual relationship between individual ashramites as members of the mystical body of Christ (Griffiths 1984: 150–151). In his deliberate conclusion, Griffiths was surely aware of the fact that was immediately related to the leading figure of the guru. The human guru is mortal, and if he is understood as an existential condition of ashram life, the moment of his death inevitably leads to the dissolution of an ashram. From this perspective, Protestant ashrams seem to be more viable in the long term, because their members intentionally sideline the guru figure.

Jointly with C. Cornille, one may, however, agree that the guru in the Christian ashram, under any name or concept, is "both the result and the agent of inculturation" (Cornille 1991: 196), which takes place there. The guru is the figure setting the ashram and the whole Movement in motion. He finds himself in a rather difficult-to-sustain position between two worlds – the world of the institutionalized Church, which he emerged from, belongs to and wants to continue belonging to, and the world of Hindu spirituality, less hampered by strict rules, that attracts him (Ibid.). Because ashrams are formed on the border of these worlds, they are not and cannot possibly be intended for everybody, even if their leaders aspired to this diligently in the late development phase of the Movement.

The figure of a guru as the founder and necessary leader of an ashram is one of the most controversial issues of the Movement ideology, in particular in the Catholic concept. Those who became gurus in ashrams were almost exclusively religious professionals. In the vast majority of cases, they were priests. Taking into account the sacred status that he obtains through holy orders, hardly any priest is willing to submit to the spiritual authority of another priest and become his disciple, standing on the same level as the disciples from the ranks of ordinary monks or lay people. At the height of the Movement, many priests, that is, potential gurus, therefore established their own ashrams where they suffered from a lack of disciples.[11] The other side of the same problem is the desire of Catholic ashramites and sympathizing bishops to have at least one Christian ashram in each Diocese and within each congregation (*Ashram Aikya Newsletter*, no. 35: 6), without, however, any suggestions being put forward as to where to get suitable gurus for them. Christianity in India, throughout its history, suffered somewhat from a lack of charismatic personalities with an authentic spiritual experience and concurrently a gift to pass it on to others. Therefore, it is the absence of significant spiritual figures that is one of the main causes of the failure of the Movement when the first and second generations of such ashram leaders left. It seems that the churches in India continue to produce more capable administrators and spiritual shepherds than religious teachers or even Christian gurus.

Sannyasa and Christian sannyasins

In ashram ideology, similar attention as that given to the guru figure is also paid to self-denial and asceticism in a broad sense. When searching for a suitable inspirational example, through the acceptance of which Christianity could meaningfully express the emphasis it places on principled detachment from ephemeral worldly worries, specifically by means of a purely Indian idiom, de Nobili and also Upadhyay, who followed his example, resorted early on to the semantically complicated term *sannyasin*. In the Hindu tradition, it can very vaguely denote virtually any ascetic who voluntarily severs all his ties with the world. However, the term concurrently describes the final and, in a sense, the highest stage of life in the intricately structured *varnashrama* system. Researchers have strong divergences over the origin and historical development of this rendition of the perfect ascetic who renounces absolutely everything to focus his attention solely on the absolute from that moment on and forevermore. Apparently, Hindu tradition itself is not quite clear on that, either (Olivelle 1993: 68–70, 117). Certain religious schools reserve the adoption of this sacred institute exclusively for Brahmans. Others, on the contrary, award the entitlement to it to all, including women. In addition, they do not even consider it the last stage in the journey of life but a possibility that is always present and which a person may have recourse to if he or she feels called to such an irreversible step. *Sannyasins* can be organized in religious orders, which are, however, based on considerably liberal principles, quite different from what is the case in religious congregations. They can also freely and without any specific target wander around the country and either gather a group of devoted disciples around themselves or live in permanent isolation out of contact with the world. The degree of asceticism that a *sannyasin* undergoes may also vary. It usually follows in the tradition of the sannyasin's teacher, who introduces him to *sannyasa* through initiation (*sannyasa diksha*). However, not even the existence of such a teacher is a necessary precondition. Like in other religious traditions, an ascetic is expected to live a life of self-denial in line with quite a standard concept, whether this is in terms of frequent fasting, avoiding sensual pleasures, prayers, meditations, staying in silent seclusion over a long period of time or observing celibacy.

In the early days of the Ashram Movement, when its banner was carried by its lay representatives and religious professionals from Protestant churches, the ascetic *sannyasin* as an ideal model for the life of a Christian ashramite was decidedly rejected. Because the ashram community was primarily seen as a spiritual family dedicated to Christ (Chenchiah, Chakkarai and Sudarisanam 1941: 217), single and married people, people observing celibacy and those living in a marriage could live side by side in most ashrams. Shared growth of a man with a woman was even considered an essential part of an ashram's rules and its meaningful order ("ashrama dharma") (Ibid., 225). The third life stage in the Hindu *varnashrama* system, the *vanaprastha* stage, was identified as an inspirational model worth following in the Christian ashram. Its framework of ideas, including both the continuing common life of the spouses and moderate asceticism and persistent spiritual efforts, seemed to correspond to the Christian conception. For some theorists and defenders of the Protestant Movement, even the vaguely outlined picture of the ancient ashram or its similarly uncertain historical development served as a source where they sought arguments for their claims (e.g. Philip 1946: 263–264). Many founders of ashrams, however, left the question open as to whether celibacy should be observed, which was perceived as particularly controversial in connection with the degree of asceticism (Jesudason 1937: 11). They put off answering this question until sometime in the distant future and placed it in the hands of the whole community, which was supposed to decide by consensus (Chenchiah, Chakkarai and Sudarisanam 1941: 226). As the history of the Movement reveals, in some Protestant ashrams, the degree of radicalism of the vow and practice of asceticism could lead to a schism or even termination of an ashram in its original, often very open, form when it became a closed monastic community.

Contrariwise, for a number of representatives of the Catholic Church, the concept of *sannyasin* together with the guru figure plays a key role in the origin of any ashram as well as in constructing any idea about life in it. The emphasis placed on absolute renunciation of the world and the severing of any ties to it is, to a considerable degree, the result of the interpretation of Christ's sojourn on earth, which is different from how the Protestant ashram environment understands it. The early Catholic ashramites, led by Monchanin and Abhishiktananda, did not build a loving community of people devoted to Christ, who committed themselves to asceticism so that they could serve others with full devotion. Their ashram was primarily intended to be a community of Christian *sannyasins*. Following the example of Christ, they figuratively depart for a desert to dwell there in solitude with God. Therefore, in their imagination, Christ appears as a perfect model of *sadhu* or *sannyasin* (Schouten 2008: 184–185), who renounces property, family ties and private life. He becomes a *brahmacharin* and a wandering ascetic, who, in his self-denial, goes even beyond the edge of death. It is in this role that he is supposed to provide Christian ashrams and their members with a model.[12]

When the Catholic stream of the Ashram Movement was at its height, which occurred with short-term Church support from the end of the 1960s to the mid-1980s, the radical concept of the Christian *sannyasa* became looser and gradually also depleted. The originally quite elitist environment of ashrams opened up to all those interested in spiritual life and the search for new forms of Indian Christian spirituality. Not only professional clergymen, be they priests, monks or nuns, found their way into ashrams, but also an increasing number of lay people, coming from many places in India and increasingly also from abroad. This more or less single-generation fascination with the phenomenon of Christian ashrams had led to deeper theological thinking through the concept of *sannyasin* and its existential dimension, meaning and role in the ashram but inevitably also in the whole Church.[13] All these aspects naturally reflected the need to establish a safely confined space where the Christian *sannyasin* could move around and also the need to set clearly defined rules concerning his religious identity. In many ashrams and theoretical works about them, *sannyasa* therefore began to be approached as the final stage in the monastic vows set out in hierarchical order (e.g. Pattathu 1997: 319).[14] These are gradually made by an aspirant to permanent residence in an ashram during his life. Through them, he dedicates himself to God more and more while simultaneously severing the ties that bind him to the world. The reason for the second and paradoxically totally opposite result of the interest in ashram life was without a doubt the willingness of some gurus in ashrams to try to meet the spiritual needs of temporary visitors. Thus, during their stay in an ashram, usually lasting only several weeks, or at the very end of it, many of them received a simplified type of an initial consecration from the hands of a guru, for which real adepts seeking permanent membership had to wait patiently for several years. The irreversible existential decision that a *sannyasin* takes up in all seriousness thus became a mere attempt at a change in lifestyle, which would continue to take place in the world. *Sannyasa diksha* somewhat turned into a blessing with which a guru could send his disciple back to that world.[15] It should be noted, however, that this trend of simplification and distortion of elements of their own spiritual tradition has been observable for many decades in many Hindu ashrams or new religious movements that take place in contemporary India.

Sadhana and *marga* in the Christian ashram

Apart from the existentially and functionally mutually contingent pair of *guru-shishya* and a certain form and type of ascetic conduct or at least ascetic approach to life, the third constitutive element of every Christian ashram is the method of spiritual effort which its members resort to. The

Sanskrit tradition, a source of inspiration for the Movement, talks in this sense about *sadhana* or the method used to achieve the desired objective. The general conception of such a method assumes that there is a particular spiritual discipline. It is perceived in a considerably holistic manner, and an aspiring person (*sadhaka*) voluntarily and actively submits to it, whether on the advice or under the guidance of his teacher or of his own free will. The selected *sadhana* can represent a specific type of religious ritual, an individual and collective prayer, contemplative meditation or mental as well as physical exercises practised over a long period of time. In the Indian environment, including Christian ashrams, this is very often some type of yoga, through which a *sadhaka* undergoes his or her systematically cultivated self-discipline. Under the influence of their founder-guru, some ashrams may follow only a single *sadhana*, which then determines the entire life in them. Others are construed rather as a space of freedom, creating ideal conditions for practising anything that makes man more perfect and leads him towards spiritual growth. When dealing with the conceptual religious notions of Hindu tradition, some ashramites incline towards the considerably loose, de facto all-embracing interpretation. According to it, *sadhana* may also be generally described as the ashram lifestyle as such, or, in other words, in this concept, the ashram itself and the life in it represent *sadhana* (Pattathu 1997: 265).

The internal and external conditions of an ashram in which and due to which a selected *sadhana* is achieved determine to a considerable extent its final form and, logically, also its efficiency. Since any *sadhana* should involve practice over a long period of time, in a concerted and persistent manner, early Protestant ashrams were already profiled as places situated outside the disturbing impacts of hectic everyday life. Serene groves on the banks of rivers or contrariwise located in the higher parts of a mountain range come to the fore as an ideal environment in this classic ashram conception. After all, returning to nature and living in tune with it is one of the most important features of the ashram myth. Very often, a modest piece of fertile land goes with an ashram. Although ashramites cultivate it, these farming activities almost never provide for their ashram financially. Almost all Christian ashrams in India are existentially entirely dependent on the generosity of their visitors and friends and disciples of the respective guru; help also often comes by way of liberal church leaders, mostly sympathetic bishops, who have expressed support for the ashram idea. On the other hand, Protestant ashrams maintain a high degree of institutional freedom. They are usually funded by the foundations and funds that were either established solely for the needs of a given ashram and therefore are also associated with its name. They may also form more complex programmes of charitable and often also missionary activities of a certain church. In the case of the Catholic and Orthodox Churches, every ashram is *de jure* set up by the Bishop to whose diocese it belongs or the superior of the respective congregation in the ashrams where the permanent core is formed by a reclusive community of monks. The economic and organizational dependency resulting from this fact determines the existence of ashrams. Their position in the diocese therefore frequently depends on the personal relationships between the guru of an ashram and the church authority superordinate to him. However, permanent financial uncertainty occurs to a large extent from a deliberate decision made by an ashram community. Its existence should be hovering on the brink of survival, as such conditions meaningfully fit into the concept of *sannyasa* and are also part of collectively experienced *sadhana*.

Nevertheless, Christian ashrams are also located in the centres of large cities if their *sadhana* is achieved in close coaction with unselfish help provided to others. Despite the hustle and bustle of the outside world, these ashrams also strongly emphasize an atmosphere of silence and peace. This creates ideal conditions for inner contemplation, which all ashramites find the time for regardless of their individual focus and everyday activities. The voluntarily adopted external lifestyle actually differs only slightly across all of the various Christian ashrams. Its emphasis is usually placed on austerity, natural simplicity or unpretentious poverty, whether in terms of food, which is nearly always vegetarian; clothes, which ashramites try to adapt to the reality of Indian villages and living space, which mostly consists of primitive huts or bare rooms with an absolute minimum of furnishings. An integral part of the internal conditions of an ashram, under which the personally practised *sadhana* of every ashramite happens, is also his role in the ashram community and the relationships existing within it. The community is always relatively small, seldom numbering more than 10–15 people. Although the level of spiritual individualism is unusual in comparison with traditional Christian communities and monastic congregations, the sharing of acquired knowledge, mutual support and openness are significant components of ashram life. After all, it is the community that essentially distinguishes the ashram phenomenon from the hermitage where a solitary ascetic dwells.

Sadhana therefore represents an individual method of every ashramite which allows him to head towards God by himself and concurrently together with the others. While this most distant aim is the only one across the ashram scene, the paths leading to it may differ considerably. In line with generally accepted Hindu tradition, succinctly formulated especially in the *Bhagavadgita*, the paths (*marga*) leading to salvation are of the following three types in principle: *gyana*, *bhakti* and *karma marga*, which means through knowledge, devotion and action. This classification is, however, purely schematic, motivated by the stubborn desire of the spirit of ancient India to define and categorize the world in its variegated complexity and sort its various components, including man, his experiences and behaviour, into clearly arranged and therefore understandable groups. No human movement towards goals is, however, schematic, and it does not take place in isolation. Its resulting form, therefore, consists of all three previously mentioned extracted types, which can be achieved in various proportions for every person and, in addition, tend to transmute during his or her life. Thus, relating to God always happens in aggregate simultaneously through knowledge, devotion and action, although only one of the paths more markedly prevails in the activities of individual ashrams and ashramites. However, there is most probably a mutually conditional dynamic relation between the individually perceived *sadhana* and common dominating *marga* of a respective ashram. This is evidenced by the relatively clear profiling of the ashrams in the Protestant and Catholic conceptions. The researchers involved in the Movement and also important authoritative documents (*Statement of the All-India Consultation on Ashram* 1978: item no. 6) that have emerged during its development therefore define three ashram types on the basis of different types of *marga*, under which any of the existing ashrams can be classified. At the end of this part, we will try to provide accuracy regarding the previously designed ashram typology and in particular to update it. Nevertheless, it is worth mentioning at this point that the direction of Protestant ashrams, which means some kind of summary of individual *sadhanas* of their individual members, was always inclined toward the path of action and to a lesser degree also of devotion. On the other hand, the ashrams of the Catholic and Orthodox Churches predominantly set out on the path of knowledge (Ralston 1987: 53). The variability in the conception of *sadhana* as well as *marga* seems to be one of the main causes of the complex historical development of the ashram idea, specific Christian ashrams and the whole Movement and, equally, also the cause of its disunion.

The briefly outlined concept of *sadhana* in the Christian ashram, as well as the practical aspects of life in it, however, ultimately constitute an obstacle to any mass development of the Movement. The "Indian lifestyle", which is so much acclaimed by ashramites, seems hardly to be acceptable for Indian Christians. In particular, the religious professionals outside the Movement are not willing to accept vegetarianism and refuse to sit on the ground while eating. They often see no point in contemplative meditation because, from the traditional environment of their church, they are only used to practising reflection, for example, on the parables and the deeds of Christ from the Gospels. For lay people from among poor Christians, the lure of the humble lifestyle pursued by ashramites is slight, as it corresponds to the standard of their everyday life, sometimes even exceeding it. By adopting it during their stay in an ashram, they do not obtain any value or spiritual knowledge. It fails to inspire them toward more focused meditation. The romanticized image of life lived in poverty and in harmony with the surrounding nature will hardly appeal to someone who has lived in the reality of poverty from birth and is forced to perceive nature as a means of survival. Although the social structure of individual ashrams is usually quite varied and we can find people with very different social roots there, it seems that throughout the history of the Movement, Catholic and Protestant ashrams attracted the interest of Christians coming mainly from cities and the middle-class intellectual milieu. At least for some of them, the ashram idea could therefore represent a form of spiritual escapism or revolt against the traditional concept of religious expression that they felt was emptied of its content.

The paradox of indigenization that is propelled by foreigners, as the critics of the Movement pointed out in its heyday, is an interesting fact in the Christian concept of *sadhana* and ashram life in general. Through the ashram phenomenon, Christendom sought to take root in India, but this initiative came in particular from the activities of priests and missionaries of non-Indian origin. Therefore, the ashram ideals seem to be de facto *videshi*, that is, foreign, ideals and a significantly Orientalized image of India. Thus, the legitimate question of whether inculturation should be pursued by foreigners, whose origin places them outside the context of the country, its culture and religion, remains open. Foreigners were also the most enthusiastic participants in ashram life and those who popularized the Movement to the extent that it came to be called the ashram fashion. Its uncontrolled development was what the second and third generation of ashramites, already of Indian origin, repeatedly warned against (Pattathu 1997: 384–385; Amalorpavadass 1985: 12). A remarkable and in some ways opposing phenomenon of the contemporary ashram scene then seems to be Indian ashramites, exclusively religious professionals, whether priests, monks or, to a much lesser extent, nuns, who regularly set off for their ashram missions to the United States and the countries of Western Europe to mediate Indian Christian spirituality there. The numerous ashrams that originated due to their activities outside the territory of India, however, go beyond the defined scope of this book.

The model example of a daily schedule in the Christian ashram

Although the daily routine of a specific ashram is determined by the selected *sadhana* and *marga*, all Christian ashrams show certain common features that affect everyday life. The practice of ashrams carried out for years and information-promotional brochures produced in their environment introducing the life and values of a given ashram to readers from among the ashram visitors nearly always determine the time schedule governing the operations of an ashram. Although activities taking place at specific times of the day are as a rule set quite clearly in these schedules, their observance is usually not rigid, with some exceptions. After all, they are neither part nor an expression of a monastic discipline, as is the case for church congregations. They are intended to serve as a tool for ashramites themselves so that their life will acquire a meaningful direction and the stay in an ashram is as contributive as possible for them. Their principle is voluntariness (Jeyaraj 2001: 22) and trust expressed in the willingness to submit to the proven method that is pursued in an ashram and supports inner calming and spiritual growth. Ashramites have an unprecedentedly high degree of freedom in adapting to a proposed schedule, always depending on their personal situation and personal needs as well as the needs of an ashram. Cases when one of the permanent members of an ashram does not participate in community life for many long months, lives in seclusion and devotes himself only to prayer and meditation are certainly not exceptional. After all, it is for the implementation of such spiritual needs that ashrams are established, and the whole community therefore fully agrees with the temporary absence of its member.

A weekday in the Christian ashram starts early, usually at around five o'clock in the morning. Roughly an hour is devoted to pursuing personal *sadhana*, whether in the form of a specific type of meditation, yoga or *namajapa* (the repetition of God's name), but always practised in solitude. Together with noon and evening, which are dedicated to inner contemplation, this period of time creates the backbone of spiritual life in the Christian ashram. It is commonly referred to by the Sanskrit term of *sandhya*, denoting three transitional moments of the day – dawn, noon and dusk, which Hindu tradition considers extremely opportune for religious activities. When it is over, the whole community meets in the ashram chapel or another meeting room to begin the day with a common prayer. In Catholic ashrams, it virtually always commences with singing or reciting the Vedic mantra *Gayatri*. However, other texts taken over or adapted from the Indian religious space and some rituals or their constituents (using aromatic essences, lighting a lantern, *arati* etc.) also make up a part of it, including in Protestant ashrams. Morning prayer may also be considerably long, always depending on the type and focus of the respective ashram. The preaching service also takes place in its course. In Catholic ashrams, this prayer then naturally turns into celebration of the Eucharistic sacrifice. The degree of its adaptation in the Indian environment, however, significantly differs from ashram to ashram. In some, it may be almost indistinguishable from a traditionally celebrated mass (with the exception of the ashram attire of the celebrants and the fact that all participants sit on the ground during the divine service), while in others, its external form, inner content and the overall set of rules represent an entirely new ritual and religious experience for an uninitiated visitor. The common prayer and mass is usually concluded with a short period of joint meditation. After that, the community goes for breakfast. In virtually all ashrams, people sit on the ground in the Indian manner during any meal, cutlery is not used and food is eaten with the right hand only. In some ashrams, silence is strictly observed during meals, while spiritually inspirational literature is read aloud in others, and in others no common rules are set. The whole morning and afternoon agenda of the ashram results from the focus of its external activities as well as from the obligations of individual members. In ashrams that are engaged in socially beneficial activities, ashramites leave for hospitals, schools, shelters, farms and so on. In ashrams that do not show any specific activity through which their interaction with the world would happen, so-called *seva*, a manual activity beneficial for the ashram, even if only symbolic, is usually expected from ashramites. In ashrams focused primarily on the spiritual growth of their members and pursuing Indian Christian spirituality, the main part of the day is dedicated to study, in which an increased emphasis is placed on the religious literature of Indian traditions but also Sacred Scriptures of other religions. The morning and afternoon programme is very often interrupted roughly in the middle of it for a short period of time, when the guru, spiritual leader or a significant visitor of an ashram converses with ashramites about a specific spiritual problem. It can be a real debate with all participants engaged in it or also simple monological preaching. The community then meets again at noon (the second *sandhya* in sequence) for another common prayer and a short period of joint meditation. In many ashrams, it is clearly scheduled which prayer texts, including those originating in a non-Christian tradition, pertain to a specific time of day. In some, however, virtually no emphasis is placed on such consistency of selection and everything happens rather spontaneously. After lunch, ashramites retire to their residential quarters and quite a strictly observed period of silence and rest begins. Here it is entirely the individual decision of every ashramite as to how he or she will spend this time – whether by relaxing or reading spiritual literature. Regarding its agenda, the afternoon programme does not differ too much from the first half of the day. It ends at dusk (the third *sandhya*), during which, as during dawn, considerable space is dedicated once again to individual contemplative meditation – another common prayer may precede it or contrariwise follow after it, this time slightly longer than it was at noon. Very often, devout *bhajanas* and *kirtanas* are sung during its course. These are once again taken or adapted from Hindu religious folklore, although the main religious language and the language of common prayer remain English in a range of ashrams, in particular those whose members come from multilingual areas of India. It is at this moment when respective local Indian languages almost always have their say. After dinner, the entire community meets once more, though not necessarily every day, for the so-called *satsang*. This plays an extraordinarily important role because it represents an opportunity for the mutual sharing of spiritual experiences. It is an open debate about the problems encountered by ashramites when achieving their *sadhana*, accepting emphatically offered impulses as well as giving them. Thanks to the *satsang*, common life in an ashram acquires a clear meaning, because during it, the individuals gathered at the feet of their teacher turn into a community with one common goal. In some Catholic ashrams, at the very end of the day, there follows adoration in a dusky chapel, which takes place either in absolute silence or by means of singing God's name. The day in the Christian ashram then comes to an end at nine or ten o'clock in the evening.

The Christian ashram in the context of the Church and society

An important intention that can be found at the root of the Movement, though remaining present throughout all of its stages more or less prominently, is that of creating a completely new identity for Indian Christians. The emergence of anything new usually leads to the transformation of the old or its complete termination. Because ashrams grew up in the context of their respective churches, in a creative dialogue with them, but most often as a moderate form of internal opposition revolting against the ingrained religious practice, the question of the relationship of ashrams to their home churches appears to be fundamental.

The Protestant environment seemed to be ideologically progressive and open to new ideas in the first half of the 20th century. Additionally, as a matter of principle, it was not so hampered by a strictly hierarchized structure, the status of which is perceived as sacred, as is the case for the Catholic Church. Therefore, the tense, often conflicting relationship between the ashram and the official church was not lived out too seriously there. No doubt, the fact that it was in particular the well-educated laity who usually became the bearers of ashram ideas played its part. They sought to create ashrams which were meant to represent an alternative to the life of Indian Christians. The status and functioning of those ashrams was to be entirely independent of the home church of their founder or founders. The ashrams that were really established through their efforts in the end expressed their affiliation to the respective churches mostly only in a formal manner. However, it is necessary to reiterate in this connection that the conditions, methods and goals of the life in the Protestant ashram were not perceived so radically as in the case of some Catholic ashrams.

It was in them where the permanently tense relationship between the ashram and the Church, in reality often happening on a personal level between the founder of an ashram and the parent Church authority superior to him, was perceived as a setback in the free development of the Movement. However, Catholic ashrams are not, and by definition even cannot be, independent institutes or phenomena which can definitively sever their ties to the Church. Many ashramites, however, vigorously resist any fixed inclusion in Church structures because they regard it as a serious threat of possible restrictions placed on the freedom and charisma that every ashram grows from. Therefore, they opt more for the long-term uncertainty arising from the vaguely set out legal status of the ashram within the Church, de facto permanently on its border. All they request from the Church is merely tolerance.[16] Because many of the Catholic ashramites come from the environment of the Church's congregations, the tension between obedience and fidelity to the home order on one hand and the inner desire to live the ashram way of life on the other is felt extremely seriously.

In the opinion of the vast majority of Catholic ashramites and ideologists of the Movement, any effort to institutionalize the ashram in the Church means to deny the ashram idea (e.g. Amalorpavadass 1985: 10–11).[17] The ashrams as conceived by them should stand completely outside Church structures because they are part of the eschatological, not hierarchized, Church (Painadath 1994: 43). As such, they transcend not only the sacraments of the Church but also the sacred order of the Church and canonical law (Griffiths 1993: 31–32).[18] The exclusivity of the phenomenon of the ashram, which is claimed here by its defenders, is anchored in the conviction of the exclusivity of the role that the ashram is to play for the Church and the whole of society. Everyday life in an ashram should constantly remind the Church of where the essence of spiritual authority and knowledge lies – not in the holy orders but in an authentic experience with sacredness, which leads to spiritual growth (Painadath 1994: 44). In its idealized form, ashram life is based on the principles of *sannyasa*. By adopting this, ashramites therefore voluntarily give up the feeling of physical as well as spiritual security that belonging to the Church ensures for them.[19] According to the most radical opinion that has originated in the ashram environment, ashramites should even stop clinging to their affiliation to a specific religion (Moses 2009: 17). After all, *sannyasa* should lead man to transcend all religious concepts. In such a decided, although somewhat ideologically inconsistent, perspective, ashrams remain part of the Church only if the Church means God's Kingdom; this is "a communion of people living together in the Spirit beyond the barriers of religions" (Moses 2007: 66). However, statements of a similar type can hardly find the support of official Church representatives. The majority Christian community in India will identify with them only with difficulty, and they are not generally accepted by individual ashram communities.

The optimistic expectation that the ashram phenomenon would create a new Christian identity that would change the whole of society as a consequence, and hence enrich India, was equally present even in the early days of the Movement. However, in an odd twist, considerations relating to the specific way of how and through whom this spiritually social revolution should happen did not start regularly emerging in the minds of ashramites until the late stage of the Catholic Movement, no doubt in response to the experienced crisis. The status of ashrams in the Church and society are very closely interrelated. After many personal disappointments regarding the hesitant support of the Catholic Church, Catholic ashramites turned their attention to the laity as the future driving force of the Movement. Concurrently, this turn stems from the change in the line of the ashram ideology that occurred in the heyday of the Movement, when Christian ashrams, originally established for a sparse group of priests, monks and nuns, suddenly opened up to everybody. In the Catholic conception, it was therefore professional clergymen who put the whole Movement in motion and who had been the bearers of its ideals for several decades. Despite the decided rhetoric, these religious professionals are only rarely able to sever their strong ties to the Church, as the briefly outlined ashram theology demands of them.[20] As a consequence, the whole ashram phenomenon is limited, doomed to always stand on the edge of the Church's as well as Christian interest, to be only an alternative spiritual and community life that is quietly tolerated or generously overlooked by the Church authorities. As believed by the late ashramites, the real revolution, which will impact the whole of society with its effect, will come only when the laity takes up the leadership of ashrams and, indeed, the whole Movement. They should become founders of entirely new ashrams,[21] both as gurus and their disciples,[22] while the influence of religious professionals in Christian ashrams should disappear once and for all. According to Vandana, only at such a moment will it be possible to talk about the Movement in the true sense of the word (Vandana 1993: 19), that is to say as about something in which numerous masses of people actively participate. From a historical perspective, it is certainly interesting that here the Catholic concept of the ashram in its last development stage returned to the starting point of the Protestants. However, a serious problem with this new horizon, which ashramites have turned their attention to since the 1990s, is the fact that the ashram ideals are strange for the Christian laity in India today.

In conclusion of this chapter, if we take a look at the ashrams that have already been dissolved, the ashrams that continue existing, and those that have only just been sketched in daring plans as communities present in the Church and concurrently in society, several different concepts can be schematically defined.[23] As part of the Movement, *ashram monasteries* are formed in which a community of monks or nuns, bound by a firm cause, pursues Indian Christian spirituality, as in all other cases. Another group consists of *ashram communities* of priests, monks, nuns and lay people, while *individual genders* of an ashram's permanent members are always consistently *segregated*. Yet others are the *ashram communities* of religious professionals and lay people *regardless of the ashramites' gender*, which, however, flourished in particular thanks to the activities of Protestant churches. Several significant ashrams managed, at least for a certain period of time, to create a *functional inter-monasterial ashram community*, and some can be described without exaggeration as *ecumenical ashrams*. The position of exclusivity is claimed by the ashrams established on the Christian initiative, which were, however, later shaped as *ashrams without confession*, intentionally overstepping any religious denomination. In their case, whether they can still be considered Christian ashrams remains the question at issue. Finally, a remarkable, although small, group is constituted by open *communities of the laity without the presence of a clergyman*. These were the ones that were perceived as an ideal unit of a future society, a sort of basic driving force of the new form of the Movement. As was expected, so-called "folk ashrams" could subsequently start emerging within the Movement (D'Souza 1993: 98–99)[24] and lead to a revival of spiritual life in India.

The typology of Christian ashrams

Although we tried to indicate the common characteristics of Christian ashrams in the previous chapters, they actually differ in almost every aspect of their origin and existence. Ashrams arise on the banks of rivers, in the mountains, in jungles and near sacred Hindu places but also in the environment of ordinary villages, on the periphery of cities or even directly in their busy centres. They may come to existence completely spontaneously, thanks to several disciples who decide to live permanently near their teacher. They can also result from a long-planned and carefully considered intent, whether at the initiative of an individual, an emerging community or a religious representative who is favourable to the ashram ideals. Some ashrams remain stable for a long period of time regarding the number of their members and in their ideological leaning. The developmental trajectories of others may be contrariwise considerably changeable, for example, ashrams which have various focuses and are consistently dedicated to clearly specified activities emerge, as well as ashrams that do not have any unequivocally set programme because, in the opinion of their members, the ashram first and foremost means experiencing the present (Painadath 2003: 130). There are ashrams that are consciously shaped through their founders as training centres of Christian spirituality, as places of ecumenical and interfaith dialogue, but perhaps also as a space for captivating prayer and healing. Ashrams that could manage to combine an emphasis on spiritual life with non-violent, yet radical, social reform still remain an unfulfilled ideal. These should be ashrams of the Dalits and the indigenous people of India, the ashrams through which the social groups oppressed for centuries will concurrently be liberated and the human spirit will be liberated and will grow.[25]

Already in the 1970s, when the imaginary reins of the Movement leadership were taken over by the Catholic Church or, to be more precise, Catholic ashramites, the first attempts appeared to systematically distinguish between ashrams and hence to create their meaningful typology. A significant theoretician and historian of the early period of the Movement, R. W. Taylor, divided the then existing ashrams into two large groups, which he referred to by the Indian terms of *khadi* and *kavi* (Taylor 1977: 19). The first group is named after Gandhi's spinners campaigns because the objective of these ashrams is to edify and reform Indian society by helping others unselfishly and self-sacrificingly. The *khadi* ashrams thus address themselves to various socially beneficial activities, and in Taylor's contemporaneous opinion, they are the sovereign domain of Protestant churches. The name of the *kavi* ashrams refers to ancient sages, mystics and poets who preferred contemplation, prayers and social seclusion to vigorous activity. By using this Sanskrit word, Taylor also hinted at the saffron-coloured apparel which is the traditional garb of ascetics and *sannyasins* in the Hindu environment. Members of the Christian *kavi* ashrams clothe themselves in just such a vestment so that they manifest their inspiration with this spiritual stream or directly experience affiliation with it. The essential difference between the two types, therefore, lies in the fact that, while historically older *khadi* ashrams identified with Indian nationalism, the *kavi* ashrams mainly identified with Indian religious tradition (Ibid., 19–20).

Taylor himself, self-critically, admits that they are considerably idealized types. In real ashrams, such a strict distinction between social service and the life of mystics is not observed, and neither is that between the civil or "sacred" clothes of ashramites.[26] The typology proposed by him, however, became exceptionally influential, a de facto standard part of any literature dealing with Christian ashrams. Its viability probably follows from the fact that the typology, by its very nature, speaks more about two possible approaches to the spiritual growth of ashramites – about the *khadi* and *kavi* spirituality. Each builds around itself a complex world of life values, goals and also methods by means of which the set goals can be reached.

Some later theorists of the Movement made efforts to refine Taylor's typology because in the context of the development of the independent India of that time, the original idea of *khadi* was waning, not only with regard to ashrams but also from general understanding. In this sense, the most influential, from among numerous varied attempts, turned out to be the classification of ashrams according to their predominant activity (*marga*), specifically *gyana*, *bhakti* and *karma* ashrams. The classification is clearly arranged, yet its drawback is that it is inaccurate regarding the numerous ashrams that are difficult or impossible to classify unambiguously in a particular group. The reason is that the differentiation based on *marga* accurately answers the question of what respective ashrams are dedicated to. However, for many of them, the more appropriate question to ask is what they actually are.

The typology presented herein is based on many years of field research in the environment of Christian ashrams actively professing the Movement or at least sympathizing with it. As part of his research, the author of this book has visited more than thirty functional ashrams – Catholic, Protestant, Orthodox and ecumenical. Also, indirectly, by studying ashram literature and through interviews with ashramites, he collected information or pieced its scattered fragments together, about several dozen other ashrams – both the existing ones and those that became extinct long ago. In line with Taylor's older concept and in accordance with the philosophical essence of the ashram as the studied object which grows from such an environment, the individual types of ashrams are referred to in Sanskrit terms (Štipl 2013: 207–208).

Seva ashrams are a permanent as well as temporary home to people who approach their life's path as a "service to God through service to people" (Grant 1994: 436). The predominant activities of these ashrams as well as the reason for establishing them consist of providing charitable assistance to others, which may be approached from a broad range of perspectives. *Bhakti ashrams* are places where the main emphasis is placed on the emotional expression of a deep personal faith in God and experiencing God's love. This happens by way of frequent prayer meetings where God is celebrated by singing devotional hymns or through the spontaneous, often highly expressive, momentary experiencing of God's presence, as is customary in particular in the environment of Charismatic (Pentecostal) churches. *Dhyana ashrams* are a spiritual refuge for all those who are urged by their inner voice to relentlessly search for the essence of human existence and the raison d'être. In these ashrams, God's name stands completely aside, and all conventional expressions of religious belief are also more or less secondary. Ashramites focus their attention fully on the very act of searching. This happens through contemplative meditation, which is very often performed in absolute silence (*mauna*), sometimes lasting for many years, in the manner of Hindu mystics. A *gyana ashram* is a type of research centre of ashram and human spirituality in general; however, in particular it aims to combine the religious ideas of the Hindu environment with Christian theology. These ashrams have excellently equipped libraries, where ashramites and persons temporarily interested in this type of ashram life may conduct their research undisturbed. *Vidyalaya ashrams* are educational centres of the Movement, akin to forest universities, where seemingly the knowledge and new discoveries from *gyana* ashrams were transformed into experimental practice and passed on to others in this unfinished form. Typically, a small community of ashramites regularly organizes short-term courses here for people interested in Indian Christian spirituality from the ranks of religious professionals and laity. Here everybody gains experience of the ashram way of life. After they leave the ashram, it is entirely up to them as to whether and how they will transfer this experience into their everyday life and common religious experience. *Matha ashrams* are monasteries transplanted into the Indian religious and cultural environment. The monks or nuns in them seek to combine the monastic traditions of Europe and India. *Kala ashrams* are experimental grounds from which original Christian art grows, expressing Gospel message through artistic traditions of India, whether it is music, dance or visual arts. Finally, *kutir ashrams* are very often impermanent abodes or rather hermitages of a single recluse, who lives in solitude for most of the time but is occasionally willing to take one or two followers as his disciples. Although these solitary Christian sadhus claim allegiance to the Movement, in the case of their *kutirs*, the question remains open as to whether they can be considered ashrams due to the absence of the *guru-shishya* relationship.

Notes

1 For the etymology of the term, the summary of its varying interpretations and the matter of the semantic link between the ashram as a place where an exclusive activity is performed, the activity itself and the theological system of the division

of human life into four stages, with specific religious and social functions attributed to them, see Olivelle (1993: 16–24).

2   A similar characteristic of the ancient ashram is proposed by a significant representative of the Protestant stream of the Ashram Movement, S. Jesudason, in his influential collective publication titled *Rethinking Christianity in India*. In addition, he also considers the following to be substantial features: the absence of a direct connection between the ashram and an existing religious organization (i.e. the freedom of its establishment and duration); setting the ashram in a beautiful natural environment which inspires the human soul, uplifting it to God; observance of celibacy by all disciples of a respective guru, at least during the time of their stay in the ashram (Chenchiah, undated: 217–218).

3   Such a concept of transcendental guru interestingly corresponds to the Christian concept of *Sadguru*, which is presented subsequently.

4   For the educational function of the ancient ashrams, see Scharfe (2002: 122–126).

5   H. Scharfe considers the term *acharyakula* more traditional and historically earlier (Scharfe 2002: 120). However, between the two, *acharya-* and *gurukula*, there was a semantic difference in the understanding of the role of the teacher – *acharya*, or the guru (Ibid., n. 33).

6   The basic hallmarks of the Christian ashram, which were mentioned in the appropriate sections of the part dealing with the history of the Movement, are not repeated in this overview. Furthermore, the overview is merely selective; it does not seek to provide an exhaustive account of all of the views on the phenomenon of the ashram as they appeared in the concepts of various Christian authors. Virtually all publications emerging from the ashram environment, whether ashram booklets, popular and scientific articles or more extensive works devoted to the Movement or the ashram phenomenon, express an opinion on the essence of the Christian ashram.

7   For many years, this work represented the most important contribution to the researched theme of Christ as the guru, but recently it has been supplemented considerably by the theologically more elaborate book by J. P. Schouten (2008).

8   The letter by Vandana to B. Griffith dated July 16, 1990; a copy of the letter is in the author's archive.

9   Other authors use the term *karakaguru* (Pattathu 1997: 313) or *upaguru* (Jeyaraj 2001: 28–30).

10 The first mention of Marc Chaduc appears in Abhishiktananda's letters in 1969 (Stuart 1995: 214). At the end of the 1960s, Abhishiktananda was already becoming a public figure not only in Catholic circles in India but also in his native France. For a number of years, many adepts from Europe had contacted him requesting spiritual guidance. Among them was the seminarist M. Chaduc, who arrived in India after two years of exchanging correspondence to become Abhishiktananda's disciple. The teacher-disciple relationship seen from the absolutized Hindu perspective considerably dominated Abhishiktananda's thinking in the last two years of his life, because in Chaduc, he had found a perfect disciple who was embracing all of the spiritual experiences that his guru had obtained over the twenty years of his life in India with incredible speed and was also able to put into practice what Abhishiktananda, in his own words, only theorized about on the pages of his books. After Abhishiktananda's death in 1973 and after a short visit to his native France, Chaduc settled down in a hermitage (*kutir*) located near Rishikesh in 1975 and began a decade-long period of silence (*mauna*) there. However, in the first months of 1977, he disappeared from his hut, probably somewhere in the Himalayas, under mysterious circumstances, and nothing is known about his subsequent fate. Marc Chaduc, under the Indian

name of Swami Ajatananda, which he adopted along with the *sannyasa* in 1973, remains an enduring inspiration for the ascetic contemplatively oriented Catholic stream of the Movement, even representing it as its living symbol to a certain extent.

11 Complaints over the lack of *sadhakas* and permanent members of ashrams are repeatedly heard in the contributions to the magazine of the ashram community *Ashram Aikya* (e.g. *Ashram Aikya Newsletter*, no. 35: 16).

12 In this sense, an interesting inspiration for the Christian environment is not only Brahmabandhav Upadhyay, who considered himself a Christian *sannyasin* in the manner of de Nobili, but in particular the somewhat younger Sikh convert known as Sadhu Sundar Singh. In the first three decades of the 20th century, the latter brought the model of a wandering ascetic preacher and mystic into Christian tradition in India. Although a large number of fantastic legends surround his person and life alike, with Sundar Singh himself probably contributing to them, he seems to be a remarkable example of the indigenous way of expressing the Gospel message in the Indian context. This applies not only to its content but also to its form in the shape of an adopted lifestyle.

13 Of particular note is the early and extremely valuable contribution by the significant theologian and Indologist K. Klostermaier (1968). Two more extensive, revealing and widely cited studies deal with the concept of the Christian *sannyasa* at Abhishiktananda and Griffiths – Vattakuzhy (1981) and Rajan (1989).

14 In the ashram monastery *Kurisumala*, this succession in the monastic life has been practised since the very beginning.

15 Beyond a doubt, it is true that every ashramite renounces something by entering an ashram or accepting the ashram lifestyle. The problem of the reckless handling of the religious terms derived from Hindu tradition or of its entire philosophical concept, however, fully manifests itself in the attempt of Catholic ashramites to introduce the term *grihastha sannyasa*. The motivation is obvious: it arises from the heartfelt efforts to engage lay people in the Movement, let them sufficiently know that they are also part and full members of ashrams and that the *sannyasa* that is so much acclaimed in ashram literature is also intended for them. Striking proof of this tendency may be the sadhu-ashramite living with his wife and three small children in the "family ashram" in Kerala, who says that he understands the adopted *sannyasa* as a way of teaching him how to lead a plain and simple life (*Ashram Aikya Newsletter*, no. 46: 10–11).

16 The letter by Vandana to B. Griffith dated July 16, 1990; a copy of the letter is in the author's archive.

17 According to C. Cornille, "the very idea of the institutional identity of an ashram is a contradiction in terms" (Cornille 1991: 150).

18 Daring as these words may be, it is nevertheless well worth mentioning that Griffiths himself was anxiously seeing to the Church support and institutionalization of *Shantivanam*. To protect his ashram against potential attacks by the Bishop to whose diocese *Shativanam* belonged, he brought it into the arms of the Italian Camaldoli congregation of Romuald. With equal care, Griffiths also saw to the continuity of his ashram. On his authority, some of his devoted disciples of Indian origin became students of theology and eventually took holy orders. Despite the repeated proclamation of meditation as the highest sacrament in the Christian ashram, Griffiths was always taking steps that would ensure there were enough priests for *Shantivanam* necessary for the daily Eucharistic celebration. This paradoxical contradiction present in Griffiths's words and actions became the target of friendly, yet strict and very accurate criticism from the pen of Vandana; see The letter by Vandana to B. Griffith dated July 16, 1990; a copy of the letter is in the author's archive.

19 The letter by Vandana to B. Griffith dated July 16, 1990; a copy of the letter is in the author's archive.
20 For perhaps the most radical concept of this severing of ties to the Church, without which the Movement has no future in the words of the author, see Moses (2009: 18).
21 It is this very type of new ashrams, believed to give the Movement a new direction, which the important Jesuit theologian M. Amaladoss calls for. He even does so at a time when the Movement has passed its prime and when there is also general disenchantment over the Christian ashram phenomenon among many ashramites (Amaladoss 2008: 176).
22 The letter by Vandana to B. Griffith dated July 16, 1990; a copy of the letter is in the author's archive.
23 This division takes into account only the permanent membership of ashrams, because temporary visitors, who can participate in virtually all aspects of the life of an ashram community, are welcome in all of them, with a few exceptions.
24 The idea of folk ashrams was first thematized at the seventh *satsang* of the Catholic ashram community *Ashram Aikya*, held in 1991. Under the influence of the deepening crisis of the Movement, it was, however, further developed by some ashramites in the following years.
25 The idea of similar ashrams appears in the Movement as a considerably late reflection on the criticism of the theology of liberation; see Painadath (1994: 43).
26 In Taylor's conception, the saffron robe is not a necessary condition even in the Catholic ashrams that shape themselves unambiguously as *kavi*. Some ashramites prefer white as the colour of their clothes because they do not feel any need to demonstrate their asceticism ostentatiously or simply because white symbolizes the purity of their lives and beliefs. On the contrary, the *kavi* attire was not unusual in Protestant ashrams. It was often accepted in particular by ashramites observing celibacy.

References

Abhishiktananda. 1990. *Guru and Disciple*. New Delhi: ISPCK.
Abhishiktananda. 1997. *Saccidananda: A Christian Approach to Advaitic Experience*. New Delhi: ISPCK.
Amaladoss, Michael. 2008. *Beyond Dialogue: Pilgrims to the Absolute*. Bangalore: Asian Trading Corporation.
Amalorpavadass, D. S. 1980. *Vision of Religious Life in Future and the Future of Religious Life*. Bangalore: NBCLC.
Amalorpavadass, D. S. 1985. *Ashram Aikya: Whence and Whither*. Bangalore: NBCLC.
Amalorpavadass, D. S. 1990. *Integration and Interiorization*. Mysore: Anjali Ashram.
Ashram Aikya Newsletter. 1999. No. 35.
Ashram Aikya Newsletter. 2005. No. 46.
Ashram booklet *Anjali Ashram*. (undated). Mysore: Anjali Ashram.
Chenchiah, Pandipeddi, V. Chakkarai and A. N. Sudarisanam. 1941. *Asramas Past & Present*. Madras: Indian Christian Book Club.
Cornille, Catherine. 1991. *The Guru in Indian Catholicism: Ambiguity or Opportunity of Inculturation?* Leuven: Peeters Press Louvain.
D'Souza, Claude. 1993. "Ashrams and the Socio-Economic and Political Needs of India." In *Christian Ashrams: A Movement with a Future?* Edited by Vandana. New Delhi: ISPCK, pp. 93–101.

Grant, Sara. 1994. "The Synod on Consecrated Life and the Ashram Tradition." *Vidyajyoti Journal of Theological Reflection* 58 (7): 435–450.
Griffiths, Bede. 1984. "Christian Ashrams." *Word and Worship* 17 (4): 150–152.
Griffiths, Bede. (undated). "Prayer in Christian Ashram." In *Praying Seminar*. Edited by D. S. Amalorpavadass. Bangalore: NBCLC, pp. 217–221.
Griffiths, Bede. 1993. "The Ashrams as a Way of Transcendence." In *Christian Ashrams: A Movement with a Future?* Edited by Vandana. New Delhi: ISPCK, pp. 30–33.
Ishanand, Bandhu. 1999. "Ashrams and Mission Spirituality." *Third Millennium* 2 (2): 122–145.
Jesudason, Savararirayan. 1937. *Ashrams, Ancient and Modern: Their Aims and Ideals*. Vellore: Sri Ramachandra Press.
Jeyaraj, Maria. 2001. *Essentials of a Christian Ashram*. Thanirpalli: Saccidananda Ashram Shantivanam.
Klostermaier, Klaus. 1968. "Sanyasa: A Christian Way of Life in Today's India?" *Indian Ecclesiastical Studies* 7 (1): 8–40.
Moses, Korko. 2007. "Christian Ashrams in the Evolution of World Spirituality." *Dhyana Journal of Religion and Spirituality* 4: 51–74.
Moses, Korko. 2009. "Rooting Christian Ashrams in the Mystical Tradition." *Ashram Aikya Newsletter* 54: 14–20.
Olivelle, Patrick. 1993. *The Āśrama System: The History and Hermeneutics of a Religious Institution*. Oxford: Oxford University Press.
Painadath, Sebastian. 1994. "Ashrams: A Movement of Spiritual Integration." *Concilium* 4: 36–46.
Painadath, Sebastian. 2003. "The Spiritual and Theological Perspectives of Ashrams." In *Solitude and Solidarity: Ashrams of Catholic Initiative*. Edited by Sebastian Painadath. New Delhi: Ashrama Aikya/ISPCK, pp. 120–148.
Painadath, Sebastian. 2007. *We Are Co-Pilgrims: Towards a Culture of Inter-Religious Harmony*. New Delhi: ISPCK.
Pattathu, Paul. 1997. *Ashram Spirituality*. Indore: Satprakashan.
Philip, P. O. 1946. "The Place of Ashrams in the Life of the Church in India." *The International Review of Mission* 35: 263–270.
Rajan, Jesu. 1989. *Bede Griffiths and Sannyasa*. Bangalore: Asian Trading Corporation.
Ralston, Helen. 1987. *Christian Ashram: A New Religious Movement in Contemporary India*. Lewiston/Queenston: The Edwin Mellen Press.
Scharfe, Hartmut. 2002. *Education in Ancient India*. Leiden: Brill.
Schouten, Jan Peter. 2008. *Jesus as Guru: The Image of Christ among Hindus and Christians in India*. Amsterdam: Rodopi.
Statement of the All-India Consultation on Ashrams, 1978.
Štipl, Zdeněk. 2013. "Christian Ashrams in India: A Bridge between Two Worlds?" In *CEENIS Current Research Series* (vol. 1). Edited by Danuta Stasik and Anna Trynkowska. Warsaw: Dom Wydawniczy Elipsa, pp. 202–211.
Stuart, James. 1995. *Swami Abhishiktananda: His Life Told through His Letters*. New Delhi: ISPCK.
Taylor, Richard W. 1977. "From Khadi to Kavi: Toward a Typology of Christian Ashrams." *Religion and Society* 24 (4): 19–37.
Vandana. 1978. "The Challenge of Christian Ashrams Today." *Word and Worship* 11 (1): 15–22.

Vandana. 1993. "Finding Our Roots before We Take Wing." In *Christian Ashrams: A Movement with a Future?* Edited by Vandana. New Delhi: ISPCK, pp. 6–22.

Vandana. 2004. *Gurus, Ashrams and Christians.* New Delhi: ISPCK.

Vattakuzhy, Emmanuel. 1981. *Indian Christian Sannyasa and Swami Abhishiktananda.* Bangalore: Theological Publications in India.

CONCLUSION
Interpretive possibilities of the Christian Ashram Movement

The objectives set by the representatives of the Ashram Movement during its development were numerous, often even considerably different and contradictory. If we evaluate individual stages of this development from a narrowly focused Christian perspective, taking into consideration only the success or failure of the Movement and therefore its contribution to Christianity itself, all we can do is to state that virtually none of the defined objectives were achieved. Christianity in India has not become more Indian. The efforts to form a new identity of Indian Christians through ashrams have failed. The monastic communities of Christian *sannyasins* have not come into existence. The inculturated liturgy has not spread outside the ashram setting and continues taking place exclusively in an experimental environment. Involving the laity in the life of ashrams has failed. Ashrams have not become the epicentre of religious and social revolution, nor a place where members of different religions meet in open interreligious dialogue that leads to the mutual enrichment and spiritual growth of all participants.

The starting position of such targeted critical evaluation of the Movement arises from the selection of the religious and cultural layer of Hinduism, which served not as the major but de facto the sole source of inspiration for ashrams. Despite the proclaimed effort to make Christianity in ashrams more Indian, the whole ashram ideology draws exclusively on the Brahmanical concept of Hinduism and focuses only on the Sanskrit religious tradition. Hence, not only are all of the other Indian religions, including the rich world of their mysticism, ignored but also popular Hinduism, which has been the mainstream of religious thought and expression in India for centuries. In particular, the Catholic ashrams with their lifestyle and adopted spiritual values really resemble "Brahmanical institutions". Although they are open to anybody and the social rules following from caste membership do not play any role in them, at the same time, there is little they can offer to common Indian classes. Ashrams do not meet their spiritual needs; neither do they prod them into a relentless quest. Nor do they present them with the answers to religious questions that would be applicable in daily reality.

CONCLUSION

The tendency toward religious and spiritual elitism has always been present in ashrams. Many ashramites from the late period of the Movement are aware of this. Through their reflections, Brahmanization or Sanskritization of ashrams thus becomes an object of boldly formulated self-criticism. According to this reflection, the Sanskrit culture, which Christian ashrams draw their inspiration from, does not have anything in common with the masses of Indian Christians. The Movement would like to enrich their lives by placing the emphasis on personal mystical experiences, but the religious and cultural background of these masses is formed through indigenous languages and local cultural traditions. In one of the late issues of the magazine of the Catholic ashram community *Ashram Aikya*, Mani Karott even presents an opinion that the main mystical tradition of Hinduism or rather the whole Indian circle of civilization is not based on Sanskrit culture but takes place outside of it or even in conscious opposition to it (Kabir, Nanak, Basavanna, Mira Bai etc.) (Karott 2009: 7). This is happening in the language and thus also the thinking of the broad public masses that can therefore actively participate in it and be its creators and bearers in the sense of it being further passed on from teacher to disciple. In his reflections, no matter how problematic their conclusions on India may appear to be from the perspective of the historian of religions, Karott draws upon the so-called spirituality of Nazareth, which turns its attention to the historical figure of Christ as the role model of a mystical teacher. He, too, was inseparably linked to the working classes. This was the background he came from, and he spoke their language when talking about his experience with God. In Karott's opinion, this is the very idea that Christian ashrams should turn to if they want to be relevant for Christianity and India. And through it, they should inculturate India – to penetrate not into the world of religious and cultural elites but that of ordinary people.

It is this absence of the relationship of Christian ashrams to the world of common people, above all the large number of Indian Christians, that yet another and perhaps the most frequently heard critical note relates to. The Movement has never managed to cope with it, and as a result, it represents one of the main causes of its failure. Through the "passive spirituality" pursued in ashrams, Christianity gives up its role as a protector of the poor and socially ostracized (in particular the Dalits in the Indian context) that has been proven by history and thus alienates all those who turn to it, hoping for liberation from oppression. Passive spirituality in the form of preaching ascetic ideals does not lead to the improvement of their lives but to stagnation; this is the stagnation of both the Christian community and the whole country. In the words of one of the most spectacular and stringent Christian critics of the Movement, Indian Jesuit George Soares-Prabhu, by promoting Brahmanic values in ashrams, tacit support is expressed for this oppression that has lasted throughout centuries. Soares-Prabhu believes that what Hinduism, in particular the social system created by it and sanctified by the religious authority, first and foremost needs today is external critical reflection, not blind admiration in the form of immersion in meditation modelled on Hindu mysticism (Soares-Prabhu in Vandana 1993: 154–155). At the same time, this critical perspective of the Dalit theology of liberation warns against turning to the long-dead archaism (Pattathu 1997: 373) that ashrams inevitably are due to their origin. This decided criticism even perceives ashrams as a totally undesirable phenomenon of contemporary Christianity in India, as evidenced by the sharp verbal attacks aimed at the Movement by the Dalit theologians. In their eyes, ashrams are a manifestation of the influence of Brahmanism, which is an enemy of the Church and of Christians.

However, the Christian Ashram Movement offers a number of other interpretive perspectives, which complete its image, dynamism and limitations in terms of temporal scope. The Movement took place within the framework of the historical development of Christianity in India, especially in the context of the changing relations of Christian churches to the religious otherness of the Indian civilization space, as they were characterized at a glance in the first part of this book. From this perspective, the Movement appears as a historical phenomenon contingent on the situation in which the churches found themselves in India in the early 20th century. This phenomenon was on the one hand influenced by the internal development of Christian churches outside India and the relationship of Europe to India at that time or, more precisely, the orientalizing idea about it. Concurrently, it was also impacted by different reactions of various components of the Indian environment, but almost exclusively Christian ones, to the activities of ashrams, the changing tendencies that the Movement was gradually revealing and also the objectives that its representatives set for themselves. The characteristic features of the respective developmental stages of the relationship of Christianity to India and its dominant religion thus contributed to the motives of the Ashram Movement and consequently also to its forms. The religious and cultural import of European missionaries, beginning with the Portuguese in the 16th century and ending with the Protestant churches in the 19th century, as well as the aggressiveness of the missions conducted by them, had resulted in a defensive reaction of the Indian environment in the form of turning to domestic religious and cultural traditions. The interest of missionaries in converts from among the Brahmans, which had remained unsatisfied over a long period of time, led to selecting the elite Brahmanical concept of Hinduism as the main source of inspiration for attempts to permeate the religious world of India. The then existing fascination with the Upanishads, with their world of ideas, no matter how vaguely it was defined, being seen by Europe in the 19th and 20th centuries as the highest stage of development of religious thought in India, sparked interest in Hindu mysticism. Attention was attracted in particular by the monistic concept of *Advaita Vedanta*. Its methods, in interacting with religious otherness, largely correlated with the inclusivist tendencies of the Christian theology of fulfilment in the 20th

CONCLUSION

century. The school system built by Christian churches and designed as a modern alternative to traditional methods of education mobilized middle-class Indian society over an extended period of time. Subsequently, church reformers of domestic origin arose from its Christian circles. In the case of Protestant churches, they were both laymen and religious professionals; within the Catholic Church, they were almost exclusively priests and theologians. In the 20th century, they made some attempts to rehabilitate the cultural and religious values of India. The often quite radical clash between their ideas about the form of Christianity and the efforts of official church leaders to maintain the firm organizational structure and internal doctrinal unity of the churches led inevitably to conflicts of opinion. It was from them that the growing need for religious and spiritual freedom of the reformers crystallized. According to some interpretations, such freedom could be achieved only in the environment of Christianity without the church. The trend of "faith without religion" is also present in the context of post-war Europe that had been coping in this manner with the impacts of the emergence of secular states. With the end of the political hegemony of the colonial Christian powers, with cultural and religious globalization and with the general loss of confidence in traditional religious institutions, this trend in India seems to be mainly the result of a conflict between two different ways of understanding religiosity. It is the Christian Ashram Movement that appears to be a model example of such a conflict because both the Christian churches themselves and a considerable proportion of ashramites are of other than Indian origin.

Another possible interpretative plane of the Movement is the purely theological perspective, through which the rich literary production of its leading figures can be analyzed. Apparently, it is, however, impossible to objectively assess today the real importance of the numerous ashram impulses for Indian theology and the impact on its future form. Nevertheless, the remarkably developed theological concept of *Saccidananda* as a representation of the Holy Trinity mystery remains its inalienable heritage, which will quite possibly lead to its rediscovery and further development one day. The same can be said about different types of approaches to the relation between man and God, whether it is the monistic concept based on the philosophy of *Advaita Vedanta*, which sees this relationship as experiencing an absolute, unqualified unity with God, or the experience of this unity when keeping the individuality of man. Also, the idea of ashram *sannyasins* revives and updates in Christianity the model of lifelong dedication to God. It had been present in the monastic tradition of Christianity throughout the first centuries of its existence, in the characters of hermits or desert fathers, but subsequently was completely replaced by monastic communities. Probably the most remarkable discovery of the theology that was nurtured in ashrams seems to be the figure of Christ as an inner teacher, *Sadguru*. In this notion, the emphasis on relentless contemplation acquires its full sense because ashramites enter a personal dialogue with the living God, who is present in them themselves. The mortal guru, whom ashramites see as an empathetic guide on this spiritual journey, then brings a completely new type and model of spiritual authority into Christian tradition. The theological perspective in assessing the Movement concurrently opens up a wide range of possibilities for religious science to explore. The theological impulses coming from ashrams can thus be compared to similar religious concepts existing in other religions, particularly Hinduism. Actually, they have already been studied by a significant number of researchers, however, until now, mainly Christian theologians.

The issues related to interfaith dialogue and its content, structure, possible extent and meaning are also associated with the approach of religious studies and thus also philosophy toward interpreting the Christian Ashram Movement. As a result, these represent the very core of the analysis of the studied problem. The concept of an interfaith dialogue originated in the environment of religiously liberalized, plural and to a large extent also post-Christian Europe. It brought to the fore the interests and needs of autonomous individuals, including the freedom of their religious preferences. The dialogue necessarily assumes a diversity of opinion, which, in the European perception, is a result of a personal religious decision. This historically conditioned religious tolerance in Europe considerably formed the plurality of its environment. However, it stands in stark contrast with the Indian perception of religion as such. It seems to be completely incompatible with the understanding of the function of religion in society and also the role of the individual in relation to the religiously firmly established society. Despite its individualistic approach to personally experienced spirituality, being open and tolerant to heterodox experiments, the Hindu world seemingly attached very little weight to individualistic free will. This, on the contrary, is crucial for the modern European concept of religious belief. It is through it that individuals can change their status towards or within society on the basis of their personal choice and hence also freely change their own religious identity but without threatening the constitutive relations within society. In India, it is as if an individual has always placed himself before God but not before other people. Therefore, the Hindu religious "pluralism" is not a manifestation of religious tolerance of a different opinion, because it does not arise from personal preferences, but stems from a hierarchically constituted society. Each of its individual classes may attain fundamentally different needs and possibilities, which result from its complex cultural and religious development (Halbfass 1988: 411). The Hindu world of religious ideas, which are in conflict due to the differences in their opinions, developed a rich tradition of religious-philosophical debates and colloquies (*vada*). However, religious tolerance is not their underlying principle, and mutual enrichment in the form of finding meaningful unity is not their goal. On the contrary, it is clearer demarcation of borders between mutually incompatible opinions (Clayton 2006: 50). It seems that a common search for unity in matters of religion is foreign to the intellectual environment of Hinduism, no matter how persuasive on the part of Christianity the motives of such a search may actually be. The Christian concept of interfaith dialogue is therefore incomprehensible and unacceptable in India, as evidenced by the minimal interest in such dialogue on the part of Hinduism (Klostermaier 1993: 265). This fact probably represents the essence of the different concepts of religiosity in Christianity and Hinduism, as well as the unsolvable problem that the Christian Ashram Movement inevitably found itself facing during its historic development.

Today, the Christian Ashram Movement seems to be a closed chapter in the history of Christianity in India. No doubt, ashrams will still exist for some time to come. The individuals to whom ashram ideals appeal for some reason will continue living in them, and the sparse ashram community of individual churches will continue meeting together, inspiring and encouraging each other, and thus keep the dying idea alive. It cannot even be ruled out that new ashrams will emerge if a mature charismatic personality turns up, seeking an alternative means of expressing his or her bearing witness to Christ, or if such a personality gathers around himself or herself a circle of disciples from the initiative of whom an ashram naturally arises. It is also possible to assume that ashram spirituality will be developed further and the theological reflections aiming to articulate the Gospel message by means of the cultural and religious idioms of India will be elaborated upon (Vandana 1983: 185). The current atmosphere of Christianity in India, however, preemptively dooms all of these considerations to the position of theological marginalia, no matter how original. Their cultivation is reserved for a place in dedicated periodicals with little influence, discussion seminars with a limited circle of participants and, quite unsurprisingly, primarily in ashrams themselves. At the time of Abhishiktananda, Griffiths and Amalorpavadass, the ashram theology may have promised to become a sovereign voice of Indian Christianity and contribute new impulses of thought to the whole Christian theology in the post-colonial and post-modern world. Today, however, it takes place only in ashrams, only ashramites deal with it and it is relevant once again exclusively for life in an ashram.

This book was intended to capture the phenomenon of the Christian Ashram Movement in its historical development and put it into the context of the generally perceived history of Christianity in India, because within its framework, the Movement acquires its full meaning. The briefly outlined interpretative perspective, through which it would also be possible to view the Movement, then opens up a wide field for further research. The interesting and in many ways still current issue of Christian ashrams is definitely worth the effort.

References

Clayton, John. 2006. *Religions, Reasons and Gods: Essays in Cross-Cultural Philosophy of Religion*. Cambridge: Cambridge University Press.

Halbfass, Wilhelm. 1988. *India and Europe: An Essay in Understanding*. Albany: SUNY Press.

Karott, Mani. 2009. "The Indian Christian Ashram Movement and the Spirituality of Nazareth." *Ashram Aikya Newsletter* 54: 4–7.

Klostermaier, Klaus. 1993. "The Future of Hindu-Christian Dialogue." In *Hindu-Christian Dialogue: Perspectives and Encounters*. Edited by Harold Coward. New Delhi: Motilal Banarsidas Publishers, pp. 262–274.

Pattathu, Paul. 1997. *Ashram Spirituality*. Indore: Satprakashan.

Vandana. 1983. "The Ashram Movement and the Development of Contemplative Life." *Vidyajyoti Journal of Theological Reflection* 47 (4): 179–192.

Vandana, editor. 1993. *Christian Ashrams: A Movement with a Future?* New Delhi: ISPCK.

INDEX

Abhishiktananda 84–85, 112–122, 124, 129–131, 133, 136, 138–139, 144–145, 150, 178, 181, 205
accommodatio 70
Ad Gentes 50, 53, 58
Advaita Vedanta 21, 74, 81, 111, 113, 117–118, 122, 202–203
Aikya Alayam 138–139
All-India Consultation on Ashrams 132–134
All-India Seminar on the Church in India Today 129, 131–134, 138, 142
Amalorpavadass, D. S. 52–54, 128, 133, 136, 140–142, 147, 173–174
Animananda 75–76, 83–84, 109
An Indian Benedictine Ashram 113–116, 118
Anjali ashram 140–143
Appasamy, Aiyadurai Jesudasen 103
Arunachala 113, 118–119
Arya Samaj 24, 80, 89–90
Ashram Aikya 134–136
Ashram Aikya Newsletter 136–137
Aurobindo Ashram 92

Banerjee, Bhabani Charan *see* Upadhyay, Brahmabandhav
Banerjee, Krishna Mohan 28
Banerjee, Surendranath 74
Bengali Renaissance 23
Besant, Annie 77
Beschi, Constanzo Giuseppe 16
Bhagavadgita 29, 147, 184
Bhakti Ashram 111–112
Bharat Ashram 89
Bharatiya puja 54
Brahmanization of Christianity 29–30, 201
Brahmo Samaj 23, 74, 87, 89

Carey, William 20
Carmelites of Mary Immaculate (CMI) 71
Catechesi Tradendae 50
Catholic Bishops' Conference of India (CBCI) 127–129, 132–133, 146–147
CBCI Commission for Liturgy 128, 133, 146–147
Chaduc, Marc 178
Chakkarai, Vengal 104
Chavara, Kuriakos 71–72, 96
Chenchiah, Pandipeddi 104
Christa Panthi 108
Christa Seva Sangha 96, 99–103, 105, 144
Christavashram 107
Christiya Bandhu Kulam 108
Christ of the Indian Road, The 106
Christukula 96–101, 105
Church Sanskrit 20–21
Congregation for Divine Worship and the Discipline of the Sacraments 128, 146–147
Congregation for the Doctrine of the Faith 62
Congregation for the Evangelization of Peoples 50, 131
Congregation for the Propagation of the Faith 62, 50
Constitution of India 31
Crown of Hinduism, The 52

Dalits 29–31, 39, 148, 192, 201–202
Dalit theology of liberation *see* theology of liberation
De, Lalbihari 73, 77
Dharmapustaka 20
dhyana 93, 126, 194
Dominus Iesus 62

207

INDEX

Duff, Alexander 22
Duperron, Anquetil 21
Dupuis, Jacques 61–62
Dutt, Narendranath *see* Vivekananda

East India Company (EIC) 8, 21, 72
Ecumenical Association of Third World Theologians (EATWOT) 147–148
Enlightenment 17, 20–21
Estado da Índia 13
Evangelii Nuntiandi 56–57
Ezourvedam 17, 21

Farquhar, John Nicol 27–28, 52
Forrester-Patton, Ernest 96–99, 133
Francis Acharya *see* Mahieu, Francis
Frykenberg, Robert Eric 9
fulfilment theology *see* theology of fulfilment

Gandhi, Mohandas Karamchand 31, 91, 100, 107, 122
Golwalkar, Madhav Sadashiv 32
Goreh, Nehemiah 28, 73, 77
Grant, Sara 103
Griffiths, Bede 119–124, 136, 144–145, 150, 174, 179, 205
gurukula 171
Gurukul Kangri 89
guru-shishya 19, 100, 119, 177, 182, 194

Handbook of Ashram Aikya 135
Henriques, Henrique 16
Heras, Henry 85, 110
Hindu Catholic 75, 77–78, 81–82, 114
Hinduization of Christianity 23, 29–30, 54, 146
Hindutva 32, 143
Hirudayam, Ignatius 138
Holy Trinity 29, 75, 78–79, 203

Indian anaphora 54, 146–147
Indian Christian liturgy 53
Indian Christian spirituality 95, 102, 105, 138, 140, 142–143, 182, 186, 188, 191, 194
Inquisition 13, 69
interfaith dialogue *see* interreligious dialogue
interreligious dialogue 48, 55–56, 61–62, 204–205
Ishapriya 144–145

Jesudason, Savarirayan 96–99, 104, 133
Jivandhara Ashram 144–145
John Paul II 50, 61
Jones, Eli Stanley 106
Jyoti Niketan 139

kavi 96, 192–193
khadi 91–92, 98, 192–193
Knox, J. 147
Kurisumala 54, 118, 120, 124–128

liberation theology *see* theology of liberation
Lubac, Henri de 28, 112
Lumen Gentium 58

Macaulaye, Thomas Babington 22
Mahieu, Francis 118–120, 124–127, 129
Mar Ivanios 7, 96
Matapariksha 20
Mathai, K. I. 107
Matridham 142–144
Mendonça, James 111–112, 114
monasticism 72, 90, 94, 109–110, 113, 116, 124
Monchanin, Jules 85, 111–121, 124, 133, 178, 181
Muir, John 20

National Biblical, Catechetical and Liturgical Centre (NBCLC) 128, 133, 140–141, 146–147
National Missionary Society (NMS) 95, 98
Neill, Stephen 8–9
neo-Hinduism 27–28, 79, 87–89, 93–94
Nestorians *see* Saint Thomas Christians
New Dispensation 23, 74
Niyogi Report 31
Nobili, Roberto de 15–17, 26, 68–71, 76–77, 86, 180
Nostra Aetate 55

Oupnek'hat 21

Padroado Real 12
paramaguru see *Sadguru*
Paul, K. T. 95
Pelvat, Charles 83–84
Pentecostal 30, 36, 116, 194

INDEX

Pietism 17
Pignedoli, S. 131
Prasad, Ishwar 142–143
Prayer with the Harp of the Spirit 126

Rahner, Karl 28, 52
Ramabai, Pandita 24
Ramakrishna Mission 82, 90
Ramana Ashram 92
Ramana Maharishi 113
Rashtriya Swayamsevak Sangh (RSS) 32
Redemptoris Missio 61
Rethinking Christianity in India 87, 103–105
Ricci, Matteo 68
Rogerius, Abraham 18
Rogers, Murray 139
Roy, Ram Mohan 23, 35, 73
Rudra, S. K. 94–95

Saccidananda Ashram see *Shantivanam*
Sacrosanctum Concilium 53, 128
Sadguru 95, 177–178, 203
sadhana 92, 141, 170, 175, 182–188
Sahajananda, John Martin 124, 150–151
Saint Thomas Christians 10–13, 33, 35–36
Saraswati, Dayananda 24
Sat Tal 105–106
Satyagraha Ashram 91
Saux, Henry Le see Abhishiktananda
Savarkar, Vinayak Damodar 32
Schwartz, Christian Friedrich 19
Sen, Keshab Chandra 23, 73, 74
Serampore see Shrirampur
Shankara 78, 111
Shantiniketan 89
Shantivanam 110–124, 128, 130, 144–145, 178–179
Shivananda Ashram 92, 144

Shrirampur 20
Singh, Sundar 24
Soares-Prabhu, George 201
Stephens, Thomas 15–16
Syrian Indian Christians see Saint Thomas Christians

Thakur, Rabindranath 74, 89
theology of fulfilment 23, 25–29, 52, 55, 62, 98–99, 114, 122, 148, 150
theology of liberation 30–31, 63, 107, 148, 202
theology of religious pluralism 61–62, 98, 150
Tilak, Narayan Vaman 24, 95–96, 101, 177
Toward a Christian Theology of Religious Pluralism 62
Tranquebar 18–19
Twelve Points of Liturgical Adaptation 54, 128, 145

Upadhyay, Brahmabandhav 20, 24, 35, 70, 73–84, 86, 109–110, 113, 135–136, 180

Valignano, Alessandro 68
Vanavasi Kalyan Ashram 32
Vandana 102, 139, 144–145, 150–151, 172–175, 178, 191
Vande Saccidanandam 79–80
Vishva Hindu Parishad (VHP) 32
Vivekananda 74, 82, 90

Winslow, Jack Copley 96, 99–102
World's Missionary Conference 27

Xavier, Francis 14

Zaleski, Ladislaus-Michael 84
Ziegenbalg, Bartholomäus 18–19